Shiva Mahapuran Complete

Dedicated to my late father Raja Ram Bhandary.

By: Raghav Ram Bhandary.

Om Nama Shivaya

Sri Shiva Maha Puran.

First Section: (Page 15 – 24)

Bidyashowr Sanhita:

Yamuna River:

Brahmdev Advice:

Sanatkumar Meets Vyas Jee:

Lingeswor Introduction: Brahma Vishnu Debate:

Shiva's Decision:

Destroying Brahma Pride:

Shiva's Advice:

Shiva's Advice to Brahma and Vishnu:

Manner to establish Shiva Linga:

Description of Holy Land:

Details of Good Manner:

Details of Holy Fire Rituals and Other Holy Rituals:

Place Time Definitions:

Worshipping Earth:

Importance of Om Nama Shivaya:

Relation and Liberation:

Defining Worshipping:

Method To Worship Shiva Linga Made from Earth Material:

Number of Shiva Linga:

Eatables Offering to Shiva and Bel Tree's Greatness:

Greatness of Shiva's Name:

Greatness of Bone Ash (Bhasma):

Greatness of Rudrarakshya:

Second Section: (Page 25 – 31)

Rudra Sanhita:

Discussion between Sages:

Nerada's Victory over KaamDev:

Destroying Ňáradh's Pride:

Naradh Ask Question to Brahma:

Establishment of Brahma:

Defining Om:

Shiva's Advice to Vishnu and Brahma:

Age of Brahma, Vishnu, and Rudra:

Worshipping Shiva:

Advice to Gods:

Method to Worship Shiva:

Offering Different Flowers to Worship Shiva:

Establishment of World:

Creation of World:

Shiva's Kailas:

Third Section: (Page 32 – 44)

Rudra Sanhita Sati Khanda:

Defining Sati:

Defining Shiva Parvati:

Brahma Kaam Sanbad:

Kaam Rati Wedding:

Sandhya's Meditation:

Shiva's Blessing to Sandhya:

Describing Sandhya:

Kaam Dev. Receives Blessing from Brahma Dev:

Brahma Dev. and Vishnu's Discussion:

Legend of Goddess Jagdamba:

Worship of Goddess Durga by Dakshya:

Conversation between Brahma Dev. and Naradh Jee:

Sati's Meditation:

Uma Gets Groom:

Shiva Sati Wedding:

Shiva Being Angry With Brahma Dev:

Defining Variety of Brahma Dev:

Shiva and Sati's Footmark in the Himalayas:

Defining Art of Moksha (Liberation):

Sati's Doubt:

Sati and Shiva Division:

Dakshya against Shiva:

Daksha's Yegya:

Sati Devi Goes to the Daksha's Yegya:

Sati Devi Sacrifice Herself at Daksha's Yegya:

Creation of Bir Bhadra and Mahakali:

Vishnu's Advice to Dakshya:

Virbhadra Cuts Daksha's Head:

Brahmadev's Character:

Shiva Let Dakshya Be Alive Again:

Fourth section: (Page 45 – 62)

Rudra Sanhita Parvati Khanda:

Himalayas Wedding:

Previous Story:

Praising Uma:

Himalaya's Devoted Meditation:

Parvati 'Dream:

Shiva and Himalaya's Conversation:

Shiva and Parvati Conversation:

Birth of Bajranga and Blessing for Son:

Birth of Tarkasoor and His Meditation:

Tarkasoor Disown Heaven:

KaamDev Goes to Shiva's Place:

KaamDev Turned to Ashes:

Narad's Advice to Parvati Jee:

Meditation of Parvati Jee:

Description of Maya (Illusion) of Shiva:

Seven Saints Goes to Himalaya's Place:

Advice of Great Saint:

Saints Counseling Himalaya:

Padma and Piplad 'Story:

Seven Saints (Saptarishi) Meets Shiva:

Himalaya Sends Marriage Auspicious (Lagnapatrika):

Shiva Invites All Gods to Wedding:

Wedding Procession:

Compromise between Gods and Hills:

Unique Play of Shiva:

Blessed to see Shiva's real face:

The description of wedding possession of Shiva:

Brahmdev Became Lust:

Kaam Dev. Gets Life Back By the Grace of Shiva:

Description of Loyalty to Husband:

Shiva Returns to Kailas:

Fifth Section: (Page 63 – 69)

Rudra Sanhita Kumar Khanda:

Beginning:

Birth of Kartikya (Kumar):

Characteristics of Kartikya (Kumar):

War between Gods and Devils:

Bravery of Tarkasoor:

Killing of Tarkasoor:

Characteristics of Ganesha:

Ganesha battles with followers of Shiva:

Cutting Ganesha's head:

Rebirth of Ganesha:

Glory of Ganesha:

Wedding of Ganesha:

Sixth Section: (Page 70 – 90)

Rudra Sanhita Yudha Khanda:

Description of Tripurasoor:

Battle between Bhadra, kali and Shankhachud:

Shiva kills Shankhachud:

Curse of Tulsi:

Killing of Hiranyachya:

Killing of Hiranyakasipu:

Story of Blinded Son:

Freedom of Sukracharya:

How Sukracharya received Mrit Sanjivini Vidya:

Varasor:

Characteristic of Usha:

Battle of Barasoor and Usha's Wedding:

Description of Battle of Sri Krishna:

Barasoor Being Garapati:

Description of Killing Gajasoor:

Killing of Nirhya:

Destruction of Devils Bindal and Utpal:

Seventh Section: (Page 91 – 108)

Sat Rudra Sanhita:

Five Figure of Shiva:

Describing Shiva's Idols:

Ardanariswor Shiva:

Nandikeshowr Incarnation:

Bhairav Incarnation:

Sarav Incarnation:

Blessing to Bishwonar:

Grihapati Incarnation:

Yegyashowr Incarnation:

Shiva's Ten Incarnation:

Establishment of Eleven Rudra

Durbasa Character:

Hanuman Incarnation:

Mahesh Incarnation:

Brishavtar Incarnation:

Characteristics of Piplad:

Story of Baisyanath Incarnation:

Dijyashowr Incarnation

Yetinath Hansaroop Incarnation:

Krishna Dashain Incarnation:

Avadooteshowr Incarnation:

Vikchubarya Incarnation:

Sureshowr Incarnation:

Brahma Chari Incarnation:

Sunat-Natrka Incarnation:

Dijja Incarnation:

Asawthama Incarnation:

Kirat Incarnation:

Debate between Arjun and Kirat:

Eighth Chapter: (Page 109 – 128)

Koti Rudra Sanhita:

Description of Twelve Jyotirlinga and Upalinga of Sada Shiva:

Meditation of Ansuya and Atri:

Glory of Atrishowr:

Glory of Nandikeshowr:

Glory of Mahabal Shiva:

Reason for Linga Incarnation:

Release of Andhakasoor:

Story of Batuk's Glory:

Establishment of Somnath:

Establishment of Malikarjun Shiva Linga:

Establishment of Mahakalleshowr Shiva Linga:

Glory of Mahakal:

Glory of Omkareshowr:

Glory of Sri Kedareshowr:

Establishment of Bhimeshwor Shiva Linga:

Glory of Shree Bishwoshwor Shiva Linga:

Glory of Maha Rishi Gautama:

They blame Maha Rishi Gautama for Killing a Cow:

Establishment and Glory of Trayambakeshowr:

Glory of Baidyanatheshowr:

Establishment and Glory of Nageshowr:

Glory of Rameshowr:

Story of Sudeha and Sudharma:

Establishment of Ghusmesh Shiva Linga:

Vishnu receives Sudarshan Chakra:

Benefit of Pronouncing Shiva's Name (Shiva Shashra Nam):

Stories of Devotees of Shiva:

Rules to Follow While Fasting on Shivaratri:

How to End Shivaratri Fasting:

Nisad (Degraded) Character:

Chapter: Nine: (Page 129 – 147)

Uma Sanhita:

Conversation between Sri Krishna and Upmanyou:

Description of Shiva's Devotees:

Greatness of Shiva:

Description of Shiva's Maya:

Descriptions of Sinners:

Description of Hells:

The greatness of Donating Food:

The greatness of Donating, Water, and Meditation:

The greatness of Holy Books:

Description of Donation:

Description of Hell (Patal):

Ways to get out of Hells:

Description of seven lights:

Describing Horoscope, Graha Mandal, and Loka:

Moksha through meditation:

Formation of body and responsibilities inside the womb:

Impurities of the body and sorrow:

Knowledge about death:

Way to escape death:

Lord Shiva and definition of death:

Description of Shadow Man:

Description About Creation of the Universe:

Description of Kashyap Generation:

Birth of Vyas Jee:

Description of Maha Kali and killing of Madhu Kaitav:

Death of Dhromlochana, Chanda Munda, Ratktabij, and Sumbha Nishumbha:

Creation of Uma:

Description of Sri Vidya of Sati:

Description of Kriya Yog:

Chapter ten: (Page 148 – 152)

Kailas Sanhita:

Conversation of Sri Vyas Jee with Saunak Jee:

Goddess Parvati Asks Lord Shiva About Prarav:

Describing Prarav:

Sanyasi Rule:

Sanyasi Mandal Rule:

Bamdev:

Description Of Shiva:

Worshiping The Idol:

Shiva Element:

Description of Creation:

Rules to Make Disciples:

Description of Yog Knowledge:

Rules For Yog Knowledge:

Yogis Death:

Eleventh Day Ritual:

Twelve Day's Ritual:

Eleventh Chapter: (Page 153 – 165)

Vaiviya Sanhita:

Story of knowledge:

Description of Shiva's Devotion:

Age of All Three Gods:

Description of Armageddon:

Description of Creation:

Creation of Rudra:

Creation of Shiv-Shiva:

Creation of Maithuni Culture:

Staying at Mandarachal:

Creation of Kali:

Kindness over Lion:

Meeting of Lord Shiva and Gauri Devi:

Devotion of Upmanyou:

Advice of Upmanyou:

Description of Vyas Incarnation:

Devotion towards Lord Shiva:

Importance of Om Nama Shivaya Mantra:

Mantra for Kali Yug:

Types of Dikshya (Teachings):

Religion to Practice All the Time:

Way to Worship:

Way to Worship Lord Shiva:

Avaran way of Worshipping:

Benefits of Establishing Shiva Linga:

Attraction of Brahmdev and Vishnu towards the Linga:

How to create Shiva Linga:

Way to do Yog:

Stories of Munis:

Moksha of Munis:

OSGN

Om Nama Shivaya

Shree Shiva Maha Puran:

Pratham Khanda

First Section

Bidyashowr Sanhita:

Yamuna River:

Once upon a time all the great sages from different parts of the world gathered for a special occasion at the meeting point of Ganga and Yamuna River. In the same occasion the great sage Shree Shoot Jee who was a disciple of Shree Vyas Jee also arrives for the same occasion and all the other great Sage give their respect to Shree Shoot Jee. They regarded Shree Shoot Jee as one of the great soul. So all the sage present started asking different questions to Shoot Jee. One of the Sage started saying that in this deadly Kali Yug, people with incomplete positive feelings are suffering everywhere, Based on these what is the best solution for them so they can clean their incomplete feelings with complete pure feelings which can lead to achieving Shiva which is complete enlighten.

After hearing the question Shoot Jee says great souls, you are to ask me such a question. Shoot Jee explains how one can destroy Kali sins by reading Shiva Maha Puran. Shiva Maha Puran is superior then Veda if one reads one over the other. By reading or listening to Shiva Maha Puran, one can achieve liberation. Vyas Jee explains that by reading one or half a line of religious poetry mentioned in Shiva Maha Puran with the positive vibe, one will liberate. One who follows Shiva Maha Puran daily will have their name and personality live forever.

In Shiva Maha Puran all elements of life Religion, Meaning of life, Duty of life and Liberation of life, are explained in details. Also, there are stories of Shiva and all kinds of wisdom with science mentioned in Shiva Maha Puran. Shiva had mentioned one hundred thousand lines of religious poetry in Shiva Maha Puran. Which were Bidyashowr Sanhita, Rudra Sanhita, Binayak Sanhita, Uma Sanhita, Matri Sanhita, Eka Das Rudra Sanhita, Kailas Sanhita, Shot Rudra Sanhita, Koti Rudra Sanhita, Sahasra Koti Rudra Sanhita, Manaviya Sanhita, and Dharma Sanhita. These were the original religious poetry titles that Shiva had mentioned in Shiva Maha Puran. So for the benefit of all human beings in Kali Yug he only let the following chapters of Shiva Maha Puran in the revised version and the titles for the chapters in modern day Shiva Maha Puran are Bidyashowr Sanhita, Rudra Sanhita, Shot Rudra Sanhita, Koti Rudra Sanhita, Uma Sanhita, Kailas Sanhita, and Vaiviya Sanhita. If anyone reads a few lines of literature mentioned Shiva Maha Puran, then he/she will be free from the cycle of death and birth. Also Shiva Maha Puran is beneficial to the whole human kind.

Brahmdev Advice:

Shoot Jee said when there was an end of the previous era and start of this new era then six great saints started thinking about what is the furthest and to find the answer they went to Brahma Jee. So the Brahma Jee advise them that the one who created everything in this Universe is the furthest and also the superior. Who is no other than Shiva? So if we hear, think and mention the name of the Shiva, then we will achieve ShivYog. Shiva means infinite, and Yog means union. So ShivYog means union with the infinite. Brahma Dev. advice to the saints to perform (Yegya) holy rituals which involves fire for one thousand years in the name of Shiva.

Sanatkumar Meets Vyas Jee:

So all the saints present at the time asked Shoot Jee, what does he mean by hearing (shrawan), thinking (Manan) and mentioning (Kirtan)? Then Shoot Jee replied with a smile and said if you worship's name, figure and you would do all the worshiping from the heart then it's called (Manan) thinking. So pronouncing he's name is (Kirtan). By pronouncing he's name will also clean our thought process. Hearing from heart the name of the Lord is Hearing (Shrawan).

So the Shoot Jee tells a story about Vyas Jee who was his Guru. Once upon a time Vyas Jee was in deep meditation of Shiva at the banks of Sarswoti River, then Sanatkumar arrives there and ask Vyas Jee, why he was doing these types of deep meditation? Then Vyas Jee replied for liberation (Mukti) of life. Then Sanatkumar said I also used to think the same way and used to meditate like you. But one day Nandi came to me and advise me that only by doing Shrawan (Hearing), Manan (Thinking), and Kirtan (Mentioning) of Shiva will achieve liberation (Mukti). So after that I started doing these activities in the name of Shiva. So Sanatkumar advice Vyas Jee to perform Shrawan, Manan, and Kirtan in the name of Shiva rather than doing deep meditation. After giving the advice to Vyas Jee, Sanatkumar left. Then the saints asked Shoot Jee how come people who don't perform Shrawan, Manan, and Kirtan can also achieve liberation?

Lingeswor Introduction:

Shoot Jee explains people who cannot perform Shrawan, Manan, and Kirtan can establish a Shiva Linga and worship the Linga. So by worshiping a Shiva figure or Linga can also achieve liberation. Shiva himself told Vyas Jee that by worshiping an idol of a Lord also can achieve liberation. Shoot Jee says that Shiva is both with definite Shape and also formless. So by performing worship to Linga also can achieve liberation.

Brahma Vishnu Debate:

One day Vishnu and Brahma Dev. came across each other. After some time they started debating who is superior. Both of them acted as they were more powerful and superior to one another. They both did not know who each other were and how they came to exist. After debating for a while they couldn't decide who is superior, so started a war between the two of them. All the other gods and goddess started feeling nervous and worried when they saw the two great s Vishnu and Brahma engaged themselves in a war for proof on who are superior, then one another. So all the divine powers went to Shiva and complain about Vishnu and Brahma about wasting their negative energy on each other, which was affecting everyone. When all the divine powers reach Kailas, Shiva called them to come close to him as he already knew about the battle between Vishnu and Brahma.

Shiva's Decision:

After the hearing what other gods and goddess had to say about the battle between Vishnu and Brahma. Shiva told gods and goddess don't panic, I will go with my Shiva Guru (Followers) to the place where they were battling. So Shiva along with his followers (Guru) went to the battle place and watched it from inside the clouds and listen to what each Vishnu and Brahma had to say about each other. After knowing they were battling for who is superior and also their pride for against each other. So Shiva converts himself into a pillar Linga in front of Vishnu and

Brahma, which had no end or start. After seeing the pillar Linga, they stop battling and thought about the pillar Linga. So they decided who ever find what the pillar Linga was first, then he will be superior. After agreeing, they both take a different shape of animals. Brahma went towards upwards of the pillar Linga and Vishnu went downwards of the pillar Linga.

They both travelled for a few hundred years and couldn't find the start or end of the pillar Linga. After some time later Brahma finds a Ketaki Flower, and then he takes the flower and say he had found the start of the pillar Linga. So Brahma takes the flower and meets Vishnu at the same place where they started the race.

Then Brahma told Vishnu that he found the top of the pillar Linga and found the flower of Ketaki, after hearing that Vishnu honored Brahma by touching his feet. Seeing this, Shiva came in front of them from the pillar Linga. Then Vishnu gave his respect to Shiva by touching his feet. After seeing the greatness of Vishnu Shiva was so impressed by him that in return he respected and honored Vishnu as he is one of them.

Destroying Brahma Pride:

Shiva became angry with Brahma, and so he established Bhairav from the middle of his eyebrow. So Bhairav respected and honored Shiva and asked for his command. Shiva asked Bhairav to show the magic of his shinning sword. After that Bhairav cuts heads of Brahma after cutting about five heads, then Brahma lays himself on the feet of Bhairav and ask for forgiveness. Also Vishnu touches Shiva's feet and asks for forgiveness for Brahma. Then Bhairav told Brahma that he misused his trust and lied to achieve, and that is not the right way to do. Then Brahma goes to the feet of Shiva and asks for his Forgiveness. Then Shiva told Ketaki flower that he wouldn't be used in as a flower while worshipping Shiva. Also Shiva told Brahma Dev. that he would only be worshipped as a priest of a Guru while anyone is performing any kind of Yegya (Holy rituals involving fire). So this is how Shiva blessed everyone in that event.

Shiva's Advice:

Vishnu and Brahma worshipped Shiva with great devotion. So Shiva was pleased and pleased with both Vishnu and Brahma he told them it's a great day and in the coming days they would know it as Shivaratri. It would be one of the holiest days. So on this day whoever worships on Shiva Linga they will liberate. People who don't worship throughout their life but worship the Linga on Shivaratri, then all his sins gets destroyed and will gain holy blessings for the whole year. Also, people who will worship Shiva Linga along with Uma on the month of Mangsir that devotee will be as loveable as Kartikya to Shiva. The benefits of worshipping a Shiva Linga on Shivaratri are unlimited. Shiva also tells Brahma and Vishnu that where the Pillar Linga that place will be known as Arunachal and they will liberate people who die naturally on this region. People who will worship this pillar Linga will achieve all four types of liberation.

Shiva's Advice to Brahma and Vishnu:

After hearing Shiva had to say Vishnu and Brahma asked Shiva what is nature's first five acts or deeds. Then Shiva said that all his work is a secret till now, but he will let them know the how it all works. There are five elements first is Creation second being situation third is Destruction fourth is Disappearance or movement and fifth is showing Favor or Liberation. These are my five Karmas that are present and practiced in the Universe. So establishing a world is karma known as nature. To run the nature smoothly is the situation. To destroy is destruction. To change the things in the world is disappearance or movement. And to get rid of everything that the world has to offer is showing favor or liberation. So Shiva told Vishnu and Brahma that these are my holy five karmas.

To manage these five karmas I have five faces, four faces on four directions and one in the middle. We know only this information to the wise beings. No one can achieve these five karmic elements that easily, only one who controls himself will achieve all five holy karmic elements. Both of you have forgotten your Karmas and now if you want you can start saying Om name only from now on. This by repeating continuously like a ray of Sun will remove pride and achieve peace from within. Shiva was facing north when giving advice to Vishnu and Brahma. Then Vishnu and Brahma gave their highest respect to Shiva. After which Shiva told Vishnu and Brahma that he has to explain all five karmic elements of life also I gave you a magical formula to attain liberation. If you honestly from the heart keep spelling the magic formula, you will know me. This magic formula will let you achieve great fortune and wisdom. By spelling this magic, formula continuously can have my position.

Manner to establish Shiva Linga:

Shoot Jee explains that one can establish Shiva Linga on the banks of Ganga River or other holy Rivers also at any place that one thinks is suitable. When establishing Shiva Linga, one has to think and remember that they would worship it daily till the end of time. Shiva Linga made of earth materials should establish according to one's wish. One should make small Shiva Linga if it's portable and big one if non portable.

By worshipping Shiva Linga or an idol of Shiva will achieve final liberation. Some devotees also put an idol of Ma Uma along with Shiva's idol and worship both of them. One should learn from the Guru about the ancient tradition of worshipping Shiva. One should take a shower, wear bone ash, light incense or light and then worship Shiva.

One should repeat the holy five letters Om. To achieve an end goal, one must receive guidance from a Guru. Guru should be Brahman and Kindly wise. When Brahman spells out holy five letters, it should be like Om Nama Shivaya and others except Brahman should spell holy five letters as Om Shivaya Nama. One who spells this magic formula fifty million times with no feeling of want will be Shiva himself. Brahman should also spell Gayatri Mantra one thousand eight times every day. Also by spelling only OM for one thousand times a day will clear negative feelings and thoughts which leads to clean feelings. Only by spelling OM mantra at a Shiva temple can achieve end goals much faster than spelling at somewhere else. One hundred hands away from Shiva Linga are a holy land and also known as Shiva's area. Shiva's area is holy land.

After hearing about this all the saints requests Shoot Jee to tell more about Shiva's area or holy land. How anyone can achieve liberation by staying or building an ashram near any holy land. How the Shiva's area or holy land was invented at the beginning please teach us about it in a karmic order.

Description of Holy Land (Shiva's Area):

The banks of River Ganga and other holy Rivers there is holy land or Shiva's area. Also, Sarswoti River is also a holy river and people who live nearby it will achieve Brahma position. Ganga River which starts from the Himalayas has hundreds of faces and is so pure and holy that even the worst of the worst sin can be cleared by showering in it. To live by the River Ganga is the holiest thing to do. There are places like Kashi, and other holy sites ideal to live in. Taking a bath and fasting at the banks of different holy places will achieve respect as much as Ganesha. Whoever lives by Narmada River which has twenty-four faces can achieve respect as great as Vishnu. People who live by Rivers like Tamsha, Rewa, Godavari, will be off the sin even if they kill Brahman. Beside these rivers other like Krishna and Benri Rivers embodied from Vishnu Lok and Tungabhadra embodied from Brahma Lok. Also other Rivers, Sarswoti, Pampa, Kanya, Shweta, Kaberi are also holy rivers which gives holy blessing by taking a bath on it. All these rivers and its banks are as respectful as Shiva Lok and by performing holy rituals on the banks of this holy rivers are blessed by Shiva and other gods and goddesses.

Details of Good Manner:

Saints asked Shoot Jee what is the way or means that leads a person to heaven or hell also explains us the difference meanings of religious and non-religious activities. Also teach us the mean and way of defeating non-religious element with religious elements. Then Shoot Jee starts with hay great saints, all beings should get up before the sun shines and meditate your respected divine power or Sun. When doing meditation, one should face east to receive better results. One should finish his work in toilet before Sun rises. Take a shower and offer holy water to Sun. After wear a clean clothes and give respect to loved ones. After which take a sit and starts spelling your mantra, Brahman should spell Gayatri mantra and other beings should spell mantra given to them. One should spell mantras three times a day.

One should also divide his earnings into three parts, and one part of the earning should go towards religious karma. Should live on simple food, also don't consume things that makes person emotional and produce negative vibe. Desire will rise from negative vibe, and that will prioritize us to do more sin in the world.

Details of Holy Fire Rituals and Other Holy Rituals:

Saints requests Shoot Jee to explain them, the fire Sacrifice ritual (Agni Yegya), God Sacrifice Ritual (Dev. Yegya), Brahma Sacrifice Ritual (Brahma Yegya) and Guru Puja.

Shoot Jee said to offer Joined Object to Fire is Fire sacrifice ritual. The Fire Ritual is of different types. The first one is oblation to fuel a fire as a sacrifice. Second one is to stay virgin till one gets married. The ashes from the fire ritual during the marriage ceremony should keep safely.

Shiva made Sunday the first day of the week, and they base other days on karmic orders. By worshiping on Sunday is beneficial to destroy one's sins. To earn wealth, one should worship on Monday, to get rid of diseases and to get peace one should worship Tuesday and also Goddess Kali and other Goddesses should also be worship on Tuesday. They should worship Vishnu on Wednesday, for long life one should worship on Thursday, and on Friday one should worship if he wants materialistic objects. On Saturday one should worship Rudra for a beautiful wife.

Place Time Definitions:

The saints asked Shoot Jee what is the best place, time, and character to worship? Then Shoot Jee says that while performing Yegya fire rituals offering to if the house is pure you will see the positive results all around it, but it gives ten times better result if the place is Cows cottage, ten times even better if it is River's bank, even ten times better if it is by the Pipal, Bel, Tulsi Plants, and Temple, Banks of holy rivers, Ganga and other Saptanadi's bank, ten times better than that would be by the ocean, ten times better than that would be top of the mountain and the most fruitful results will be to perform Worship at the place you feel is the best.

Worshipping Earth:

Shoot Jee starts by saying that one should worship Symbol or Image made from mud which can lead to all wishes come true of men and women. To make a symbol or image of, one should get mud from inside the river, lake, pond etc. and mixed it with good smell producing powder and also mix cow's milk to it and after playing with a mud for a while make an idol of you want to worship. Specially one should make a statue of Ganesh, Parvati, Shiva, Vishnu, and Sun and start worshipping it. Person who worships Shiva on the statue made from mud with pure feeling can achieve whatever he wishes for. On Shiva Linga made by others are used to worship, then three kilograms of sweets has to offer. If Shiva Linga made by yourself, then offer five Kilograms of sweets has to be offer.

Importance of Om Nama Shivaya:

The shape of the world build by nature is boat shaped. Wise Pundits call it the sound of OM. OM sound always present in the heart of great saints. By repeating the word, Om continuously destroys all the sins one has committed. OM is also the union of Shiva and Power. So by keep repeating the Om for a long time will also provide liberation. Most of the magic formula (Mantra) present in the Veda and other holy scripture the OM is use. One should repeat the magic formula Om Nama Shivaya about fifty Million times, then one achieves liberation. Great souls used to say that to know about Shiva Lok one has to have the blessings from Shiva. Any person who hears this magic formula (Om Nama Shivaya) from a Brahman Guru and pronounce it five hundred thousand times then he will increase his life span. This magic formula is itself a Shiva, and whoever accepts these will be Shiva himself. A person who reads Shiva Maha Puran while always get the blessings from Shiva and will also achieve liberation.

Relation and Liberation:

Saints asked Shoot Jee what is relation and liberation? Then Shoot Jee said that nature has eight relation because of these Soul got the name Life. To get out of these eight relations is liberation. Thinking, wisdom, Pride, and Panchatan (Five Senses) are the eight relations of nature. These bodies of ours are building from these eight elements of nature. Body creates karma and karma creates body, so this process goes on and on. We have three bodies Mass body (Sthool), Earthly body (Shukshyam), and Reasoning Body (Karan). So mass body does the business, Earthly body worships the organs and reasoning body is to deal with soul. We become happy and sad because of the activity of these three bodies. This process rotates like a wheel, and one can get out of this cycle only by worshipping Shiva. Shiva is out of these eight relations of nature. For all these eight relations of nature are under the control of Shiva. First one should worship Ganesh and then only worship Shiva's Linga.

Defining Worshipping:

Saints said Shoot Jee you are a great person to explain the greatness of Shiva Linga. Now you have to tell us about greatness of Shiva Linga made from earth material (Paarthiv Shiva Linga) as you have heard from your Guru Vyas Jee.

Then Shoot Jee says dear saints, I am impressed by your devotion towards Shiva. Now I will tell you about greatness of Shiva Linga made from earth material. Some say that Shiva Linga made from earth material is the supreme of Linga. By worshipping the Shiva Linga made from earth material, many saints has achieved liberation. By worshipping a Shiva Linga made from earth material saints and devils both have achieved liberation to their soul. In Truth Era (Satya Yug) they made Supreme Shiva Linga up of Precious Jewel, and in Second World Age (Tretya Yug) Shiva Linga made from Gold was supremely Linga. So in Third World Age (Duarpa Yug) Shiva Linga made from Platinum was the supreme of the Linga and in Kali Yug the present time Shiva Linga made from earth material is the Supreme of the Linga. In these days and age by worshipping Shiva, Linga made from earth material is more beneficial and fruitful than doing meditation for Years. Person who makes Shiva Linga out of earth material and worships it all lifelong will go to Shiva Lok after death from this body.

Method To Worship Shiva Linga Made from Earth Material:

Shoot Jee says now I will teach you the method of worship Shiva Linga made from Earth material. First one should be familiar with the magic formulas (Mantra) of Veda and perform meditation in the right manner and perform Brahma Yegya (Fire ritual) then one can worship Shiva Linga made from Earth material with proper manner mention in the Veda.

Number of Shiva Linga:

Shoot Jee starts with several Shiva Linga made from Earth materials depends upon wishes of the people. People who want education should worship one thousand Shiva Linga made from Earth material and people who wants wealth should worship five hundred Shiva Linga. People who wants liberation should worship ten million Shiva Linga, people who wants land should worship one thousand Shiva Linga, People who goes to different holy places (Tirtha) should worship two thousand Shiva Linga made from Earth material. So whoever wants whatever kinds of wish they should worship that many number of Shiva Linga made from Earth material in the manner mentioned in the Veda. Worshipping Shiva Linga made from Earth material will bring positive results as much as performing Ten million holy fire rituals (Yegya). By worshipping a Shiva Linga you will worship the whole Universe and everything on it. To get out of the Worldly affair, one needs to worship Shiva Linga as a best and quick way compare to other ways of getting liberation. One should not worship Shiva Linga without wearing Rudrarakshya beads and Bel leaves.

Eatables Offering to Shiva and Bel Tree's Greatness:

Eating eatables offered to Shiva can destroy one's sins. One who receives and consumes eatables offered to Shiva, then he receives holy blessings and results could receive as much as one billion holy fire ritual (Yegya) performed. Houses worships and distribute eatables offered to Shiva to others. Those houses will always pure energy. So whenever anyone has time to eat an eatable offered to Shiva, he should eat it with the feeling of love. Even a Brahmin killer will be free from his sins after consuming eatables offered to Shiva.

Shoot Jee starts now let me tell you about the greatness of Bel leave. This thing called Bel leaves, it's the form of Shiva himself. Even gods have praised a lot about Bel leaves and they can find it on most if not all the holy places of the World. On the root of Bel tree Shiva lives in the form of Linga. So any person who pours water on the roots of the Bel tree will earn credit of taking a bath at all the holy rivers in the World. Also, anyone who does worshipping with colored flowers incense etc. will go to Shiva Lok after death. Person who lights light by the side of Bel tree will destroy all his past and present sins, and also he becomes genuinely intelligent. If a person cooks rice pudding underneath the Bel tree and feeds Shiva devotees, then he will never have to be poor.

Greatness of Shiva's Name:

Saints requests Shoot Jee to explain us the importance of bone ash (Bhasma), Rudrarakshya, and Shiva's name.

Shoot Jee explains that when bone ash, Rudrarakshya, and Shiva's name all three elements stay together than it's like Triveni (three rivers meeting point). Shiva's name is engaged with river Ganga, Bhasma (bone ash) is engaged with river Yamuna and Rudra with river Sarswoti, all these three rivers destroys all the sin of one bath on it. So one should always accept all three elements. By repeating the Shiva's name a mountain they will destroy full sins. It will liberate person who always keeps saying from this World.

Greatness of Bone Ash (Bhasma):

Shoot Jee said Bhasma are of two types. First one is Maha Bhasma, and a second one is Swolop. There are three kinds of Maha Bhasma which are Source (Shrot), Awareness (Smriti), and third one is Worldly (laukik). Among these Bhasma Source (Shrot Bhasma) and Awareness (Smriti Bhasma) are for Brahmans only. For others there is Worldly (Laukik Bhasma).Bhasma should be collected from the ash of a holy fire ritual (Yegya). One should wear Bhasma and only perform evening worship. Person who wears Bhasma and worships or meditates that person can control his death. When wearing a Bhasma one should spell the magic formula (Mantra) Om Nama Shivaya.

Greatness of Rudrarakshya:

Shoot Jee said **Rudraksha** is Shiva's one of the most loveable thing. By wearing it and spelling magic formula (Mantra) with it will destroy all the sins one has committed in present or past lives. Shiva himself told the story of Rudraksha to Mata Parvati. Shiva told **Mata Parvati** that in the previous era I was meditating for thousands of years. Suddenly I felt a kind of like scared and at the same moment I opened my eyes from the meditation. From the drop of my tears, the Rudraksha tree started growing. All people from four caste system should wear Rudraksha bead. While spelling out the magic formula (Mantra) one should do it with Rudraksha bead, it will be produce beneficial result. If one wears Rudraksha beads during the day, then we will destroy all the sins committed at night, and if someone wears it during a night, then all the sins committed during the day will destroy too. By Putting Bhasma and wearing a Rudraksha Beads and spell the magic formula (Mantra) Om Nama Shivaya, then that great soul will never have to go to hell. Also, they don't have to face sudden death situation. Such a person will always be healthy. Rudraksha with three faces can give liberation. Same wise we regard four faces Rudraksha as Brahma. Rudraksha with five faces is his Rudra, and this Rudraksha fulfills all wishes, and it also grants Liberation. So usually Rudraksha can found from one face to up to fourteen faces.

Om Nama Shivaya

Rudra Sanhita:

Second Section.

Discussion between Sages:

All the saints at the time thanked Shoot Jee for letting them know the Bidyashowr Sanhita, and requests Shoot Jee for more stories about Shiva, rising of Uma, Marriage of Shiva with Mata Uma, domestic culture and other stories.

Shoot Jee says all of your saints are great because of your query to know more about Shiva is a great thing and it is as pure as River Ganga. One day Naradh asked Brahma the same question, then Brahma explained to Naradh.

Nerada's Victory over KaamDev:

Shoot Jee says once upon a time Naradh Jee was meditating deeply at a beautiful cave by the Himalayas. His meditation was so deep and powerful that King of God Indra became scared of Naradh Jee that he sends Kaamdev to destroy the meditation of the Naradh Jee. After trying for quite some time with angels dancing and singing next to where Naradh Jee was meditating for Shiva. So KaamDev gave up the idea to destroy Naradh Jee meditation because it was a Tapo Bhumi, where once Shiva meditated himself and he defeated Kaamdev, who also came to destroy Shiva's meditation. So KaamDev had no power to destroy anyone's meditation because Shiva meditated in that region. After some time Naradh Jee came out of meditation and he finds out that he won over KaamDev who came to destroy his meditation. After that, Naradh Jee had a pride that he won over Kaamdev, which doesn't happen that often. So he let Shiva about his victory over Kaamdev, so Naradh Jee goes to Kailas. So Naradh Jee reaches Kailas, and he gives his respect to Shiva and tells the story to Shiva how he won the battle with Kaamdev, who came to destroy his meditation. After hearing from Naradh Jee Shiva told him it impressed him with Naradh Jee but not to tell this story to any other gods, especially to Vishnu. Then Naradh Jee couldn't control himself because of happiness and pride that he went to Vishnu Lok to meet Vishnu and told him the story how he achieved victory over Kaamdev and how his Maya didn't work on Naradh Jee. So Vishnu told Naradh Jee that Kaamdev usually bothers only non-devotees, so why would Kaamdev bother Naradh Jee? After hearing this Naradh Jee became angry with pride and said he defeated Kaamdev so he is more powerful than other gods. After showing off his pride to Vishnu, Naradh Jee left Vishnu Lok and went somewhere else.

Destroying Ňáradh's Pride:

Then Shoot Jee says Vishnu with his power created a beautiful town in the same direction as Naradh Jee was going. The king of the town was Shilnidhi, and he had a beautiful and talented unmarried daughter. Same day as Naradh Jee reached the town, there was an engagement ceremony for the princess. Different kings and prince came for the engagement ceremony. So Naradh Jee also went to the palace where the ceremony was taking place. So when the king saw the Naradh Jee, he gave his respect to him and asked to take a seat. After that the king called his daughter and asked Naradh Jee what kind of husband will she have? Then Naradh Jee looked at the princess and impressed by her beauty so told the king she will have one of the best and talented husbands.

After saying that Naradh Jee left from there and he had this idea if could have that princess as a wife. So he thought if he gets a face of Vishnu then he could have the princess as his wife. So he goes back to Vishnu and addressees Vishnu as Hari and tells him about the princess and how he impressed by her beauty and wants to make her his wife. Then Vishnu told Naradh Jee that he will have a face of Hari at the time of engagement of the princess. So Naradh Jee being thrilled after hearing Vishnu goes back to the palace where the engagement ceremony was taking place. So Naradh Jee takes a seat and his face looked that of the monkey. Because Hari also means monkey in Sanskrit language. Vishnu also came to the engagement ceremony with the looks of a king and weds the princess and goes away.

Then Naradh Jee finds out from the doormen of Vishnu that his face looks like that of a monkey, and it really made Naradh Jee angry with Vishnu. He curses the two doormen of Vishnu that they are born in Earth as demons. Then he went to Vishnu and was in a furious mood. So as soon as he sees Vishnu Naradh Jee curse him so he has to be born in earth as king and has to go through the pain of not having his wife with him. After that Vishnu happily accepted the curse of Naradh Jee and got rid of the Maya which lead Naradh Jee to behave differently. After realizing that it was all Maya of the, Naradh Jee felt shameful that he cursed Vishnu. So Naradh Jee apologizes to Vishnu and ask for his forgiveness. Then Vishnu tells Naradh Jee that it all happen with the will of Shiva and there was no reason to apologize for it. So don't worry, just repeat the name of Shiva, it will destroy it.

Naradh Ask Question to Brahma:

After that, Naradh Jee goes to worship Shiva Linga around the World. Then he meets the doormen of Vishnu to whom he had cursed. The doormen ask for Ňáradh's forgiveness and also ask him how they will get off the curse that Naradh Jee had spelled on them. Then Naradh Jee tells the two doormen that he thought of Maya that had created to destroy Ňáradh's pride. So he is sorry that he cursed them and tells them they will birth in Brahmin family but they will be of demon features. They will be the great devotee of Shiva. Their name will be famous all over the world. And when Vishnu takes birth in earth as Sri Ram, then he will be the one who will liberate them by killing them in a battle. That's how you will get rid of my curse, Naradh Jee tells the two doormen. After that Naradh Jee reaches Brahma Lok where Brahma stays. So after giving his respect to father Brahma he asked Brahma Dev. what is the kindness and happiness of Shiva?

Then Brahma Dev. told Naradh that he asked very pleasant, full question which will do good to the world. So listen carefully, Brahma Dev. tells Naradh Jee. On previous annihilation everything got destroyed. Things like earth, water, stars and so on all got destroyed. Only thing there was sky and everything else vanished in the sky, so it was like zero, where nothing existed. Only thing that existed was Shiva, who was also in like zero situations. The situation in which Shiva stays on zero situations is same as worshipping the idol of Shiva. Idol of god and goddesses are always in zero situations. Then Shiva created, never ending energy from his formless body. Later on that energy known as Mata Janani (Goddess of Nature). After that Siva and Mata Janani created Shiva Lok. Which later known as Kashi. So any person who dies at Kashi region will achieve liberation.

While Shiva was roaming around the Shiva Lok, he thought of inventing another male character just like him. So Shiva created a male just like him and named that male character as Vishnu. Then Shiva told Vishnu to meditate, and he also gave Vishnu all the knowledge of all four Veda. After meditating for years, water started coming from all parts of Vishnu's body. So Vishnu vanishes inside the same water and then many elements got created. So those elements expanded and created five senses. After that, the Universe started creating by itself.

Establishment of Brahma:

Brahma Dev. said while Vishnu was sleeping in the water by the wish of Shiva, a Lotus flower grew from the naval of Vishnu. And on that lotus flower they established me, said Brahma to Naradh Jee. At, the time of establishment Brahma had four heads. I could only see the lotus flower all around me. Then I didn't have the knowledge of the, so I had a wish to find out who established me. Then I started going down on the steam of the lotus flower and I went down for hundreds of years but couldn't find the base of the flower. Then I heard the voice from the Lotus to meditate. Then I meditated for twelve years and I saw Vishnu in front of me when I opened my eyes. Then I asked Vishnu, who are you? Then Vishnu told Brahma Dev. that he is his creator and Brahma Dev. should surrender himself to Vishnu and that will end all miseries. Then we both had a huge argument on who is superior? So we started a great battle between us. Then in the middle of the battle large Linga came in front of us. We both stopped the battle and started worshipping the Linga.

Defining Om:

Brahma Dev. said they heard Om three times. Vishnu also saw the letter Om written on the large Linga. Then we started thinking how this Linga came there suddenly? Then a great saint appears before us. So when they saw the saints they wonder, and Vishnu finds out it is Shiva. The letter Om can only know that Shiva. This letter Om is the real truth, nectar, the whole Universe. The same letter Om is responsible for Brahma Dev. to be born from Vishnu's naval. The figure of Om is Vishnu, and form is Shiva. Om created heaven as upper parts and lower part created earth. After that thirty-eight letters, Mantra got established. Later on that Mantra known as Maha Mirtyunjaya Mantra. Along, with this mantra they established another Mantra Nama Shivaya and other three Mantras for the first time. All together Five Mantras from five faces of Shiva. After that, both Vishnu and Brahma started repeating those Mantras.

Shiva's Advice to Vishnu and Brahma:

After meditating and repeating the Mantras by Vishnu, it thrilled Shiva. Then he gave a lesson of Veda to Brahma Dev. and Vishnu. The Vishnu asked Shiva what makes him happy? Then Shiva replied to Vishnu that he very impressed him and shouldn't worry about anything. He should make a Shiva Linga from earth material and worship that. By worshipping the Linga it will destroy all your sadness, and it applies to anyone who worships Shiva Linga regularly. Shiva also told Vishnu that the person who will come out of him will call Rudra and there is no difference between Shiva and Rudra. Shiva told Brahma Dev. that he is the creator of the World and Vishnu will be the Controller of the world. So Mata Sarswoti who is also part of the nature will be the wife of Brahma Dev. and other part of the nature Mata Laxmi will be the wife of Vishnu. And I am with Uma, the other part of the nature.

Age of Brahma, Vishnu, and Rudra:

Shiva told Vishnu that they would worship him in all three Lok. He also said that the world Brahma will create which will always have Vishnu as a source of getting rid of one's problems. Shiva also told Vishnu that he will appear in the world many times to kill the demons and help the saints. He told Brahma Dev. that to help Vishnu when he needs help. Also Shiva told Vishnu if you ever need help just do the Kirtan of Rudra and I shall take away all your problems. Now let me tell you the age of all three elements of us.

One day comprises sunrise to sunset, thirty days of that would be a month. Similarly, twelve months would be one year. One hundred years will be one day for Brahma and one year of Brahma would be one day of Vishnu, and one year of Vishnu would be one day of Shiva. Then Shiva blessed Vishnu and left. Since that day the worshipping of the Shiva Linga begins.

Worshipping Shiva:

Brahma Dev. said to Naradh Jee that he will tell the method of worshipping Shiva Linga in a brief manner because if he tells it will take more than a few hundred years. Every day, everyone should worship Shiva. First thing one should do as soon as one wakes up is worship Guru and then worship Shiva after that one should worship Vishnu and they should follow this process every day. After that, one should finish all the bathroom needs.

While bathing at a holy place, one should follow the instruction on Veda. First one should worship Ganesh and then only worship Shiva. Then establish Shiva in front and call Shiva. After that, one can start worshipping Shiva.

One should meditate about the traditional-looking Shiva. After that, one should start spelling Om Nama Shivaya Mantra and pour water on Shiva Linga. After that one should put paste of Sandalwood to the Shiva Linga, followed by Mantras from Veda and flowers and other sweets and fruits. After that start spelling Mantras from Veda and give your highest respect by joining your two hands. One also needs to bow his head to the Shiva Linga and give respect.

Advice to Gods:

Brahma Dev. told Naradh Jee that once all the gods including Brahma Dev. worshipped Vishnu and asked him whom should they worship to take away their problems? Then Vishnu told them I had told you before too, but let me tell you again it is Shiva to whom you or anyone should worship to get rid of problems and unhappiness. People who want happiness should always worship Shiva regularly. Whether the human being, god, or demons all needs worship Shiva if they want their wishes to come true. Also, people who worship Shiva regularly will also achieve liberation after death.

After hearing all this advice from Vishnu Brahma, Dev. and other gods worshipped Shiva. So Vishokarma made different Shiva Linga and gave to all the gods and goddesses to worship. After that, Brahma Dev. told everybody the method of worshipping the Shiva Linga and also that one should continue to worship Shiva Linga throughout one's life.

Method to Worship Shiva:

Brahma Dev. said now let me tell you the best method of worshipping the Shiva please listen carefully. When it two hours left before the Sunrise get up and worship Shiva along with Mata Parvati. One should meditate imaging both the Shiva and Shakti. One should worship with the feeling that Oh Shiva you are the one who lives in the heart of all human beings please wake up and show me the way towards truth. Please lead my life towards that ultimate truth. One should have such a feeling while meditating or worshiping Shiva. Also, one should think and thank his guru after worshipping Shiva. Then one should take a shower and finish other work in the bathroom. Then offer some water to our ancestors while thanking them. Then wear clean clothes. Then start worshipping Shiva to fulfill all your wishes. One should also Worship Ganesh before worshipping any other gods or goddesses. Then while worshipping Shiva, one should also worship Mata Parvati. Then take a flower and feel that they would be happy with your worship so than after that offer flower to the Shiva and Mata Parvati.

Offering Different Flowers to Worship Shiva:

Brahma Dev. said it should offer flowers like Lotus to Shiva while worshipping if one needs to earn wealth. So twenty Lotus flower is equal to one (pathi), one thousand Bel leaves would be half (Pathi). One should also offer rice, incense, sandalwood, etc. to Shiva Linga. If one wants to be free of diseases should offer fifty lotus flowers, to get a beautiful girl one should offer twenty-five thousand lotus flowers should offer. To achieve education, one should offer Ghee. One should also spell the Mantra Om Nama Shivaya while offering flowers and other things. One should offer many flowers to Shiva except Ketaki and Champa flowers.

Establishment of World:

Brahma Dev. said to Naradh Jee that after Shiva left Brahma dev. meditated Shiva and start creating the world. First thing I created was water. After that I created birds and animals, after that I created gods and goddesses. Then with the advice from Shiva I created Human beings. After creating five different creations, I created nature.

Creation of World:

Brahma Dev. said after creating the world with humans I created sky, air, fire, water, Himalayas, Oceans, trees and etc. After that I created different Sages from different parts of my body, including Naradh Jee.

After that they separated in two parts, one half became male and the other half became female. So it went on and they married to each other and start having children. Then Sati was born, then later on Sati becomes Uma of Shiva. So Sati gave her life in the holy fire ritual performed by her father. Later she was reborn as Mata Parvati, and with hard meditation and worship she remarried Shiva. So with the help from Shiva I created the world Brahma Dev. told Naradh Jee.

Shiva's Kailas:

Shoot Jee says that Brahma asked about when Shiva did went to Kailas and how he became a friend with Kuber? Then Brahma said there was a town where Yegyadutt named Brahman used to live with his wife and eight-year-old son named Gunniti. Gunniti had bad habits of gambling and other things. One day he stole his father's ring and lost it while gambling. His father finds out about all the bad habits Gunniti, then he disowns his wife and Gunniti. After that, Gunniti leaves his home and goes away. He ends up in Shiva Temple where he regrets his bad habits that hurt and separated his parents. He was starving and had eaten nothing all day. So he steals all the sweets offered to Shiva on Shivaratri day from the temple. Later on everyone finds out that Gunniti stole sweets offered to Shiva, so they beat him to death. Since he died at the Shiva Temple while consuming eatables offered to Shiva, he went to Shiva Lok after death instead of hell.

Brahma Dev. said when I got establish I had a human son, named Polsatya after that he had a son name Baishrowa who ruled in Alkapuri with the blessing from Shiva. Gunniti was his son. So Shiva made Gunniti the Kuber, a Lord of wealth. He established Kuber in Alkapuri and Shiva stayed in Kailas near the Alkapuri.

Om Nama Shivaya

Rudra Sanhita Sati Khanda:

Third Section.

Defining Sati:

Naradh Jee asks Brahma Dev. how a superior Shiva got engaged with Sati. Then Brahma Dev. said once I had a daughter who was so beautiful even I had a feeling. So seeing these Shiva told me to meditate and get rid of feelings like that. Then I wanted to involve Shiva in Maya. So I had my son Dakshya, who then had a daughter named Sati. It was the same Sati who became and meditates for years to have Shiva as a husband. So after the very hard meditation and worship, Sati marries Shiva.

Because of Maya of Shiva Daksh, the father of Mata Sati started having pride over Shiva. So he started talking bad mouth about Shiva and organized a Maha Yegya (a holy fire ritual), where he invited everyone except Shiva and Mata Sati. Even without getting the invitation, Mata Sati goes to her father's house to observe the Yegya (holy fire ritual); there she hears bad words about Shiva from her father Daksh. She also saw nothing offered to Shiva in that Yegya, so she takes her life right there. Hearing this news Shiva became furious and took out the hair from the head and Bir Bhadra was born from the hair of Shiva. So Shiva orders Bir Bhadra to go kill Daksh and destroy the Yegya that he was performing. So Bir Bhadra kills Daksh and destroys everything at the Yegya. By doing so, it created chaos all around the World. So everybody started Worshipping Shiva, and that made Shiva happy again. As a result, he made Daksh alive again and Sati's body got crashed in the Himalayas as a Volcano. Later on, Sati was reborn again as a Daughter of Himalaya, this time named Parvati. So again with hard meditation and worshipping she marries Shiva.

Defining Shiva Parvati:

Shiva became more powerful after wedding with Mata Parvati as she is also a form of Shakti (Energy). From left side of Shiva's body Vishnu was born and Brahma was born from left side of Shiva. From the Brahma, Vishnu and Mahesh have three figures. Brahma Dev. created Gods, Demons, and Human beings. I also created women. I also created some great saints, said Brahma Dev. After creating all of them, I felt the Maya of Love for them. Then a good-looking man who also smells good came in front of Brahma Dev. and asked for his order. Seeing him, I asked him to manage the world of Education and wealth. So I named him Pushabaar. I asked him to manage wellbeing and happiness of all human beings said Brahma Dev. So all my sons who are great saints will assist you saying this Brahma went away.

Brahma Kaam Sanbad:

Brahma Dev. said that other saints named him Manmath (God f Love) because he established love in the heart of Brahma Dev. when he first saw him. It was his second name. Then Brahma Dev. told him that Dakshaprapati will offer a girl for you to wed. Her name will be Sandhya. The Kaam established five cycles, which are Thrill, Charm, Fascination, Withering, and Killing. Also, Kaam's wife Sandhya was so beautiful that anyone can easily fall in to her even Kaam. Kaam who can control anyone with his five cycles. Then Kaam put even Brahma Dev. under his five cycles. Then Shiva told Brahma Dev. that how cans Kaam control him, he is superior then these five cycles of Kaam. Then I along with Dakshya all started sweating, then from the sweat a beautiful girl was born. She could charm the whole Universe so she named Rati (love, Delight). Since Kaam was giving us a problem, then I spelled Curse on Kaam that one day Shiva will destroy you, said Brahma Dev. After I spelled a curse on Kaam, he apologized to me and I told him that one day you will be destroyed by Shiva and by his grace you will be born again. After saying that, Brahma Dev. Disappear from there.

Kaam Rati Wedding:

Then after everyone left then Daksh asked Kaam whether he will marry his daughter Rati? So Kaam gets married to Rati and thrilled after the wedding. Even Daksh the father of Rati was very pleased to see Kaam and Rati together. Kaam forgot all about the curse Brahma Dev. spelled on him. It thrilled Kaam to have Sandhya as his wife and so was Sandhya thrilled to have Kaam as a husband.

Sandhya's Meditation:

Then after seeing desire from her own brothers and others, Sandhya did meditate and wash her sins. Then she went to the Chandra Himalaya and meditated. Then Brahma sends one of his son Vasistha to teach Sandhya how to properly meditate. Then Vasistha told Sandhya that she should pronounce the Mantra of Shiva to get rid of all her problems. He told her to pronounce Om Nama Shankara ya Om. Vasistha told Sandhya to keep repeating this Mantra and worship Shiva that will take away all your problems. This is how great Saint Vasistha teaches Sandhya the right way to meditate.

Shiva's Blessing to Sandhya:

After Vasistha Jee left, Sandhya meditated according to the way he taught her. She constantly meditates for Shiva with the Mantra mentioned by Vasistha Jee for years. Then Shiva came in front of her from the sky. Then Shiva asked Sandhya for her wish. So Sandhya said I want my first wish as a human being should not be lustful as soon as they are born, and second wish is that I want to be popular as the husband, caring and loving.

So Shiva agrees to fulfill Sandhya's wish and Shiva told her that from now on I will divide human beings into four categories childhood, youth, manhood, and old age. So human being can only be lustful on manhood stage only. Also, you will be known as virtuous women in this world said Shiva to Sandhya. He also said that her husband would be very lucky and wouldn't die for seven lives.

Describing Sandhya:

Brahma Dev. said after that Sandhya went to Megha Tithi Yegya (holy fire ritual). There by the blessing of Shiva no one saw her, and she jumps to the holy fire. Nobody saw her jump on the holy fire. So her body got destroyed by the holy fire. So fire took her body to Sun and so upper part of the body became morning time and lower part became evening time of the day. When the holy ritual (Megha Yegya) finished, the saints found a beautiful baby girl on the ashes of the holy fire. So saint took her and named her Arundhati. They took Arundhati to their ashram and start raising her there.

When Arundhati was five years old all the three s Brahma, Vishnu and Shiva came to the ashram and wed Arundhati with saint Vasistha. So Vasistha had a son with Arundhati named Satapadik.

Kaam Dev. Receives Blessing from Brahma Dev:

Brahma Dev. said I was lust after seeing Sandhya and it is because of the Maya of Shiva. So Shiva made fun of me, and I felt I should find women who can make Shiva feel lust. So I was thinking about that if I will ever find such a woman in the entire Universe. I was discussing the same subject with other saints and right then Kaam with his wife Rati arrived there. Then after raising their married life I asked them to give birth to a girl which can make Shiva feel lust. So Brahma Dev. asked Kaam and Rati to give birth a daughter who can make Shiva feel lust by her beauty. After that, Kaam said I will make Shiva feel lust, but you have to produce the women for me. After trying many time to make Shiva feel lust was unsuccessful and Kaam said to Brahma Dev. that it was not possible to make Shiva feel lust so he better try it himself.

Brahma Dev. and Vishnu's Discussion:

Brahma Dev. said to Naradh Jee after Kaam Dev. gave up trying to make Shiva feel lust. Then my entire dream became scatter. Then I thought of different ways to make Shiva feel lust, and then I thought of Vishnu.

As soon as I thought of him, Vishnu came in front of me. Then I started praising Vishnu, and after that he asked me why did I think of him? Then I said I had tried to make Shiva feel lust with the help of Kaam Dev., but I was unsuccessful. Then Vishnu asked me why did I think of making Shiva feel lust, what is the real reason behind this? Then I told the entire story to Vishnu how he felt lust for Sandhya and how he wants to see Shiva also feel lust for someone. So I want to see Shiva get engaged in a domestic affair.

Then Vishnu told Brahma Dev. that he cannot make Shiva feel lust so he better give up this idea and asks him to meditate of Goddess Bhagwati to fulfill his wish. So Vishnu tells Brahma Dev. that he should ask one of his sons Dakshya to meditate of Goddess Bhagwati and please her. So she would take birth as his daughter, and Shiva will wed Goddess one day. After saying all this, Vishnu vanishes from there.

Legend of Goddess Jagdamba:

Brahma Dev. said after that I was in deep meditation of goddess Durga. So I started praying to goddess Durga that she fulfills my wish that Shiva will be married. I continued to meditate and pray to goddess Durga, so goddess Durga came in front of the Brahma Dev. Goddess Durga was beautiful and bright as Sun. Then I praised the goddess Durga in different ways. After that Goddesses Durga is pleased with Brahma Dev. and asked him, why was he praising and worshipping her so much? Then Brahma Dev. said Goddesses Durga you are the only one who can manage Shiva as a wife and I would like to see you born as Daksha's daughter and marry Shiva that is my wish. This is the reason I worshipped and praised you. I was ashamed by Shiva when I had a feeling of lust when I first saw Sandhya, so now I like to see Shiva also engaged in married life with you. There is no one in this Universe which can make Shiva feel attracted towards beside your Brahma Dev. told Goddess Durga. Then Goddess Durga told Brahma Dev.

that it will not occur till Shiva himself wants these to happen because Shiva himself is the of all Maya in this World. So goddess Durga told Brahma Dev. that she will have to get a positive response from Shiva for this to happen. After that goddess Durga accepted Brahma Dev.'s request and agree to born as Daksha's daughter and marry Shiva. After granting the wish to Brahma Dev., goddess Durga vanishes from there.

Worship of Goddess Durga by Dakshya:

Brahma Dev. said that Dakshya meditate of Goddess Durga for three thousand years. Then Goddess Durga appeared in front of Dakshya. Goddess Durga already knew about the wish of Dakshya, even though she asked Dakshya what is his wish for meditating for so long. Then Dakshya said that that Goddess Durga should bear and marry Shiva, so that Shiva will also get engaged in a domestic affair like other gods.

After hearing the wish of Dakshya Goddess Durga told Dakshya that she will bear as his daughter and with hard meditation and worship, she will marry Shiva. After blessing Dakshya Goddess Durga vanished from there.

Conversation between Brahma Dev. and Naradh Jee:

Brahma Dev. said to Naradh Jee that after that Dakshya tries to start the creation of the world. Dakshya tried many ways to create a world but he couldn't successes at first so he went to Brahma Dev. for advice. Then Brahma Dev. told him a way to create the world. Then Dakshya marries Virani and he started accepting Maithun (copulation) religion. So with Virani he produced ten thousand sons. Dakshya asked his sons to go start the creation of the world. But with the advice of Naradh Jee instead of creation of the world, they started meditating and gave their life to meditate. Then Dakshya again produced hundred thousand sons. They also gave their life for meditation instead of creation of the world because of Naradh Jee, so Dakshya curses Naradh Jee that he cannot stay in one place for too long. So Naradh Jee also accepts the curse spelled to him.

Brahma Dev. said the Dakshya had sixty daughters from his wife, and they got married to different personalities respectfully. Then Dakshya again meditation of Goddess Durga and this time she came in as a child. Then Dakshya named the child Uma. Dakshya and his wife started taking care of Uma.

Sati's Meditation:

Brahma Dev. said when Sati (Uma) grew up then they worried her father Dakshya that whom he wed Sati with. Sati told her mother that she wants to marry Shiva and after getting permission from her, Sati started worshipping Shiva at home. Sati worshipped Shiva, especially in the month of Asoj (September). For one year she worshipped Shiva continuously, and all the gods and goddesses also went to witness how Sati will please Shiva. After seeing how sincerely she worshipped Shiva, then Brahma Dev. along with Vishnu went to Shiva. So they started praising Shiva, after seeing this Shiva was very pleased with Vishnu and Brahma Dev. he asked them what they want from him. So Brahma Dev. and Vishnu told Shiva that for the better good of all gods, goddesses, and humans Shiva should marry someone and settle down. Then Shiva told Brahma Dev. and Vishnu that he is unaffected by female character and meditation is the only thing he wants to do so there is no need for me to get married, said Shiva.

After requesting again and again to Shiva BY Brahma Dev. and Vishnu, then Shiva told them that first they have to give her the knowledge, and she has to gain the energy on her own to handle the different energy of Shiva. Then Brahma Dev. told Shiva that Uma knows other than Goddess Durga and I now know she is now as Uma (Sati) the daughter of Dakshya. Sati is also doing hard meditation to have Shiva as a husband, Brahma dev. told Shiva. At the end, Shiva agrees to marry Sati on their requests.

Uma Gets Groom:

Brahma Dev. said the Sati started fasting for Shiva. Then Shiva is pleased with Sati, and he appeared in front of her. Shiva told Sati that he was very pleased with her and asked her wish so he could bless her. Then Sati told Shiva that he should bless whatever he feels like. So Shiva told Sati to marry him. After hearing that, Sati told Shiva that he should wed her with her father's permission and also follow all the wedding processes. Then Shiva blessed Sati and vanished from there. So Sati let her parents and others know about how Shiva became pleased with her, ready to marry her. Hearing this Sati's father, Dakshya was very pleased along with his wife. So it thrilled everyone to hear the news that Shiva would marry Sati.

Shiva Sati Wedding:

Brahma Dev. told Naradh Jee that when Brahma Dev. arrived at Kailas, then Shiva questioned the proposal that Sati kept forward. Then Brahma Dev. said that his son Dakshya it delights Dakshya to give Sati to Shiva, and everyone is happy about it. Then Shiva goes to Daksha's house to wed Sati on one auspicious Sunday with all the gods' goddesses and animals.

So Dakshya also with all the process worshiped Shiva and others and performed the holy ritual ceremony to wed Shiva with his daughter Sati. So the wedding took place and from animals to gods everyone was happy that Shiva married Sati.

Shiva Being Angry With Brahma Dev:

After the wedding Vishnu went to Shiva and said hey, you are the father of the Universe and Sati Devi is the mother of the Universe, so now you two have to do well for the world.

Then everyone deceived by the love Maya of Shiva and Devi Sati. When Brahma Dev. saw Devi Sati, then he felt lust. So when Shiva found out about it he was very mad and wanted to kill Brahma Dev., So with the Trishul (Weapon) Shiva almost kills Brahma Dev. and right then Vishnu praises Shiva and tells him how all three of them Shiva, Vishnu and Brahma are same and there is no difference between them. After trying for quite some time, Vishnu could make Shiva happy again and forgive Brahma Dev.

Defining Variety of Brahma Dev:

Brahma Dev. told Naradh Jee that when Shiva forgave him and not kill him, then all the other gods and goddess were so happy that they started praising Shiva. So Brahma Dev. also started praising Shiva along with other gods and goddess. Shiva became happy with the praise by gods and goddess and in the meantime Shiva put his hands on head of Brahma Dev. and he felt so embarrassed he asked for forgiveness from Shiva. Then Shiva told Brahma Dev. to meditate, and that's how he is forgiven and also shines.

After all these, then Shiva and Sati Devi went to Kailas. There Sati Devi asked Nandi and other followers of Shiva to stay far from Kailas. So after that Shiva and Sati Devi started pleasing each other. So twenty-five years gone by and it thrilled Brahma Dev. that now Shiva also got engaged in domestic affairs.

Shiva and Sati's Footmark in the Himalayas:

Brahma Dev. said one day when it was raining on monsoon season Sati Devi Said to Shiva hey since monsoon had started now you can live wherever you feel like in Kailas, Himalaya, and Kashi. After hearing that from Sati Devi Shiva said to her that monsoon won't reach them in Kailas or any other place as long as they are together. So Shiva told Sati Devi tells me know which Himal you want to go? Giri Raj Himal is the best since there is peace and lots of Yogis come there to meditate also on the caves, daughters of gods hide out. Then Sati Devi told Shiva I want to live in the place where there is no one and peaceful. So Shiva took Sati Devi to the Himalayas and where they lived happily for ten thousand years pleasing each other.

Defining Art of Moksha (Liberation):

Brahma Dev. said once Shiva was in a very pleasant mood, then Sati Devi asked him what is that which will liberate anyone from this world. Then Shiva told Sati Devi that science is the element along with Brahma Dev.'s meditation. Devotion is the mother of science. People are against devotion can never achieve science. Shiva told Sati Devi that he himself is under the rule of devotion. So there are two types of devotion, good devotion and bad devotion.

In all four Yug (Ages) devotion has a special achievement. Especially in Kali Yug devotion is quite fruitfulness. So people who does good devotion towards me I am under their control, Shiva told Sati Devi.

Sati's Doubt:

One day Shiva along with Sati Devi went to Dandakaranaya Jungle. There Shiva showed Sati Devi a place from where Rawan took Sita. There Ram and Laxman were wondering around looking for Sita. Then Shiva appeared in front of Ram and gave his full respect to Ram. Then Sati was in surprise why Shiva being the Lord of the Lords had to respect so much to an ordinary person like Ram. Then Sati Devi asked Shiva why did he gave his respect to Ram and please explain me so it will clear my doubt.

After hearing the question from Sati Devi, Shiva explained that Ram is actually Vishnu. And he came to earth as a human being to protect the saints and devotees from demons and cruel kings. After that, Sati Devi still didn't believe that Ram was actually Vishnu. So Shiva told Sati Devi to take the test of Ram to find out if he is Vishnu?

Then Sati Devi incarnates as Sita and goes in front of Ram and after seeing these Ram asked Sati Devi where is Shiva? And why she is roaming in the jungle in Sita's appearance. After that, Sati Devi felt kind of shameful. Then Sati Devi appeared in her own form and asked Ram why did Shiva respects him so much.

Sati and Shiva Division:

Sri Ram said once upon a time Shiva asked Vishokarma to build a beautiful palace in Shiva Lok. Shiva asked to make a beautiful cow-stall. Shiva had also invited Brahma Dev., Indra, and other Gods and Goddesses along with angels. Then he asked Vishnu to take the responsibility of running the World smoothly as he is the caregiver of the world and everyone in it. Shiva himself put Vishnu on the throne and declared him as a caretaker of the World.

After that Shiva went to Kailas So Vishnu told Sati Devi that he has taken birth as human as Ram and he has come to the jungle with his wife Sita and brother Laxman. Also, the demon took Sita away from Ram. So Ram told Sati Devi that he and his brother are looking for Sita desperately in the jungle. He told Sati Devi the entire story and went back to the jungle looking for Sita. Then Sati Devi knew that Vishnu was the closest devotee of Shiva. Sati Devi also fell guilty that she tested Ram's intention.

After that Sati Devi came to Shiva, and she was looking a little nervous. So then Shiva asked Sati Devi if she had tested the intension of Ram. Then Sati Devi lied and replied that she did not test the intention of Ram. So Shiva already knew everything, so he just felt divided inside his heart with Sati Devi after she lied to him. But he didn't mention any of that to Sati Devi. So they went back to Kailas, and Shiva went to perform meditation for years after that. When he came out of the meditation, Sati Devi was right there waiting for him. So after that Shiva told good stories to Sati Devi and after telling true stories for while Sati Devi became pure from inside. So after that Sati Devi also felt happy like before.

Dakshya against Shiva:

Brahma Dev. said once upon a time yogis gathered in PRAYAG organized an enormous YEGYA holy fire ritual. All gods and goddesses along with great saints were present there. Shiva along with Sati Devi also arrived at the YEGYA, so everyone there gave their respect to Shiva and Sati Devi. In the meantime Dakshya the father of Sati Devi also arrived at the same YEGYA, so everyone also gave their respect to Dakshya, but Shiva ignored him. So that made Dakshya angry, and he started saying whatever he feels like about Shiva he also cursed Shiva. That made Nandiswor (bull ride of Shiva) angry, and he cursed back at Dakshya and the Brahmins that they will not understand the real meaning of Veda and will always fight among one another for it. After that Shiva made everyone quiet and so after that everyone including Shiva and Sati Devi went to their respected homes.

Daksha's Yegya:

Brahma Dev. said to Naradh Jee and others that Dakshya organized a Yegya (holy fire ritual) to show his anger towards Shiva. He organized the Yegya (holy fire ritual) at a place called Kankhal. Dakshya invited all the great saints, Snakes, and all the wise creatures to the Yegya (holy fire ritual) including Brahma Dev. and Vishnu Dev. But he intentionally didn't invite Shiva and Sati Devi. So everyone who came to the Yegya (holy fire ritual) took their respected seats. So Saint Dadhichi and others asked Dakshya, where is Shiva? After hearing the question Dakshya said that Vishnu is there, and he did not need Shiva to be present there. After that, Dakshya said to make his Yegya (holy fire ritual) successful to all the saints present there. So Saint Dadhichi said that his Yegya (holy fire ritual) will not be successful without the present of Shiva, and it will destroy all of them for their act to perform Yegya (holy fire ritual) without inviting Shiva. After saying that Saint Dadhichi and other Shiva devotees left the Yegya (holy fire ritual) and went to their respected ashram.

After seeing Saints and other devotes of Shiva leaving the Yegya (holy fire ritual) Dakshya made fun of them and started the Yegya (holy fire ritual).

Sati Devi Goes to the Daksha's Yegya:

After that, Sati Devi goes to the Daksha's Yegya with sixty thousand devotees. After seeing Sati Devi, her mother and sisters were excited, and they welcome her. But her father and his devotees didn't care for Sati Devi. So Sati Devi felt down after her father Dakshya said nothing to welcome her at the Yegya. So Sati Devi sees Vishnu and Brahma Dev. and she was angry that Shiva wasn't invited. So Sati Devi asked her father why he did not invite Shiva at the Yegya. How can you perform Yegya without Shiva being present? So after hearing all these from Sati Devi, Dakshya said I intentionally didn't invite you and your husband. But you came to my Yegya even without the invitation. Dakshya also insulted Shiva in front of Sati Devi.

After hearing insulted words from Dakshya about Shiva, Sati Devi became furious and said people who listen and insults Shiva will definitely go to hell. So Sati Devi with the help of Yog energy she destroys her body completely and dies at the Daksha's Yegya.

Sati Devi Sacrifice Herself at Daksha's Yegya:

When Sati Devi stayed quiet with both eyes closed, thinking about Shiva through Yog energy, she destroys her body. After Sati Devi sacrificed her life, then everyone at the Daksha's Yegya started panicking. On the other side, all the devotees of Shiva took the weapon and stayed in a line. Those who devotion started making trouble everywhere. Among the sixty thousand devotion of Sati Devi, twenty thousand gave their life in sorrow after hearing that Sati Devi sacrificed herself. Then the devotees of Shiva started making trouble for everyone there. Then one of the saint Vhrigulay produced demon name Ritu from the Yegya. Then Ritu fought with devotees of Shiva, and he almost defeated them.

In the meantime there was a voice heard from the sky saying foolish Dakshya what have you done? You insulted your own daughter and Shiva; you didn't invite and worshiped Shiva and Sati Devi instead you made fun of them. Shiva is the one who should have been invited at the Yegya, and by even seeing the physical body of Shiva the whole purpose of the Yegya would have been successful. So by not inviting Shiva to the Yegya the Yegya was unsuccessful, so without worshipping Shiva anything good will happen to you Dakshya, the voice said.

Creation of Bir Bhadra and Mahakali:

After hearing the voice from the sky, all the gods and saints became silence and surprised. No one spoke even a word. The devotees of Shiva went to tell everything to Shiva. After hearing all the stories from the devotees, Shiva became furious. So Shiva pulled one hair from his head and threw it on the rocks of Himalaya and it broke in to two pieces. From the first piece of broken hair Bir Bhadra got established and from the second piece Mahakali got established.

Then Bir Bhadra regarding Shiva asked him, what shall he do? With your permission I can finish the water in the ocean or I can destroy all mountains, also I can destroy the whole Universe or I can also disappear all the gods and saints. So whatever you suggest I will accomplish it said Bir Bhadra to Shiva.

Then Shiva blessed Bir Bhadra and said that Brahmadev's son Dakshya is performing a Yegya, so you will have to go there and destroy the Yegya. Also kill everyone is at the Yegya and don't leave Dakshya.

After that, Bir Bhadra took permission from Shiva and left to destroy the Yegya of Dakshya. Shiva also sends his devotees who were as strong as Bir Bhadra along with weapons of destruction. Bir Bhadra took a ride in a chariot that was one hundred feet long, with hundreds of lions pulling it and thousands of elephants protecting it.

Also Kali, Katyani, Ishani, Chamunda, Mundamardini, Bhadrakali, Bhadra, Bali, and Baisnuvi all nine goddesses that represent Maha Bhagavati also went along with Virbhadra to kill Dakshya. Virbhadra and Maha Kali's warrior were uncountable. So they slowly started moving with making different sounds from different things which represents good luck.

When Virbhadra started his trip, then all the bad luck signs started appearing at Daksha's Yegya. Daksha's left eye, arm, and leg vibrated. Also Earth started wavering, directions points started meeting, black spots spotted on Sun, stars started falling down, and eagles crowded the Yegya place, and also started making loud noises. Then it appeared dark everywhere. Also Vishnu and other gods feared the situation. In the meantime voice again came from the sky that hey Dakshya you are a great sinner and fool and now you have to suffer for what you have done. Because of you all these gods you have invited will also feel sad or unhappiness.

After that, Dakshya was sacred and went towards Vishnu and started worshipping him.

Vishnu's Advice to Dakshya:

Dakshya said hey Vishnu I am terrified please protect me. You are the supreme of this Yegya, so please protect my Yegya from being destructed said Dakshya to Vishnu. After hearing the request from Dakshya, Vishnu told Dakshya that how could he forget Shiva? It results from his action in another word Karma. When you insult Holy personalities, then you will face difficulties in every step. So its better that you worship Shiva with a pleasant attitude, Vishnu told Dakshya. Because of your doing my affects are not being useful, said Vishnu to Dakshya. After hearing that, Dakshya felt dry in his mouth and throat and he just sat down on the floor.

In the meantime, Bir Bhadra arrived there with his warriors. So they covered the whole area of the Yegya and earth started shaking ocean started flowing in all directions. After seeing that scene, Dakshya started vomiting blood from his mouth. Then he again went towards Vishnu asking for protection. Then Vishnu told Dakshya that Bir Bhadra is the devotee of Shiva and he will destroy and kill any Shiva's enemy, so no one can stop him. Along with you, he will also kill me because I came to your Yegya without consulting with Shiva. So I am also scared of Virbhadra, said Vishnu to Dakshya.

Then Bir Bhadra attacked the Yegya and Indra and other gods fought with Virbhadra, but Indra and other gods couldn't do much against Bir Bhadra. Then for the sake of Dakshya Saint Vrighu defeated some ghost warriors of Bir Bhadra. That made Bir Bhadra and Mahakali furious, so Bir Bhadra defeated all the gods and saints present at the Yegya. After that Vishnu stepped in and starts fighting with Bir Bhadra.

Virbhadra Cuts Daksha's Head:

Bir Bhadra thinking about Shiva attacks Vishnu with the Trishul on his chest. After which Vishnu feels unconsciousness and falls on Earth. Again Vishnu attacks Bir Bhadra with his Sudarshan Chakra, but Bir Bhadra stalls the chakra on Vishnu's hand. Then Vishnu couldn't move or do anything. So the Saints with magic formulas from the Veda unfreeze Vishnu. After that Vishnu picks up his Shankar Dhanush (Shiva's Bow) that also Bir Bhadra breaks it in two three pieces. After that Vishnu disappeared and went to his Lok (Place). So after Vishnu left, Bir Bhadra grabbed Yegya's God and destroyed him. He also destroyed and killed so many other gods and saints. After that he found Dakshya hiding inside the Veda, so he grabbed Dakshya and separated his head from his body. After destroying everything at the Yegya, Bir Bhadra went to Kailas to meet Shiva, and he told Shiva everything. So after hearing Bir Bhadra Shiva was happy and made him the head devotee among the other devotees of Shiva.

Brahmadev's Character:

Brahmdev said after Bir Bhadra destroyed the whole Yegya (holy fire ritual) all the gods came to me and told me the entire story on how the Yegya got destroyed by Bir Bhadra. Then after hearing their stories Brahmdev said I had a feeling that how can I help all these gods, also how to make Dakshya alive again and how to complete the Yegya. So doing all the things I had a feeling about, I went to Vishnu Lok to meet Vishnu. So I started worshipping Vishnu at Vishnu Lok. So Vishnu was happy with the worshipping, and he said that Dakshya has done a great sin by not o0ffering any portion to Shiva while conducting the Yegya. So we all gods also have committed a sin by taking part in that Yegya, said Vishnu. So all of you need to go to Shiva and apologize for what we all have done, otherwise it will destroy the whole Universe. After hearing Vishnu we all went towards Kailas along with Vishnu to apologize to Shiva for what we did said Brahmdev. When we reached Kailas we saw Shiva meditating under a huge Bel tree. So we respected Shiva and start praising Shiva with his different names, said Brahmdev. We started apologizing to Shiva for what we did and request Shiva to let the Daksha's Yegya be complete so that we would dedicate a portion to Shiva. Requested by Vishnu, Brahmdev and other gods to Shiva.

Shiva Let Dakshya Be Alive Again:

Brahmdev said hey Naradh after all the gods praised Shiva then Shiva said I am sad by your action but I am happy by your praise. Daksha's Yegya (holy fire ritual) is not destructed by me but because of his own bad karma. People who wishes ill for others will have to bear the kill himself. So now Dakshya will be alive again, but with the head of a goat. After that Shiva let Dakshya be alive again with the goat's head, and as soon as he was alive he started praising and singing holy songs to Shiva. By this also Brahmdev along with Vishnu started praising Shiva. After that Dakshya finished the Yegya with other gods and goddess. After they finish the Yegya everyone wished well to Shiva and went to their respected homes. Shiva along with his devotees went to Kailas.

Om Nama Shivaya

Rudra Sanhita Parvati Khanda:

Chaturtha Khanda

Fourth section.

Himalayas Wedding:

After the Sati Devi gave up life on the Yegya fire, then she took birth again at Himalaya's home because Mainka wife of the Himalaya had worshipped Sati Devi with great devotion.

Then Naradh Jee asked Brahmdev to tell more about Mainka, about her birth and about her wedding with the Himalaya. Then Brahmdev said in the North direction there was a king named Himalaya. Who was a very talented and successful King? I knew him as Sailraj Himalaya as a very popular king. So to the extent his family he got married. So he sends his people to the father of Mainka Pritigarn to offer his daughter to the king Himalaya, they also said by doing so it will benefit all the gods and goddess. After the hearing the request Pritigarn lets his daughter Mainka wed king Himalaya. So at the wedding Shiva Vishnu and Brahmdev with all the gods and goddess were present, and they all left for their respected homes after the wedding?

Previous Story:

Brahmdev said to Naradh Jee that his son Dakshya had sixty daughters among a daughter named Swadha to Priteshowr to marry her. Then Swadha gave birth to three daughters, among them eldest one was Mainka, Second eldest one was named Dhanya, and they named the youngest Kalawati. So Brahmdev said at one time all three sisters went to Swaitdeep to worship Vishnu. There was a big festival been organized over there and lots of Saints from different places had gathered there. At the same place a Saint Sanatkumar also arrived and everyone gathered at the function stood up and gave their respect to Saint Sanatkumar. But the three sisters didn't care to respect Saint Sanakadi and seeing that angered Sanatkumar. So he cursed the three sisters that they now have to sacrifice the Heaven and get birth as a human being on Earth. He told the three sisters that because of their ego they didn't respect him, and as a result he had to curse them. After that the three sisters begged him to take back the curse and showed their devotion and respect towards the Sanatkumar, but he couldn't take it back. But he explained them the real reason behind cursing them, he said the oldest one among you will marry to Himalaya and give birth to Parvati who later on will marry Shiva. The second oldest among you will be born as a daughter of King Janak who will be Goddess Laxmi as Sita. So the youngest one of you will marry Brishbhanu and give birth to daughter MahaMaya Radha.

After that Sanakadi said even though you all will be born on Earth you will still be able to get all the luxury of Heaven and after saying all that the Saint disappears and the three sisters also went to their home.

Praising Uma:

So after marrying Mainka, Himalaya took her to his home. After that they went to different places and enjoyed lots of luxuries in Life. Vishnu along with other gods came to Himalaya, and by seeing that Vishnu came to meet him that really made Himalaya thrilled and joyous. So Himalaya told Vishnu he is very fortunate that the Vishnu came to meet him and offer him the Hartley gratitude to wards Vishnu for the opportunity and asked him the reason for a visit. After that Vishnu said that you are aware about the sacrifice made by Jagdamba Sati Mata at Daksha's Yegya. So now you have to prepare yourself for giving birth to Mata Jagdamba as your daughter, so it will accomplish the wish of all gods and goddess after hearing that Himalaya said (THATASTU) sure.

After that all the gods and goddess praised Ma Jagdamba in different ways and after praising for some time Ma Durga appeared in front of all the gods and goddess and everyone was happy and delighted to see her. So everyone bow their head down and gave their respect to Ma Durga. Then everyone apologize to Ma Durga and praised her even more and said please make the Sanatkumar prediction right by taking birth in Earth and marrying Shiva as where she belongs happily and so everyone can enjoy Ma Durga magic on them for eternal happiness. After hearing many requests from all the gods, Ma Durga told them that she will again take birth in Earth as Himalaya and Mainka's daughter and will marry Shiva. The reason for birth is to unite with Shiva and also Himalaya and Mainka have been continuously worshipping and praising Ma Durga and also Shiva feels the absence of Ma Durga by his side so for all these reasons I will take birth again said Ma Durga. She also told them to now praise Shiva as he feels the emptiness of Ma Durga without her presence he hasn't rested or closed eyes. So after that everyone was happy and delighted to hear Ma Durga.

Himalaya's Devoted Meditation:

Brahmdev said after the gods told Himalaya and Mainka that Ma Durga will take birth as their daughter, they praised and meditate upon Ma Uma Devi for twenty-seven years and also did fasting and worshipping for Ma Uma Devi. So then Ma Durga Devi appeared in front of them and asks them for their wish and so they said they want one hundred sons and daughter as Uma Devi herself. After hearing the wish, Ma Durga granted them the wish and disappeared from there. After ten months Mainka the first son for them took birth in their home.

Mainka and Himalaya continuously keep meditating and worshipping Shiva and Ma Durga even after that. On an auspicious day Mainka became pregnant and after ten months Ma Sati Shiva took birth as their daughter.

Then Uma Devi took birth as a daughter of Mainka and cried as soon as she took birth, and by hearing her voice everyone was thrilled. Then her Nawran was conducted on the eleventh day of her birth, and her parents donated various luxurious items to the public on the day.

So Jagdamba which is Uma daughter of Himalaya and Mainka also started growing up like a regular human being by doing different things which kids does. So one day Naradh Ji visited the Himalayas Palace and after seeing Naradh Ji at their palace they took good care of Naradh Ji and asked about the future of Uma Devi. Then Naradh Ji said that this girl is very fortunate and her husband will be the one who was no father or mother and no other things can attract it.

So after hearing Naradh Ji parents of Uma Devi became a little sad, but then Naradh Ji said all the qualities that I described are present in Shiva so Uma Devi should worship Shiva to have him as her husband.

Parvati 'Dream:

Brahmdev said one day Mainka told her husband King Himalaya that Parvati has grown up and we should look for a suitable husband for her. After hearing his wife Mainka then King Himalaya told her that whatever Naradh Ji has said has always happened and so she should ask Parvati to worship Shiva to have him as her husband. So after hearing what Himalaya had to say, Mainka felt sad and tear up her eyes by thinking hard meditation that her daughter has to do to have Shiva as her husband?

After seeing her mother being very sad, Parvati told Mainka that last night on her dream she saw wise saint and he told her to meditate and worship Shiva to have him as her husband. So after hearing what Parvati had seen in her dream, Mainka explains everything to her husband Himalaya.

Shiva and Himalaya's Conversation:

Brahmdev said hey Naradh after some time Shiva along with Nandi and his other follower went to that place where Holly River Ganga was falling down from Brahmaloka. After reaching their Shiva meditated there and so he sits and get into deep meditation. After hearing that Shiva is meditating, their King Himalaya went to meet and greet Shiva. After reaching their King, Himalaya respected and worshiped Shiva. Then Shiva told King Himalaya that he came there to meditate and arrange for him, that no one comes to disturb Shiva there. Then King Himalaya said to Shiva that hey please don't worry I will arrange everything here so that no one will come to disturb you. So he arranged everything accordingly and went back to his palace.

Brahmdev said hey Naradh after a few days King Himalaya went back to where Shiva was meditating this time he took Parvati and fruits and flowers along with him. After reaching their Himalaya gave his regards and respect to Shiva, then requested to Shiva to keep Parvati as his server to serve him while he is meditating in the Mountains.

After hearing what King Himalaya had to say, Shiva opened his eyes and saw Parvati and was impressed with her beauty and described her as beautiful as the moon. Shiva also told Himalaya that if she stays there, then because of her beauty he could not meditate with peace of mind, so Shiva asked Himalaya to take her away from there. After hearing Shiva's decision quite upset and surprised Shiva Himalaya.

Shiva and Parvati Conversation:

After hearing Shiva Parvati said hey whatever you have said to my father, I would answer them for him. So Parvati said hey the one who knows everything the decision you took to meditate is itself is power energy, and it is the same energy which is believed to be the karma of Nature. It is that energy in nature which is taking care of everything in the Universe. So you decide who this nature energy is and also who you yourself are. If there was no nature then how the body would worship the energy and how everything would perform.

After hearing what Parvati had to say, Shiva said Parvati Jee I have destroyed the nature through my meditation so I now represent an element. So then Parvati smiled said hey mind your language but if you have destroyed the nature, then how you are as it is and all the other functions of the World is still performing in a smooth manner. Is it that my Lord is not recognizing the nature. I am nature and you are the Purush (the original source of Universe). So it is because of me you are, and I am the nature, said Parvati. So after hearing Parvati, Shiva said if you think I am the of the Universe then you should desire to serve me therefore Himalaya let her come to visit me every day as I wish to mediate little more time said Shiva to King Himalaya.

So from that day Parvati visited Shiva every day and worshipped him and praise him. By seeing these entirely all the other gods and goddess went to Brahmdev to request him to find the solution for Shiva to accept Parvati and let something complete all their work of uniting them. So all the gods and goddess send KaamDev to Shiva to influence him to accept Parvati. But Shiva destroys KaamDev to ashes.

Birth of Bajranga and Blessing for Son:

Naradh Jee asked father who was Tarkasoor that was making gods fear him by troubling them. Also, why Shiva turn KaamDev in to ashes? Please describe us the reason for this play of Shiva.

Then Brahmdev said Naradh Marichi had a son named Kashyap, and he had married Daksha's daughter Diti. So had two sons from Diti named Hiranyakasipu and Hiranyayacha. Vishnu by a taking figure like Baraha and Narsingh killed both sons. Also Indra destroyed the fetus inside Diti by making in two pieces inside the womb. So the pieces inside the womb were forty-nine and as result forty nine sons were born. Which then later on turn into Marud Group, which went straight to heaven. So because of anger with Indra, Diti meditate for ten thousand years which pleased Kashyap to give birth to Bajranga. Bajranga won the kingdoms from gods by obeying his mother Diti as per her wish. Later on, Brahmdev and Kashyap Jee help release the gods from Bajranga. Also later on, Bajranga returned the heaven back to the gods as per the request of Brahmdev. So he became the follower of Brahmdev. Brahmdev also produce a beautiful female for Bajranga for him to wed her. So the wife of Bajranga asked Bajranga to have a son who can also defeat Vishnu. Then Bajranga worshipped and meditate Brahmdev to have a son who can also defeat Vishnu. Brahmdev being pleased with worship and meditation by Bajranga granted him the wish to have a son who can also defeat Vishnu. After granting the wish to Bajranga, Brahmdev went back to Brahma Lok.

Birth of Tarkasoor and His Meditation:

After some years Bajranga's wife became pregnant, and she gave birth to tall and wide body shaped boy. The day he was born everything in the World felt some kind of bad luck feeling was merging around. At the time of Nawran (Name selection day on the eleventh day of birth) Kashyap Jee named the boy Tarkasoor. After some years he grew up like mountains. Then he asked for permission from his mother to do meditation, and his mother granted him the permission to do so. Then Tarkasoor thought about defeating gods for that reason he performed hard and difficult mediation. At first he positioned both of his hands towards sky while stepping the grounds with only toes of the leg, he meditates in that position for one hundred years and another hundred years in upside down position. Because of the power of his hardship meditation gods were feeling scary and everything in heaven started shaking. So Brahmdev appeared in front of Tarkasoor and asked Tarkasoor for his wish to perform such a hardship meditation.

Then Tarkasoor asked Brahmdev to grant the wish that no creature created by Brahmdev in this World could defeat him and only son produced from Shiva 's energy can only destroy or kill him, after hearing the wish of Tarkasoor Brahmdev granted him the wish and went back to Brahma Lok.

After that Sukracharya the priest of demon took permission from Brahmdev to make Tarkasoor the king of demons and So Tarkasoor became the demons. After becoming the king of demons, Tarkasoor beat and defeat gods and used to make them his servants and who used to refuse to be his servants used to get hard punishments. Being scared with Tarkasoor, Indra gave all his valuable belongings to Tarkasoor and also Tarkasoor roamed around the World and collect all things valuable to him from others. One day he defeated the gods and took over the heaven by throwing Indra and other gods out heaven. He then kept all demons in the heaven and made heaven a place of hell.

Tarkasoor Disown Heaven:

Brahmdev said hey Naradh, then all the gods came to me to tell me the difficulties they are facing because of Tarkasoor occupying heaven and not letting them stay in heaven. Then Brahmdev said I cannot kill Tarkasoor, neither can Vishnu or Rudra. Only son born from the energy of Rudra can kill Tarkasoor, said Brahmdev. So now Daksha's daughter Sati, who has taken birth at King Himalaya and Mainka as their daughter. So she will marry Shiva, and the son from Shiva and Sati will kill Tarkasoor. So instead of wasting your time here, you guys can make an environment for Shiva to wed Sati Devi.

After saying all that to the gods, Brahmdev went to heaven to meet Tarkasoor. After seeing Tarkasoor at heaven, Brahmdev said to Tarkasoor that he had granted him the wish to be powerful, to allow him to stay within the limit of obligations, so it is better for him to leave the heaven for gods. Brahmdev also told Tarkasoor that it is better for him to rule Earth and leave the heaven for Gods. If he doesn't do so, then it could be harmful for him. After saying all these two Tarkasoor, Brahmdev left and Tarkasoor also moved to Earth by leaving heaven for gods. Then Tarkasoor made SHOORIT city as his country to rule on Earth.

KaamDev Goes to Shiva's Place:

Then Hey Naradh all the gods gathered to discuss ways to make Parvati Shiva's wife. Then Indra calls Kaamdev and asked him to go over where Shiva was meditating and produce feelings in Shiva's heart for Parvati so he would wed Parvati and have a son who then would kill Tarkasoor. After hearing what Indradev had to say, Kaamdev agreed and went to where Shiva was meditating with other Kaam soldier of his.

After reaching the place where Shiva was meditating then Kaamdev started his power of illusion to make the place beautiful with flowers and greenery. Also, rivers started flowing with good vibration sound and great smells from beautiful flowers started flowing everywhere. So the act of Kaamdev attracted everything in that jungle, but it didn't affect Shiva. In the meantime Parvati also arrived there to worship Shiva and then when Shiva opened his eyes to accept the worship then suddenly he felt emotion created by the Kaamdev and was surprise to see the surrounding changes. So Shiva thought how all this happened.

KaamDev Turned to Ashes:

Brahmdev said hey Naradh after seeing about his bad luck, Kaamdev felt being unsuccessful and was frightened and started staring at all the directions. By seeing these all the directions also got scarred, and that made other gods also terrified. After seeing and knowing Kaamdev was responsible for the acts that Shiva had felt made Shiva furious that opened Shiva's third eye in-between the eyebrows. As a result, Kaamdev dropped to the ground and started burning in to ashes. After seeing these, Parvati went back to her house with her maids. Also, the wife of Kaamdev Rati cried loudly in shock after her husband Kaamdev burned and turned into ashes. By this observation everything and everyone in the World felt sad and depressed. All the gods came to give their condolence to Rati to take it easy and also they worshipped and praise Shiva by singing his glory. The Shiva told all the gods and Rati that now Kaamdev only be born again at the end of DWAPAR (Third) YUG being the son of Krishna from Rukmani. The SAMBAR named devil will throw him in the ocean. So the Rati can now settle in the city of SAMBAR, where she will meet her husband again.

The gods requested Shiva not to do so because Rati won't be alive till then to meet him again. It is also gods who send Kaamdev over there for the work they had asked Kaamdev to accomplish. So gods told Shiva to forgive them and protect all of them by keeping them there. The Shiva said then Kaamdev will soon be alive and will become my follower and I will also take care of all of your problem which you all are dealing right now. Also Shiva told gods and other present they're not to mention about this to anyone. So Shiva asked all of them to go to their respected home without worrying about anything.

Narad's Advice to Parvati Jee:

After KaamDev turned into the ashes, Parvati Jee thought more about Shiva because of the incident she witnessed. So even while eating, drinking and sleeping Parvati, Jee thought about Shiva. Then one day Naradh Jee arrived at Himalaya's palace and they all respected and gave regards to Naradh Jee as he was their guest. Naradh Jee being very pleased with the service he was provided while he was a guest at Himalaya's palace so he told King Himalaya and his wife to worship and praise Shiva and he left from there and went to where Parvati Jee was and told her you wished to marry Shiva without meditating and also your ego was also being involved in that wish. So without meditation you could not marry Shiva, therefore from now on if you want to marry Shiva then start meditating with these words as sentence "OM NAMA SHIVAYA". So after you meditating with those words you will marry Shiva said Naradh Jee to Parvati Jee and Naradh Jee left from there.

Meditation of Parvati Jee:

Then Parvati Jee meditated to receive Shankar as her husband so went to her father and mother and asked for their permission to perform a meditation to have Shiva as a husband. Then King Himalaya told Parvati Jee that there is no need to go to jungle to meditate because they do not make jungles for women to stay there, so instead of going to jungle to meditate they told her to meditate at home. After hearing what her parents had to say, Parvati Jee became upset and felt sad. By seeing the sadness in her face, her parents finally grant her the permission to go to jungle and meditate. So after that Parvati Jee went to the same place where Ganga Jee Holy River flowed and also the place where Shiva turned Kaamdev into ashes. She used to sit on the same place every day and meditate the words" OM NAMA SHIVAYA". In hot days she used to sit on warm objects, and in cold days she used to sit on top of cold water and do meditation. Parvati Jee meditate like that for three thousand years and by its effect gods started visiting the place where she was meditating. No other female had done such a hard meditation for so long, so because of the energy it created gods used to go there to feel blessed to be near her. After some time, all three Lok (Universe) heated. So all the gods, demons and all other creatures went to Brahmdev and told him about the situation, So Brahmdev along with all others went to Vishnu and told him about it, So then Vishnu told everyone that it is because of effect of Parvati Jee 's meditation. So Vishnu told all of them to go to Shiva, and all the gods got scared because of what happened to Kaamdev. Then Vishnu told them not to be afraid as Shiva is also Bholenath, one who forgives other all the time. So don't be scared and all of you just go over to Shiva and explain him everything. After hearing what Vishnu had to say, they all went to where Shiva was. All the gods put Naradh Jee at the front and then gave their highest regard and respect to Shiva.

Acceptance of Shankar (Shiva):

All the gods started saying hey father of the Universe we all came to take protection from you as we are suffering very much because of Tarkasoor the devil. He has removed us from our own places and making us suffer because of different conditions because of Tarkasoor. So hey Shankar, please marry Girja (Parvati) and have a son from her who then can only kill Tarkasoor. So please Shiva rescue us from suffering because of Tarkasoor by having a son with Parvati, who will kill Tarkasoor said Vishnu to Shiva. The Shiva said I have already destroyed KaamDev so there is no Kaam left in me so I would not marry Parvati said Shiva and he despaired.

After getting advice from Nandiswor (Half bull half human, a vehicle of Shiva) the gods again worshipped Shiva and after sometime Shiva again appeared in front of them. So all the gods again requested Shiva to marry Parvati to have a son from her who then would kill Tarkasoor and rescue all gods.

Then Shiva said I am bondage to devotion of a devotee so for that reason I would marry Parvati said Shiva. Even though there is no Kaam (Lust) left in me but for the sake of devoted I will marry Parvati and by doing so would help all of you to get rid of Tarkasoor. So now without worrying go back to your respected homes and wait said Shiva to other gods and saints.

Parvati Test:

Brahmdev said hey Naradh after Vishnu along with other gods left, then Shiva called Saptarishi (Seven saints) and told them at Gauri Shikhar (Gauri Hill) there is Parvati meditating to have

Shiva as her husband. So all of you seven saints go to Gauri Shikhar and take a test of Parvati about her love towards me and after that come here and tell me everything said Shiva to Seven saints. Then the Seven saints went to Gauri Shikhar and after seeing Parvati they told her what she was doing there. After hearing the questions from the saints, Parvati told them that Naradh Jee told her to meditate hardly to have Shiva as her husband and for that reason she was meditating to have Shiva as her husband.

After hearing what Parvati had to say, seven saints laughed at her and told her that not to believe in Naradh because he never tells the truth and always makes stories to make others in a difficult position? They also gave a few examples of how Naradh had destroyed families and lives of other beings by showing and telling them about dreams and hope which never happened. So they told Parvati to go home and be happy with her family instead of meditating there in the jungle for something that she may not achieve.

After hearing the seven saints, Parvati smiled and told them that actually Naradh opened her eyes and she will to more and more hard and difficult meditation to have Shiva as her husband. If she cannot have her as her husband then she would stay Kumari (Virgin) and will worship and praise Shiva and end her life being a devotee of Shiva. After hearing what Parvati had to say seven saints then blessed Parvati and went back to where Shiva was waiting for them?

After hearing all the details from seven saints, the Shiva took a figure of Brahman and went to Gauri Shikhar where Parvati was doing meditation. After reaching there and seeing Parvati meditate Shiva who was in the figure of Brahman asked Parvati what she was doing there and why she is not at her home? Then Parvati told Brahman figured Shiva that she was the wife of Shiva in the previous life and had killed herself by jumping on the fire back then. Also in this life she meditates to have Shiva again as her husband, but it feels like it is not working for her so she told Brahman that again in this life she will give up her life by steeping in the fire. As soon as she told Brahman she then steps inside the fire but this time fire became cool as ice so nothing happened to Parvati.

Shiva and Parvati Conversation:

Hey Naradh, then Parvati told Shiva who disguised himself as Brahman that she is determined to have Shiva as her husband from both the body and mind. I also know it is a very difficult task but my hope and belief system has not it has not hampered system so I will keep trying said Parvati to Shiva. Then Shiva who disguised as Brahman told Parvati because of Guru's favor I know Shiva very well be the one who rides old ox also always remains naked he assumes addictive drugs also rubs ashes all over the body and wears a poisonous snake as neck ornament and also he has rough and twisted long hairs looks like a beggar. Even Sati, his first wife, had to cry tears and also could not wear and eat nicely. So it is better you take your mind out of him told Shiva to Parvati. He also told her she is beautiful and can have anyone like Vishnu or even god Indra as her husband. He doesn't think Shiva is suitable for her to have as her husband said the Brahman to Parvati.

After hearing the Shiva who disguised as Brahman Parvati became angry and told him the way you insulted Shiva, the seven saints also came here and told similar things. It is Shiva who by protecting all Vishnu Brahma and other gods are having good times in their life. Shiva is the father of the Brahmanda (Universe) and who can even know what he is. All eight siddhi (enlightens) lie and enjoy in his lotus feet. People who insults Shiva will never be happy so from now on don't insult Shiva said Parvati to Brahman and after that Parvati stay quiet and started to meditating about Shiva. Again the Shiva who disguised as Brahman was about to say something harsh then in the same time Parvati told her friend Vijaya that insulting Shiva is not only sinful but even hearing about is sin, so please take this Brahman away from here otherwise I will leave from here. After saying that Parvati stared to get ready to leave the Shiva came in his own figure and told Parvati hey where are you going? There is no divine energy in all of Universe who can debate you, and I took lots of your test. You have already with your devotion made me your prisoner. You are my eternal wife and I am under you and I have never left you, said Shiva to Parvati. After hearing Shiva Parvati became thrilled.

Parvati then said hey my, why did you forget about me like that? You please accept me as your wife and become my husband said Parvati to Shiva. Now I will go to my house and tell all these to my father and you also tell my father you want to accept me as your wife so ask him for permission. Also tell my parents my accepting him as their son-in-law have a blissful life by letting me wed you.

After saying all these two Shiva Parvati stayed quiet and Shiva said bless you (Thatasthu) to Parvati and went back to Kailas. After reaching Kailas Shiva told Nandiswor and other ghosts and souls who all stays with Shiva as his prime devotee that he has married Parvati and after hearing the news all of them thrilled.

Also Parvati goes to her home then Himalaya along with his wife Mainka other relatives and priest's l goes a little far to receive Parvati to welcome her back home. After meeting her everyone praises her by saying jay hos jay Hos.

Description of Maya (Illusion) of Shiva:

Hey Naradh said Brahmdev after seeing that level of devotion on Parvati for Shiva god Indra and other gods thought Himalaya will be immortal and will be Shiva yogi after letting Parvati wed Shiva and by doing KanyaDan (Sacrifice of a Daughter by performing her wedding to the groom). So this is not right and we should stop this process of KanyaDan by Himalaya, said the gods. All the gods went to Guru Brihaspati and told him about the issue they were facing because of wed that would happen between Shiva and Parvati. Then Guru Brihaspati told the gods that this issue is out of his capability to solve it. Then the gods went to Brahmdev with their issue, then Brahmdev also told them the same thing as Guru Brihaspati. After that gods went to Kailas to meet Shiva and told him about how it is not fair for them for Himalaya to be immortal. After knowing what's on the mind of god's Shiva went to Himalaya's place with a figure of (Baisab) other being. After reaching their Shiva in some other being figure said lots of bad things about Shiva which then make Himalaya and Mainka parents of Parvati not to do KanyaDan process.

Seven Saints Goes to Himalaya's Place:

After Shiva went in disguised figure to Himalaya and Mainka and lots of bad things about Shiva himself, then Mainka really got scared to let her daughter Parvati to wed Shiva. Then so she said to Himalaya that she will not allow Parvati wed Shiva and will never allow that to happen and started crying loudly.

On the other side at Kailas Shiva invited seven saints at Kailas and explained them everything and asked them to go over to Himalaya's place and advice Himalaya and Mainka to let Parvati wed Shiva. After hearing Shiva, seven saints went straight to Himalaya's place. Also Himalaya after seeing seven saints at his doorstep, he invited them inside and gave his respect and regards to the seven saints and asked them what he can do for them.

Advice of Great Saint:

Hey Naradh said Brahmdev, then seven saints requested King Himalaya to let her daughter Parvati marry Shiva because Shiva is the father of the Universe and Parvati is the mother of the Universe. By doing KanyaDan OF Parvati to Shiva you will succeed this life of yours, said the seven saints to Himalaya. After hearing the seven saints King Himalaya said I know you all are telling the truth but little ago a Brahman had come and he told us all the bad things about Shiva and because of that my wife Mainka is very sad and still crying in a room said Himalaya. After hearing that seven saints send Arundhati to the room where Mainka was being sad and crying. By reaching their Arundhati tries to solve the issue by counseling Mainka. Arundhati gives many examples and advice to Mainka to make her feel better about letting her daughter Parvati wed Shiva. Also, the seven saints do the same thing of counseling and advising King Himalaya. They also told Himalaya about the story of King Anirnaya who by being scared wed her daughter to the Brahman to save himself and his family.

Saints Counseling Himalaya:

Brahmdev said during that time Himalaya after hearing name of King Anirnaya, he wanted to hear the whole story about him. So Himalaya asked the saints to tell him the story of King Anirnaya. Then Vasistha Rishi (One of the seven saints) told the story to King Himalaya. He said the first fourteenth human was named Indraswarni, and they loved him devotee of Shiva. He was the master of all seven rays of light. He made BHRIGU JEE ACHARYA (Priest) and performs one hundred Yegya (Holy ritual). He also had five queens, and with them he had one hundred sons and one daughter. That girl was pretty, and her name was Padma. So that girl Padma was very much loveable to king and queen.

Some other day Piplad named saint was meditating in the jungle. In the same jungle he saw a man was having fun with his own wife at a distance. After seeing the couple having so much fun saint, Piplad also felt a very strong feeling of lust. Saint Piplad had develop having a female partner, but he did not know how to. One day saint Piplad saw Padma taking a bath at the river and after seeing Padma Piplad became attracted to Padma. The saint Piplad asked around to others about Padma and other people told him she was the daughter of King Anirnaya and they also joked around him by saying why don't you ask her hand for the wedding with the King. After hearing made saint Piplad feel shy. Then Saint Piplad had a desire to have Padma as a wife and he could not control that feeling and so after finishing his daily rituals in the morning saint Piplad went to the palace of King Anirnaya and asked the King to let her daughter Padma be wed with him. After hearing that King Anirnaya stayed quiet. After some time the saint Piplad said he King gives your daughter to me or else I will finish the life of you and your whole family.

After hearing what the saint Piplad had to say, King cried and thought how I can give my young daughter to this old saint. At the same time royal priests and royal Guru also arrived there and started to counseling the King. After that the wise King Anirnaya let his daughter Padma wed saint Piplad. So after wedding Padma saint, Piplad became thrilled and went back to his ashram with his wife Padma. The King Anirnaya left the palace to live in the jungle, and queen also despaired. So this is how King Anirnaya had saved all his family by letting saint Piplad marry his daughter. So king Himalaya you also do the same thing and let your daughter Parvati marry Shiva. By doing so all the gods cannot harm you and you will also become immortal that way, said the seven saints to King Himalaya and his wife Mainka.

Padma and Piplad 'Story:

Brahmdev said Naradh after hearing the brief story about Padma and Piplad then King Himalaya asked where did Padma and Piplad went after that? How did they live and survive asked Himalaya to Vasistha Rishi (Saint)? Then Vasistha rishi told King Himalaya that Piplad was really an old saint, and he took Padma to his ashram were they started living. One day Padma was taking a bath at Swarnada River, then Dharma Raj came to test Padma with by looking like a prince of some country. Dharma Raj who disguised himself as prince told Padma that she is beautiful and it is not suitable for her to waste her life with an old person like Piplad. Instead, he offered her to make his queen and stay in a palace and enjoy life rather than having a difficult time with old Piplad. After saying all that he moved forward to grab Padma, then Padma being furious cursed him for saying things like that to a married woman. Padma told Dharma Raj that it will destroy him for what he said to her.

After hearing Padma curse him, Dharma raj came to his real figure and apologized to Padma for his cruel words and he also told her he was only testing her. After that Padma told Dharma Raj that a curse given by husband oriented wives never go waste. So now you will now have four legs in Satya Yug, three in Tretya Yug and two in Duarpa Yug and none in Kali Yug and after Kali Yug when Satya Yug starts again then will have four legs again. After hearing that Dharma raj became thrilled and blessed Padma for being so husband oriented, also told she that now her husband Piplad will turn into a young man and you will have ten sons from him said Dharma Raj. After blessing her Dharma, Raj went back to his place. Also Padma when reached home found her husband Piplad very young and attractive. So slowly one after another they had ten sons, and they also raised all of them.

Seven Saints (Saptarishi) Meets Shiva:

Then after hearing the story from Vasistha rishi Himalaya told seven saints that now all the misunderstanding about Shiva has disappeared from my mind, so now I am ready to let Parvati wed Shiva. King Himalaya also told the seven rishis that all his wealth, family, sons, daughters all dedicated to Shiva. He also then that now he would arrange a grand wedding ceremony for Shiva to wed Parvati. After hearing that seven saints blessed King Himalaya and Parvati and left their place. After that, seven saints along with Arundhati went to where Shiva was. There they told Shiva all the details about what happened and also that King Himalaya is now ready to let their daughter Parvati to wed Shiva. Then they also said to Shiva to get ready to wed Parvati and also asked him to invite all the real gods to the wedding.

Himalaya Sends Marriage Auspicious (Lagnapatrika):

Then King Himalaya invited all his relatives and also Ganga Jee to make marriage auspicious for to send it to Shiva. Shiva welcomed and respected the priests who took the marriage auspicious paper to him from King Himalaya. Then King Himalaya invited most of the mountains like Bindyachal, Trikut, Chitrakut, Benkat, Shreegiri, and Ganga River and they all came to King Himalaya's place as invited. Himalaya gave his high respect to all of them and arranges nice places for them to stay.

After that, King Himalaya invited Vishokarma to make suitable places for them to stay while they were there to attend the wedding. Vishokarma also designed a grand wedding pavilion. The wedding pavilion was ten thousand times seven thousand two hundred meter tall and forty thousand times four miles wide. Also Vishokarma made different many statues of animals, birds, gods, goddess all around the wedding pavilion with gold and other valuable ornamental stones. Anyone who sees the pavilion would keep watching it as it was so attractive.

Shiva Invites All Gods to Wedding:

Shiva then called Naradh Jee and told him to invite Brahmdev all other gods, Siddha Rishis, Gandharva and others to the wedding and also make sure they come with their respected spouses in their official vehicles (Bahan). So after receiving the invitations Brahmdev, Vishnu and other gods all came with the way it instructed them. Then when everyone arrived, they decorate Shiva for the wedding. Shiva's third eye became his crown, Moon became the mark on the forehead as sandal, the snake on the neck of Shiva became his earring, and the ashes from funeral shone all over his body. The skin of tiger and deer became his clothes. The Vishnu told Shiva that now you apply the method of performing a wedding and do as per the method which later on humans will also apply the same method to get married. Shiva also did the same thing. After that Brahman started spelling VEDAS and Swastani and after completing all process then all the invited guests along with Shiva starts the wedding procession to reach the bride's house.

Wedding Procession:

Brahmdev said hey Naradh Shiva called Nandiswor and other followers of Shiva to start the procession of the wedding. Then there were millions and millions of followers of Shiva gathered to start the procession along with other invited guests. I asked some followers of Shiva to stay in Kailas for the security of Kailas. Vishnu was in the middle of the procession in his vehicle who was Eagle. Also, I was in the procession with VED and other holy books with me said Brahmdev. Along with Shiva was Chandidevi as the sister of the groom walked in the wedding procession towards the King Himalaya's place.

The Shiva after discussing with Vishnu send Naradh Jee to Himalaya to see how everything was prepared there. But Naradh Jee after reaching the wedding place and seeing how everything is decorated so well by Vishokarma forgot to return to inform Shiva by being so impress by the preparation. So when the wedding procession reached the Himalaya's place, then Himalaya's son Mainka and Naradh Jee welcomed all the guests of the wedding. When Naradh Jee described how well the preparation for the wedding has done, the Indra got sacred for what he had done in the past. After knowing that Indra being scared, then Vishnu told him not to be scared because Shiva was with them and no illusion (Maya) of Himalaya will work on them. So keeping Himalaya's son in front Shiva with all the guests entered the city of Himalaya where the wedding would take place.

Compromise between Gods and Hills:

Knowing that the wedding procession of Shiva has almost arrived then King Himalaya along with other hills went further to welcome Shiva along with other guests who came with the wedding procession. When King Himalaya saw the guests in the wedding procession, he was shock and surprise to see something like two sides of the ocean coming together. Similarly, the Hills from Himalaya's side compromised with Gods from Shiva's side that came as guests of Shiva to attend the wedding of Shiva and Parvati. Then Himalaya sends his sons to receive Shiva and other guests, and all of them went to meet King Himalaya. Then Mainka The mother of Parvati also wanted to meet Shiva before the wedding.

Unique Play of Shiva:

Mainka said at this I want to see the figure and face of Shiva who is here to marry my daughter Parvati. On the other side Shiva also felt of Mainka. All the gods and angels were in the front, dancing and singing. Then Mainka thought Vishnu probably is Shiva, so approached Vishnu if he was Shiva then Vishnu said no and pointed towards the middle of all ghosts and other followers of Shiva, Shiva who was in the middle with five heads and ten hands and huge body, Shiva was looking like something scary then. After seeing Shiva Mainka fainted because of the shock of seeing that figure of Shiva.

Then Brahmdev said that after that all Mainka's servants and other relatives ran around saying she fainted. So later on when Mainka woke up she cried and said she will not let her daughter Parvati get married to Shiva. Then Vishnu tries to calm Mainka saying that is not the real figure of Shiva and you really haven't seen his real true figure so that's why you are crying foul here. But she wouldn't listen to Vishnu and again cried even louder. Then King Himalaya told Mainka that not to act like these in front of all the gods and demons who came in with wedding possession, as a matter of fact she only saw one face of Shiva whereas he has too many other figures that he can change himself into. After that Mainka said ok if Shiva comes here with his real true figure then I will let my daughter Parvati to marry him otherwise I will object said Mainka.

Blessed to see Shiva's real face:

Brahmdev said then I asked you Naradh and Vishnu to go over to Shiva and please him to come in his real figure. So Vishnu and Naradh Jee went over to Shiva and they started praising the Shiva with many devotions and singing his glory made Shiva to appear in his real figure. Then Shiva appeared in his real true figure then Naradh Jee told Mainka to look at Shiva then she realized a reflection of almost ten Suns, wearing a half Moon in the head, wearing many priceless stone elements, Smiling all the time, white-colored skin, all the gods serving him as he was coming towards the wedding house. After seeing that figure of Shiva, Mainka agreed for the wedding.

Mainka then said Hey Parvati you are very lucky to have Shiva as your husband and also we are very proud of him too. We are very pleased to have you wed Shiva said Mainka to Parvati. Then Mainka asked Shiva to forgive her for the entire crude act she showed to him because of different circumstances. She asked Shiva to forgive her sin which was created by showing her anger towards Shiva. After that all the women of the area came to worship Shiva, and they also blessed Parvati who then would be the wife of Shiva.

The description of wedding possession of Shiva:

When Shiva reached the door of Himalaya's palace with the wedding possession, then Mainka went inside the house and prepare necessary essentials for to conduct door entrance worship for Shiva and the wedding possession. Right then, when Mainka arrived at the door to worship Shiva to let him welcome inside the house, Shiva got off from Nandi the bull and stood in front of Himalaya and Mainka. Then Shiva was as beautiful as Kaam Dev. and had fair skin, three eyes one in the middle, wearing a necklace of Jasmine flower which was smelling superb, wearing a crown with valuable stones attached to it, wearing a Bengal and other elements made with valuable stones, wearing clothes of different designs, smelled like sandalwood, very young looking, smiling and very attractive to look at. So Mainka was very pleased to see that figure of Shiva, and she happily worshipped Shiva to welcome him to wed Parvati. Then Parvati with all dressed up and nice make up came out with her friends to go to the temple to worship Kul Devata (Main god of the whole family).

Then Himalaya with all respect to tradition and culture served Shiva with all respect and harmony. Then with ancient tradition Shiva showered and worn beautiful and valuable ornaments and clothes. After that Ganga Acharya (Main Priest) asked Himalaya to bring Shiva to Kanya Daan room (a tradition of handing the girl for a wedding). So Himalaya asks Shiva and Vishnu and other gods to please visit the Kanya Daan room for traditional wedding function. Then Shiva rides the Nandi the bull to the Kanya Daan room.

After some time the auspicious time to do Kanya Daan arrived and so Mainka, the wife of King Himalaya came into the room with clean water in gold vase and sit left to King Himalaya. Then Himalaya asked Shiva for his ancestors' history about his families. …….?

Brahmdev Became Lust:

Brahmdev said hey Naradh after I concluded then the Kanya Daan all the priests asked Brahmdev for permission to conduct a wedding ceremony by establishing fire at the ground. So by doing fire and Brahma wedding according to rituals, the entire priest present started reading all the Vedas and pronouncing the words from the Vedas in front of the fire. Then Parvati also arrived there, and they gave her Lava (flower from the grain of rice) and she had to put that Lava into the fire at different times. Parvati took a circle of fire and put some Lava at the fire and again took a round of fire up to three times and put Lava on the fire every time. After that Sila (stone) worship was conducted and after that Shiva put Sindor on the middle part of the head of Parvati, he also put Tillari (Necklace) on the neck, and after that he made Parvati sift sitting position to conduct Bamangi (ritual done at the time of wedding), also he played Pasa (a board game) and also feed her Mahur (special ritual food). Then all the priests finished pronouncing all ritual words, so they perform Godan (a ritual conducted at the time of wedding). They made commitment for each other and was put Tilak (a ritual to put the ash of the fire put on forehead as blessing). After that wedding ceremony was conducted and then Parvati left to go with friends, when Parvati was stepping up the steps she pulled her dress little and then Brahmdev saw the feet of Parvati which as a reaction created a feeling of lust in Brahmdev. Right then Shiva noticed all that and became furious. To please the every other gods and saints present at the wedding started praising Shiva for quite some time and after a while Shiva became happy with praising and forgave Brahmdev. After that hey Naradh said Brahmdev I pushed my negative feelings of lust into the ground on mud with my legs, then lots of atoms got produced from it and then thousands of child saints were born from those atoms. They were very talented and smart kid saints. Then they stand up and started calling me hey father hey father then you Naradh came and asked them not to disturb me and go away said Brahmdev. Then all of them gave their highest respect to Shiva, and they went towards Gandamandan Mountain to perform hard meditation.

Kaam Dev. Gets Life Back By the Grace of Shiva:

Hey Naradh right then Rati came with ashes of Kaam Dev. and said hey today on your wedding day everyone is happy and pleasant, so why should I be in sorrow for loss of my husband Kaam Dev. said Rati to Shiva. She also cried loudly and said all sorts of sorrow stories without the present of her husband. After seeing her crying in sorrow, Goddess Sarswoti felt bad and asked Shiva to forgive Kaam Dev. and let him be alive again. So everyone there started requesting Shiva to forgive Kaam Dev. and let him be alive.

After hearing request from Goddess Sarswoti Shiva looks at the ashes of Kaam Dev. and he became alive. After which Kaam Dev. gets up and bows to Shiva and Shiva asks him for a wish. So Kaam Dev. says that hey let me stay with you to serve you and always serve you to let your devotees have my affection present in them always. The Shiva said I am very pleased with you, and now you go to Vishnu and stay in his place by obeying as per his instructions.

After seeing dedication from King Himalaya Shiva told him that his devotion is true and there is no one like him who is so devoted in all three Worlds and also Shiva said that he is very impressed by him. Shiva also said it's been so many days he is been staying at Himalaya's place so it's time to go back to Kailas. After hearing that King Himalaya requested Shiva to stay two days more, and he agreed. After a few days Seven Saints told Himalaya and Mainka that ShivShiva have left today back to Kailas so prepare everything to let them go back said Seven Saints. After hearing Seven Saints Mainka went to Shiva and said that Parvati have been his internal energy for generation to generation so please take her and if she does anything wrong, then forgive her said Mainka to Shiva. Then Shiva said she is my responsibility and you not to worry at all about anything. Then after that they left for Kailas.

Description of Loyalty to Husband:

When Seven Saints announced that Shiva will go back to Kailas with Parvati, then King Himalaya asked Mainka to prepare Parvati. Then Mainka made Parvati look beautiful, and she was making her ready right then an old lady appeared before the two of them. She then gave a lesson to Parvati about how to be loyal (Patibrata Dharma) towards her husband. She said hey Parvati always eat only after your husband eats, sleep only after he sleeps, never be angry with your husband, always obey your husband, never stay in other's house with no reason, always take care of things of your husband, you should be smart in domestic works inside the house, without the permission of husband go nowhere, if you want to go to devotional places then just do good deed to your husband and you will feel devotional, without the permission of husband don't fast or do unnecessary worship and other things, whatever you may do never harm your husband, however he may be never ever give him up, also never use bad words for your husband, goodness or badness never be upset with your husband, think of your husband bigger than Brahma, Vishnu, and Mahesower. Never use harsh words with your husband, also in front of mother-in-law and sister in laws never speak loudly or laugh loud. Once upon a time a Brahman killed by an animal was excused by a loyal wife after the request from all three major Gods. But you are the first female goddess, so you are a caretaker of the whole Universe. I know I didn't have to give you these lessons, but I gave it for to carrying on a tradition. After that the old lady sat back to witness goodbye moment at a wedding.

Shiva Returns to Kailas:

Brahmdev said hey Naradh after that according to the words of an old lady, Mainka put Parvati at a carrycot and sees her off by saying bye.

While saying bye by everyone blessed Parvati for good life and also King Himalaya and Mainka also blessed Parvati and also gave her priceless ornaments and dresses and other things.

Then King Himalaya went towards Shiva and Vishnu and wishes them also he walked with them up and then said bye to them return home. Whereas Shiva and others went to Kailas with Parvati. After reaching Kailas everybody was fed with a good meal, and after that everyone left for their respected home.

Om Nama Shivaya

Rudra Sanhita Kumar Khanda:

Fifth Section

Beginning:

Naradh Jee asked Brahmdev hey father now you tell us that story of Parvati when she and Shiva had Kumar as a son. Shoot Jee tells Sanak the story as Brahmdev would say it to Naradh Jee.

When Shiva came back to Kailas after marrying Parvati they looked like a match made in heaven and then they worked for god's demands. After that Shiva assigned work for everyone in Kailas among his core followers, and they went to the jungle with Parvati for the honeymoon. They were in the jungle for thousands of years celebrating honeymoon. Since it was been while since Shiva and Parvati had gone so all the gods gathered and went to Vishnu to ask what about. Then they asked Shiva since it's been so long that Shiva and Parvati have been married and they still have had no son, so what to do next? The Vishnu said not to lose patience and also not to disturb Shiva for anything. Then suddenly the entire Universe shook because of an affection of the honeymoon of Shiva and Parvati. Then all the gods along with Vishnu went to the jungle outside where Shiva and Parvati was having honeymoon and they started praising Shiva by singing his devotion.

Birth of Kartikya (Kumar):

Even though Shiva is the super god and he while making love to Parvati wasn't giving it up till it would satisfy her. But since it had been few ages and also all the other gods were praising Shiva to come out to hear what they want to tell him about terrorizing done by Tarkasoor. After sometime Shiva came to the door as it is and was pleased to see Brahmdev, Vishnu and other gods all praising Shiva, so after that the gods told Shiva how Tarkasoor was terrorizing everyone. The Shiva asked who has the potential energy to hold his sperm, then after sometime Shiva drops his sperm on Earth. After that by advice of other gods Fire consumes the sperm and in the meantime Parvati also comes out at the door looking for Shiva and observes everything. After seeing that all the efforts have been wasted, so she becomes furious with gods and curses all the gods, they become asexual. She also tells them they will never be happy to have the pleasure in their life. She also curses fire saying he cannot understand any elements of Shiva and also he will always serve gods. After saying all these, Parvati went inside the temple.

The Shiva was went inside the temple. After that, Parvati gives birth to Ganesh from the dirt of her body. Also, all the gods started having a severe stomach ache because of the curse and they couldn't bear the pain so they started praising Shiva. So Shiva became happy with their praising and appeared in front of the gods were in lots of pain. So Shiva advice they to throw up all the reproductive sense and they will feel better. So all the gods threw up all their reproductive sense, and they felt better after that. The Shiva told fire that he was furious of him and now he needs to inject that sperm which he swallowed to some female said Shiva. After that Shiva went away to be with Parvati. Then all the gods decides that fire has to inject the sperm in the month of MAGH (between the months of Jan to Feb) in Prayag. So in the month of MAGH Fire establish himself in Prayag. So wives of seven saints came to take a shower in Prayag and since it was freezing, they went towards the fire to get the heat from it and while getting heat from the fire they came close to the fire. Right then the fire through the heat wave injects the sperm on them in their bodies. After that those women became pregnant and knowing that their husband abandoned them. So they went to the Himalayas to meditate but they couldn't bear the pain so by eating KUVINDO'S seeds they drop the sperm on the Himalaya. Also the Himalaya couldn't bear the pain, so he drops it on the holy River Ganga. Ganga also couldn't bear the pain so by waves she also throws it to the side on the bushes. There on the bushes a beautiful boy takes a birth from it. That boy had six months and as soon as he was born Shiva and Parvati felt superb and went to visit him. Also flowers started pouring from sky all over the boy. Happy waves flourished everywhere and also at the same time devils got scared because of the birth of this boy.

Characteristics of Kartikya (Kumar):

Brahmdev said hey Naradh, then there a great saint Bishomitra came and Kumar asked Bishomitra to do giving him a name but asked him to keep it secret by not letting others know. After that, Bishomitra did the process for giving a name to Kumar. As a gratitude Kumar Kartikya gave knowledge to Bishomitra.

Then there Soyet named saint arrived there, and he hugged and kissed Kumar Kartikya also he blessed Kumar with not to face defeat ever. Saint Soyet also gave weapon named Amogh Sastra. Then with Amogh Sastra (Weapon) he climbed mount Kauncha to the top. From there he went straight to the heaven and there he met six women known as Kartikya. They with love all of them breast feed Kumar to all six mouths with each of them. They also took care of Kartikya till he grew up and gave him powerful advice and good clothes to wear with great ornaments.

So time went by and one day Parvati asked Shiva about his Amogh sperm which gave birth to a boy. The Shiva told Parvati that the boy was growing up in heaven with seven Kritkas as seven women. He also told her they even breast feed him and also love him as their own child.

After hearing that from Shiva, Parvati send a big and great chariot along with **Nandi** to invite Kumar Kartikya to Kailas. Vishokarma built that chariot. So Nandi with his so many followers went in the chariot to get Kumar Kartikya from the heaven where he was living with seven Kritkas as his seven mothers. When Nandi along with all his followers reached there, he told Kumar Kartikya about the invitation from Parvati. Then Kumar Kartikya talks to his seven mothers about living their home to go to Kailas. So he finally makes them understand the situation and leaves with Nandi to go to Kailas. After reaching Kailas Kumar Kartikya bow down in front of Shiva and Parvati to give them the respect of being his parents. He also respected all other gods present there. Then all the great rivers like Ganga Jee and others came to look Kumar Kartikya. At Kailas Kumar Kartikya started playing in the arms of Parvati. That moment Parvati organized a big function to celebrate being with Kartikya. Shiva pronounced magic words from VEDA to welcome Kartikya in Kailas, which he did for nonstop one hundred hours. Twasta an artist made beautiful town and build big and really beautiful **palace** in that town for Kartikya by the order from Vishnu.

Once a Brahman came to Kartikya and told him he had one Goat and he lost it somewhere without it he cannot finish the ritual worship which he was doing (Yegya). The Brahman also said to Kartikya that he was very brilliant and strong so maybe he would look and find the animal that the Brahman lost and without sacrificing that animal it will not complete his ritual worship. So Kumar Kartikya asked one of his followers to go look for the lost animal. Then his follower found the Goat in Vishnu Lok, and he had made so much trouble at the Vishnu Lok. When they brought the Goat from the Vishnu Lok, then Kumar Kartikya rides that Goat. When he sat on the Goat, the Goat took a whole circle of Earth with Kartikya along with it and stopped right at the same place where he was lost. Then the Brahman after seeing his lost Goat with Kartikya asked him to return the Goat to him to complete his ritual worship. Then Kumar Kartikya told the Brahman that this Goat need not die so not to take him and just go home arrange some other ways to conclude your worship. By my true words your ritual worship will complete on its own so just conclude the worship sacrificing no animals said Kartikya to the Brahman. After hearing the Kartikya, the Brahman went home without the Goat.

War between Gods and Devils:

Brahmdev said the war broke between gods and devils, and it was a big war. The king of devil Tarkasoor used all his energy to attack king of Gods Indra. From the attack, Indra got injured and couldn't do anything to protect self. So he along with all other Gods got injured by the attack from the devils. So devils made all the gods run away from the war field and they captured Heaven and ruled Heaven as how they wished. By seeing all these Bir, Bhadra got furious. Then with the help from his followers Bir Bhadra reached where Tarkasoor was and beat Tarkasoor without mercy. Then all other brave devils came to fight with Bir Bhadra, and they fought for quite some time. The devil named Tarak made Bir Bhadra run away from the fight. Then all other remaining Gods also started running away from the war field. After seeing this entire Vishnu, he fights with Tarkasoor.

Bravery of Tarkasoor:

Brahmdev said hey Naradh there was a big war going on between gods and devils, and after observing everything I went to Kumar Kartikya to ask him to kill Tarkasoor. Because I had blessed Tarkasoor that no other gods can kill him so only you will kill Tarkasoor, said Brahmdev to Kumar Kartikya. Then Kartikya got up from his seat and said I will fight Tarkasoor. Then Kumar Kartikya walked towards Tarkasoor. By seeing Kumar Kartikya coming towards Tarkasoor, he said hey gods don't you have shame to send a little boy like this to fight with me? You gods have no shame and will do anything even by sending such a young boy to fight me said Tarkasoor. Then Tarkasoor said hey little boy run away from here and go home otherwise I will kill you in no time. After Tarkasoor insulted gods like Vishnu and Indra, his power decreased within him. Then he fought with Indra and ignored Kumar Kartikya. Also, he was still very difficult for gods to defeat him due to the blessing from Brahmdev.

Killing of Tarkasoor:

Brahmdev said hey Naradh after that thinking and praying Shiva inside his mind Kumar Kartikya leading thousands of soldiers went to attack the forces of Tarkasoor and started moving forward towards Tarkasoor. After seeing that all the gods started praising Kumar Kartikya also, the saints praised him. The fight broke between Kumar Kartikya and Tarkasoor. The fight continued, and it injured both of them. All the gods witnessed the deadly fight between Kumar Kartikya and Tarkasoor. Both of them became tired and injured and right then Kumar Kartikya meditating on Shiva and Parvati attacked Tarkasoor with a unique weapon and it killed Tarkasoor. He felt on the ground with pieces and died right there. After he died, all the gods were happy that they won the war between gods and devils. They all felt very blessed and peaceful. After that, Parvati blessed Kumar Kartikya with love from the mother. Also, right then, Kumar Kartikya also killed the devil Barasoor with the bow and arrow. He was destroying and giving pain to Kranch Mountain and its residences that used to live there.

Characteristics of Ganesha:

Naradh Jee says to Brahmdev, Father of the Universe, you have told us the story of Kumar Kartikya now please tell us about characteristics of Ganesha.

Then Brahmdev said once the friends of Parvati Jaya and Vijaya said to Parvati that Shiva has too many followers and we don't have any right over them. So Parvati should create her separate followers for her. Then one day Parvati was taking a bath and Nandi was guarding the entrance and Shiva entered inside and saw Parvati taking a bath. Then Parvati felt shameful for it and thought about the advice of Jaya and Vijaya about creating followers who would obey her more than anything. Then one day when Parvati was taking a bath, then she made a beautiful boy out of the dirt from her body and wore him good clothes and ornaments. After that she put him on the entrance to guard it till she takes a bath. She also told him that without her permission no one should be allowed inside. So you are my son and your name is Ganesha, she told the boy and blessed her many times.

Next day Parvati again put Ganesha at the entrance to guard it to let no one enter inside while Parvati is taking a bath. Then while Ganesha was guarding the entrance Shiva came and tries to go inside and Ganesha stops him by saying Mother Parvati has asked him not to allow anyone inside. The Shiva gets a little angry with the behavior of Ganesha.

Then followers of Shiva came to Ganesha, and Ganesha told them it will not benefit them if they oppose him. So go away said Ganesha to followers of Shiva. Then the followers told Ganesha that they are the followers of Shiva and cannot back out. So then Ganesha said then I am also the follower of mother Parvati so I will also not back out. After that followers of Shiva went towards Shiva and told him what Ganesha told them. So Shiva told the followers to remove Ganesha from there and that's all I care said Shiva. Again, Ganesha did not move from the entrance and allowed no one inside. After hearing the shouting and other sounds mother Parvati sends her friends to look outside to find out what was happening outside. After seeing everything friends of mother Parvati came back to her and told her the whole story on how Ganesha is stopping everyone from entering, including Shiva. After hearing the story about Ganesha mother, Parvati smiled and said he is doing a good job. Outside Shiva told his followers to fight with Ganesha to remove him from the entrance and stayed silence.

Ganesha battles with followers of Shiva:

Brahmdev said after receiving instruction from Shiva all his followers went to fight with Ganesha. Ganesha was also ready to fight all of them. Then Ganesha said today you all will see and feel the bravery of Ganesha. After hearing what Ganesha had to say, all the followers of Shiva also went to attack Ganesha. Ganesha alone fought with all the followers of Shiva. Many followers of Shiva attacked Ganesha, but they couldn't harm him, instead they were all beaten up by Ganesha. After witnessing such an incident all the gods gathered around Shiva to ask him why was the fight broken? The Shiva told the gods that there is a boy in front of my door and he won't let anyone enter inside the entrance. If Brahmdev wants, he can solve this problem, said Shiva. Then after that Brahmdev goes towards Ganesha to talk, but Ganesha grabs him by his beard and starts pulling them. Ganesha also picked up a weapon to attack Brahmdev, but Brahmdev runs away and save himself from Ganesha and tells Shiva about it. After hearing what Brahmdev had to say, Shiva becomes furious? Then all the followers of Shiva again go to attack Ganesha at the same time. But all the followers of Shiva including Kumar Kartikya were defeated by Ganesha. So Shiva himself then goes to fight with Ganesha. Also Vishnu and his followers also went with Shiva.

Cutting Ganesha's head:

Brahmdev said to Naradh, after listening to you Shiva went to fight with Ganesha. All the great Gods and including Vishnu with his big force fought with Ganesha. Vishnu couldn't defeat the Ganesha, so he left. Then Shiva fought with Ganesha and fought for quite some time. Then Ganesha praying to Mother Parvati attacked Shiva with the weapon. So that made Shiva furious and furious. So Shiva with his TRISHUAL attacked Ganesha and separated his head from the body. After that, Naradh went to Mother Parvati to tell her the news that Shiva separated head from the body of Ganesha. After telling her the news, Naradh disappeared in to thin air.

Rebirth of Ganesha:

Brahmdev said hey Naradh after hearing the news from your Mother Parvati became furious and said all the gods and their followers killed by son. Now I will finish them all, I will start a great war to finish all said Mother Parvati. Then from her energy Mother Parvati created one thousand energies to finish all the gods, their followers and saints. Now you eat whoever you find among gods, and their followers said Mother Parvati to the one thousand energies that she created. Then those energies entered the bodies of the devils and start eating gods wherever they find them. Everywhere the energies created by Mother Parvati started being visible. Those energies grabbed gods and started eating them by swallowing them. After seeing all these all the gods including Shiva, Vishnu and Brahmdev also all thought now they would all die. Then all the saints praised Mother Parvati, the Chandika figure. They started saying Mother Parvati even your husband Shiva is present here with us all and your energies are finishing us all so please stop it. Then Mother Parvati said if my son is becomes alive again and becomes divine then I will stop it. Then all the saints with the gods gathered around Shiva and Shiva said if it will save the creation, then will make him alive. So Shiva said go to South and whatever animal you find cut its head and bring it here and I will reattach it to the body of Ganesha and he will be alive again.

After hearing what Shiva had to say, all the gods went towards south direction and they found one tooth elephant. So they cut the head of the elephant and brought it to where Ganesha was and Shiva attached the head of the elephant to Ganesha's body and he was alive. After that they took Ganesha to Mother Parvati, and she was thrilled, and the entire problem vanished. It also thrilled mother Parvati was also to see Ganesha alive.

Glory of Ganesha:

When Mother Parvati found that Ganesha alive, then she was thrilled and pleased. She hugged him and made him wear good clothes and other ornaments. Then Mother Parvati kissed Ganesha on the chic and blessed him with enlighten. She also told him whoever worships you with Sindor (Right lead) it will remove all their obstacles as a blessing said Mother Parvati to Ganesha. Then Shiva put his hands on Ganesha's head and told everyone that he is his second son. Then Ganesha stood up and gave respect to Shiva and also other gods and goddess. He also apologizes to all of them. Then all the gods blessed him with saying that he would be the first god to be worshipped and only after worshipping they should worship Ganesha other gods. Then

Shiva worshipped Ganesha then Brahmdev, Vishnu, Mother Parvati and also all other gods worshipped Ganesha. So Ganesha became the first god to be worshipped before worshipping any other gods.

Wedding of Ganesha:

Brahmdev said hey Muni to Naradh Jee as time went by so did Kumar Kartikya and Ganesha also were grown up. They used to play together and so on. One day Shiva and Mother Parvati were sitting quietly, and they thought about the marriage of Kumar Kartikya and Ganesha. So then Kumar Kartikya and Ganesha somehow knew about the thought of their parents and so asked them to do their wedding first. Both Kumar and Ganesha asked their parents to have their wedding first before the other one. Then Shiva told them whoever among you two circle the Earth will first will have their wedding first. Then Kumar Kartikya runs to circle the Earth while Ganesha thought he wouldn't be able to run as fast as Kumar. So Ganesha asks his parents to sit together, and he started worshipping them first, and after that he circled them seven times. After that he told his parents he won the race by circling them seven times. So there was a debate and Ganesha said according to procedure in other holy books he should have won the race. Then at the end Shiva and Mother Parvati agreed with Ganesha. Then Prajapati came to meet Shiva while looking for the groom for his two daughters named Siddhi and Buddhi. Then Shiva and Mother Parvati agreed to let Ganesha wed with Siddhi and Buddhi both. Then Vishokarma wed Ganesha with Siddhi and Buddhi in a huge function where everyone was invited.

After so many years, Ganesha had two sons. One from Siddhi named Cheyam and Laav from Buddhi. Then only Kumar Kartikya came back from circling the Earth, and on the way Naradh Jee told Kumar Kartikya all the stories. So that made him sad, and he went to Kaunj hill to meditate.

Om Nama Shivaya:

Rudra Sanhita Yudha Khanda:

Sastha Khanda.

Sixth Section:

Description of Tripurasoor:

After the death of Tarkasoor all three sons of his went to Uttarakhand of India to perform harsh meditation. They were first one Bidubmali, second one Tarkchu and third one Kamalcha. All three of them were brave winners, and against the gods. All three of them to impress Brahmdev did hard meditation in a place called Sumaeyru. They meditate for thousands of years with hard meditation, so then Brahmdev appeared before them. Then they gave their regards to Brahmdev and told him that if it thrill him with their meditation, then please bless us with being immortal. By being immortal we if we like we should be able to control all three Lok. Bless us with that, said the three sons to Brahmdev. After hearing them, Brahmdev told them to start praying and devotion toward Shiva. Also, no human can be immortal, so ask for some other blessings, said the Brahmdev to the three sons. Then the three sons asked for a three fortresses that no one can break or damage and also it should have wealth and many luxury items and it shouldn't end. So Tarkchu asked for golden fortress, Kamalcha asked for silver fortress and Bidubmali asked for metal fortress. Then Brahmdev said bless you and wish them the same. So the three fortress got build according to their wish, and it situated them in heaven, sky, and Earth. So all three sons of Tarkasoor relaxed and enjoyed their own fortress. Then they also grab all three Lok to rule by themselves.

So after that because of effects of three fortress all the gods being very humiliated went to Brahmdev and told him their sadness. Brahmdev then told them to go to Shiva and so they all went towards Shiva. When they reached there, they started praising Shiva by singing his glory. The Shiva asked them what happen. Then all the gods said because of three son Tarkasoor they have no place and the three sons have occupied all three Lok. Till they do not destroy the three fortresses please make us place and policy on what to do now said the gods to Shiva. The Shiva told gods that all three sons of Tarkasoor are my devotees and they always have worshipped me so I can't kill them. But all of you go to Vishnu to find the solution to your problem said Shiva to gods. Then do what Vishnu tells you to do said Shiva. Then all the gods along with Brahmdev went to where Vishnu was. The Vishnu listens to what the gods had to say and told them to organize a holy fire ritual called Yegya in Sanskrit. So according to the order of Vishnu all the gods organized a Yegya and from the fire of that Yegya different brave ghosts came out. And Vishnu asked those ghosts to destroy the three fortress. Then the ghosts went to destroy the three fortress but they couldn't do anything. Most of the ghosts died and remaining ones went to Vishnu to tell him they were unsuccessful in their mission. Then Vishnu told gods that because of their devotion toward Shiva and the three sons' always worshipping Shiva have made them sort of immortal. So first we have to make them no devotional towards Shiva and also will have to make them stop worshipping Shiva only then we will be successful in removing all three fortress to kill them said Vishnu to gods? After saying all these Vishnu said let me think of some ways to help you but now all of you rest.

Implementing Idea of Atheist or Unbeliever:

The Vishnu creates an atheist or unbeliever human. Whose clothes were dirty and head was bold. Vishnu named that human unbeliever. That human who was named atheist or unbeliever was holding a wooden board in one hand and broom in another hand. Then unbeliever covering his face with cloth stands in front of Vishnu. Vishnu told Unbeliever that since he was born from Vishnu's body, he can complete the task. You will be a great illustrator full of Maya energies, said Vishnu to Unbeliever. So you compose a sixteen thousand sentences to describe religion, heaven and hell. You must prove in the book that everything is right there within the reach. After telling the Unbeliever what to write in those sixteen thousand sentences, Vishnu vanishes.

After that the Unbeliever started preaching the religion which had all the religions and also there was no differentiate between being male or female. Which was the Maya based book that Unbeliever composite based on the knowledge given to him by Vishnu. Then he had four devoted disciples who accepted the religion that Unbeliever invented. Then all four disciples covering their nose with a wooden bowl in one hand and broom in another hand started walking around and preaching others to do the same through the power of Maya. Atheist or Unbeliever had created a scripture of Maya, which he was teaching all his disciples and making them believe it is the truth.

Then the followers or disciple of Atheists entered Tripura where the three brothers were ruling and preached young kids about the scripture of Maya. But there effects of Maya couldn't last long as a blessing of Shiva to Tripura. So Naradh Jee appeared before them to take the Atheist to the three brothers, and after that they all started believing the atheist or unbeliever. Soon all the people living In Tripura came under the effects of Maya played by the Atheist. So all the towns in Tripura was under the effect of Maya.

Request to Finish Tripura and Designing of Shiva's Chariot:

When Tripurasoor abandoned the throne after listening to atheists, then all the religions inside Tripura disappeared and all the citizens of Tripura ill conducted. Then Vishnu went to Kailas to pray to him to kill the demons to establish peace among all. Also Brahmdev, Indra and also other gods also went with Vishnu to please Shiva. After listening to all the praise from all the gods, Shiva came out riding Nandi. Shiva said to the gods that he already knows about the sins of the demons in Tripura so he would kill them, but from the heart they still devote them still to me and that needs to be removed from them. After that I would kill them and rest of them can be killed by Vishnu, said Shiva.

After hearing Shiva Vishnu became sad and right, then Brahmdev requested Shiva that he would be more capable of killing all the demons inside Tripura. You will not gain any sin by killing those demons so consider killing them all instead of Vishnu said Brahmdev to Shiva. I am also your priest and Vishnu is your prince and Indra and other gods are your devotees. You are the father of the Universe, and also ours said Brahmdev to Shiva. The Shiva said you all have raised me to kill the demons inside the Tripura, but I have nothing. No Chariot, no bow, nothing so how can I go to war with nothing said Shiva to the gods. Then the gods said if you will go to fight the demons, then we will build all those things for you. After saying that to Shiva, all the Gods stand still with patience.

The Shiva said provided I divine chariot, divine bow and arrow, and divine chariot driver. After hearing that from Shiva all the gods became thrilled and went towards Vishokarma. After receiving order from Vishnu, Vishokarma build a very nice chariot for Shiva.

The chariot was all made up of gold. It had sun on the right wheel and moon on the left wheel. Twelve stars were on the right wheel and sixteen arts on the left wheel. On that chariot twelve suns and sixteen positions of the moon on the right side of the chariot. All the elements of the universe were on that chariot. After getting orders from Vishnu and Brahmdev Vishokarma made the chariot with lots of devotion.

When the chariot was ready with all the specifications, the Brahmdev attached the chariot with horses made of Veda. Then they requested Shiva and Goddess Parvati to sit at the chariot. Then riding that chariot reached front of the Tripura. The Shiva told the gods that not to worry and one who fasts for betterment then that one will be liberated. Then all the gods became thrilled and praised Shiva. They also followed Shiva and Goddess Parvati with horses, lions, tigers and other rides all the way to Tripura. The liberated ones started throwing flowers from the sky to the force of Shiva and Goddess Parvati. Then after reaching Tripura, the Shiva and Goddess Parvati entered inside the Tripura along with all the forces of gods.

Killing of Tarkasoor:

Brahmdev said when Shiva got on the chariot, the chariot didn't move at all. Shiva had to wait for quite some time in the chariot. Then suddenly a voice came from a sky that Shiva has not worshipped Ganesh. Ganesh was standing on his toe and therefore delaying the procession of the chariot. The Shiva according to rules and regulation worshipped Ganesh, and after that

Ganesh was happy. So he quickly removed all obstacles from the way for Shiva to process. Then Shiva put a powerful arrow in the bow to destroy everything in Tripura. Right then all the devils inside Tripura looked at Shiva, but the Gods told Shiva not to spare any of the devils inside Tripura. So then hundreds of hot fire likes Sun arrows from the bow of Shiva killed all the devils inside Tripura. Thousands of devils who used to live inside Tripura got killed. They scared the devils who abandoned worshipping Shiva to be atheist.

When Tarkasoor was dying in the fire from the arrow, he said hey Shiva; I knew I would die from your hand. But I was not aware of the death I would get. Which is great than the death of great Sage. Then Tarkasoor requested Shiva that from now on in any of my lives I should always praise you and nothing more than anything else. So please grant me this wish, said Tarkasoor and other two of his brothers. Then except for devil named Maya all other devils died and the three brothers of Tarkasoor became the follower of Shiva.

Indra got a new life:

Once Guru of Gods Brihaspati and King of Gods Indra was going towards Kailas to meet Shiva. Then Shiva wanting to test them disguised himself with dreadlock hair and stopped them on their way. Indra didn't recognize Shiva and asks him hey dreadlock guy is Shiva in Kailas or has he gone somewhere? Asked Indra to dreadlock Shiva. Then Shiva answered nothing, and that angered Indra. Then with ego Indra said I am Indra king of gods and I am asking you a question said Indra. Then Indra said I will hit you with this weapon Bajra and you will die at once and also I will see if anyone will come to rescue you. Right then Indra picked his Bajra to hit Shiva and then Shiva grabbed Indra's hand and he was about to hit himself with the Bajra by the force of Shiva. Indra couldn't move because of pressure from Shiva, who was furious with Indra. Then when Indra felt the power of Shiva, then he thought this dreadlock guy will finish him soon. Also Indra was in a lot of pain because of pressure from Shiva grabbing his hands with the Bajra.

When Guru Brihaspati saw the superpower in the dreadlock guy, then he recognized his Shiva. Then Guru Brihaspati bowed in front of Shiva and praised Shiva. Then Indra also lied down with Guru Brihaspati in the foot of Shiva. They then ask for forgiveness from Shiva, especially Guru Brihaspati. Then Shiva said where can put this anger of mine to forgive you. So Shiva tell Guru Brihaspati that because of his request and effort he has given new life to Indra so from now on I will call your life and my anger will no longer give pain to Indra said Shiva.

Then Shiva put his anger in the ocean to rest. Then Shiva vanished, and Indra and Guru Brihaspati also went back to their homes.

Creation of Jalandhar:

When Shiva put his anger in the Ocean, then a baby boy born from that anger. And he started crying loudly at the conjunction of Ganga Sagar Ocean. The boy was crying so loud that the whole Universe could hear him crying loudly. He was so loud that the entire world became curious about his crying. He was crying so loudly that everything in the World was being disturbed. After hearing the child of Shiva cry so much, all the gods went to Brahmdev and told him everything. They also requested Brahmdev to kill the boy, so he won't be a problem for them later on. After that, Brahmdev went to the Ocean where the boy was crying. When Ocean saw Brahmdev, then he gave his respect and regard to Brahmdev and put the child on his lap. Then Brahmdev asked Ocean, whose son is it? Ocean then replied I don't know whose son this boy is, but he was born on the conjunction of Ganga and Ocean. Now you do the honor of naming the boy said Ocean to Brahmdev.

As Ocean was saying, the child grab the neck of Brahmdev and he wouldn't let go. So Brahmdev had a tough time trying to take the child's hands from his neck. While he was trying, tears fell from both the eyes of Brahmdev. So finally he took the child's hand out of his neck. Brahmdev then said listen, I will name the boy Jalandhar because he made tears fall from my eyes. He is a young boy as soon as he was born. He is capable of many qualities to defend anyone in war. He will be the leader of devils. He can even defend Vishnu in war. Only Shiva can defeat him. His wife will be beautiful, husband oriented, and will have all the good qualities. After saying everything about Jalandhar, Brahmdev left. Then Ocean called Saint Sukracharya the Guru of devils to take Jalandhar and make him the king of the devils. Brinda a daughter of devil Kalnemi. It was a big wedding, and many guests took part the wedding. Then after that Jalandhar started ruling the devils with the guidance of Saint Sukracharya.

Battle between Gods and Jalandhar:

At one time Jalandhar with his wife Brinda was sitting in a palace and Bhrigu Jee appeared before them. Then Jalandhar regarded and offer his respect to Bhrigu Jee and asked him hay Guru who cut the head of this devil Rahu? Then Bhrigu Jee said that gods had drilled the Ocean (Samundra Manthan) and took out potion from it. While drinking that potion, this Rahu also disguised as gods and took the potion. After finding out that God Indra complained that to Vishnu. Then Vishnu cut his head. After hearing that, Jalandhar became furious and his eyes turned red. So he called his honest server Ghasmar and asked him to take his message to god Indra. Then Ghasmar went to the palace of god Indra and started saying hey sinners, why did you mishandled my father Ocean and took all the priceless valuable jewelry and stones and other things from him. So if you want your wellbeing, then bring all those things you took from my father. It will destroy otherwise I will come and destroy your kingdom and you will suffer said Ghasmar to god Indra. Then Indra also said, why did that Ocean gave shelter to my enemies, the devils? Because he gave them shelter, I took everything from him. Then Ghasmar goes back to Jalandhar and describes everything to him.

After hearing what Ghasmar had to say, Jalandhar became furious. Then he started calling devils from everywhere to attack Indra Puri. So an enormous number of devils went to Indra puri. At the Heaven they arrived at Nandaban (Jungle|). So Gods also started gathering to prepare themselves for war with the devils. So war broke between Gods and devils. Saint Sukracharya was saving all the injured and dead devils by spelling Mrit Sanjivini Mantra. **Guru Brihaspati** on the other side was saving Gods with herbs from Drohangiri.

Then Jalandhar asked Guru Sukracharya how gods are being alive again? Then Sukracharya said that Guru Brihaspati is bringing herbs from Drohangiri and saving them. Then Sukracharya suggested to Jalandhar that he should throw Drohangiri in to the Ocean. So devils threw Drohangiri inside the Ocean. Then Guru Brihaspati told gods now you can't win this war. You should all try to save yourselves. He also said it is because Indra had insulted Shiva long time ago, therefore this results from war. Then all the Gods went to hide at different locations. Jalandhar then stays at the throne of Indra puri.

Battle between Jalandhar and Vishnu:

Gods who went into hiding at different locations because of the fair of Jalandhar reached Baikuntha where Vishnu lives. There they started praising Vishnu. Finally, Vishnu heard their prayer and came to them. Vishnu said don't worry Gods, just throw your fear of Jalandhar away. I will defeat him in battle, said Vishnu to the Gods. After that, Vishnu gets ready to go to the battle with Jalandhar. Then Goddess Laxmi ask Vishnu not to kill Jalandhar who is also her brother. Then Vishnu says I will not kill him, but I still have to go the battle. Then Vishnu along with Gods goes to the battlefield.

The really long battle took place between Vishnu and Jalandhar. Devils started defeating the Gods. Then Gods started running away. By seeing that, Vishnu moved forward and started killing devils in large numbers. By seeing this, Jalandhar started battling with Vishnu.

Then Jalandhar being furious started attacking Vishnu with bow and arrow. Jalandhar also broke the bow of Vishnu. Then Vishnu attacked him with Gada (Weapon of Vishnu) but that didn't affect Jalandhar so much. Instead, he stabbed Vishnu on the chest with an arrow. Then Jalandhar attacked Vishnu with Trishul, then Vishnu thinking about Shiva broke the Trishul. After some time they wrestled with each other. After battling for a while. Vishnu appeared in front of Jalandhar in spiritual figure. And told him he is very impressed with Jalandhar for not giving up the battle. Also was pleased to see his battling skills. So Vishnu told Jalandhar that it thrill him with him and ask him to make a wish. Then Jalandhar said if you are so pleased with me, then you and my sister Laxmi must stay with me in my house. Then Vishnu granted him his wish. So Vishnu and Goddess Laxmi then started living with Jalandhar in his house. Then Jalandhar took all the valuable stones and Jewelry from Gods and brought them to Earth. He also made Nishumbha devil in charge of Patal (Devil's Country). Then Jalandhar won the battle against everyone and started ruling the World.

Trick of Naradh Jee:

So Gods were all getting frustrated by Jalandhar and the way he was ruling the World. So they started thinking about Shiva. Then Shiva thought about doing well for the Gods called Naradh Jee to Kailas. Then Shiva send Naradh Jee to Jalandhar's Kingdom. There he saw all the Gods were suffering. He then told Gods that don't worry, soon your sufferings will be over. After saying that, Naradh Jee went inside the palace of Jalandhar. When Jalandhar saw Naradh Jee, he respected him and gave his regards to Naradh Jee. He then asks Naradh Jee what brings him there. How can I serve you? Is there anything that he wants? Jalandhar asked Naradh Jee. Then Naradh Jee says I just came from Kailas and there at a beautiful Jungle whose beauty is indescribable. And there I saw Shiva with Goddess Parvati sitting there. That was the most beautiful thing that I ever saw, said Naradh Jee. So I thought could there be anything more beautiful than that. So then I thought about you, and therefore I came to see you. So I wanted to compare you with what I saw. Then Jalandhar being thrilled started showing his achievement in terms of jewelry and other priceless stones which he was possessing. After seeing everything Naradh Jee then says you have all the wealth and priceless jewelries, but you don't have what it takes to make these things appear beautiful. There is no woman in this entire Universe who is prettier than Goddess Parvati. So all your wealth and priceless stones and jewelries means nothing in front of her says Naradh Jee to Jalandhar. After saying that then, he returns and disappears in the sky.

Conversation of the Messenger:

After Naradh Jee left, then Jalandhar send one of his devil server Rahu to Kailas as a messenger. When that messenger reached Kailas, then Nandi Jee stopped him at the door and didn't allow him to enter. But somehow by tricking Nandi Jee that messenger Rahu reached where Shiva was sitting with his followers. There he said loudly that that Jalandhar has demanded Goddess Parvati for himself. Right then a creature came out of the Earth whose face was like that of Lion and he started chasing Rahu and captured him. Then Rahu takes refuge to Shiva and begs for his life. Then Shiva lets Rahu be free from that creature. So Rahu then returns to Jalandhar. While that creature then complains to Shiva that he is hungry. Then Shiva told him to eat his own hands and legs. Which he does, and only his head remains alive after that. So Shiva becomes very pleased with himself and makes him the gatekeeper of Kailas who later on known as Sakirtimukh.

Battle between Shiva followers and devils:

When that messenger returned, then he told the whole story to Jalandhar. Jalandhar then asked his army of devils to prepare for battle with Shiva. The devils from all directions started gathering. There were millions and millions of devils. So all the devils were ready to battle with Shiva. So devils started heading to start the battle with Shiva. Then many bad signs occurred from sky while they were travelling to the battlefield. Right then crown fell from Jalandhar's head to the ground, which was a sign of bad luck. Even though they still continued towards the battlefield.

Then Shiva followers went to Shiva and told him about what is happening. They also told Shiva that Vishnu also is taking refuge at Jalandhar's palace. Also, all the gods are also under Jalandhar's territory. So please kill this devil, Jalandhar said, the Shiva followers to Shiva.

Then Shiva called Vishnu and asked him why he didn't kill Jalandhar. Then Vishnu said Jalandhar is actually a brother of Goddess Laxmi, so I couldn't kill him. Also, he is very brave and knows many battling skills that is also why I couldn't kill him, said Vishnu to Shiva. After hearing Vishnu, Shiva laughed and said I will definitely kill Jalandhar now.

The devils started making noise outside Kailas. Shiva also gave permission to his followers to battle with the devils. Then near Kailas battle begin between devils and Shiva's followers. Devils started attacking with many weapons. Even Earth started shaking because of the effect of the Battle. All the dead animals and solders started piling up Like Mountain. Then Sukracharya started saving dead devils by spelling Mrit Sanjivini. Then that Made Rudra furious, then a lady with long iron hands came out of his mouth. Then that lady started chewing devils on the battlefield. Then she reached in front of Sukracharya and hide Sukracharya inside her body. When Sukracharya was not there, then all the devils started running away from the battle. Ganesh and Kartikya also started killing devils in the battle.

Then Shiva's followers started killing most of the devils. They defeated most of the devils while battling. Then Jalandhar came to the battlefield. Then he started battling with Nandi, and Ganesh, and he defeated them. Then Kumar Kartikya pulled an arrow towards Jalandhar and it hit Jalandhar and made him fall in the ground. But he got up quickly again and battled. The Jalandhar also injured Bir Bhadra. Then Shiva's followers were defeated by Jalandhar and remaining force started running away from the battle to save their lives.

Battle between Shiva and Jalandhar:

Then Shiva in Rudra figure riding on Nandi entered the battlefield. The devils got scared by looking at the dangerous figure of Rudra, and so they started running out. Then targeting thousand arrows at a time, Jalandhar started attacking Shiva. Shiva then cuts off all the arrows in to pieces. Then Shiva cut off the head of devil Khadoaroma. He also cut off the head of devil Bahla. Then Jalandhar started scolding his bravest soldiers for running out of the battle. Then Jalandhar attacked Shiva with seventy arrows at the same time. While Shiva was cutting those arrows in to pieces, he also broke bow of Jalandhar. Then Shiva attacked Jalandhar with seven arrows and that injured Jalandhar. Then Jalandhar started attacking Shiva with Gada, and that also Shiva broke it in two pieces. Then Jalandhar disappeared from there and went to Goddess Parvati by disguising himself as Shiva. After seeing Goddess Parvati Jalandhar couldn't control and sperm flew from him. Then Goddess Parvati thought he was shameless, so she disappeared and went to the bottom of the Ocean to hide. Then Vishnu appeared in front of Goddess Parvati.

Then Goddess Parvati said to Vishnu that does he know what Jalandhar did today? Then Vishnu said yes, I already know about it. Then Goddess Parvati said for what he you also destroyed his wife's honesty and dignity towards him. Then only that devil can be killed.

Destroying Brinda's Devotion:

Then Vishnu went to Jalandhar's palace and stayed in a garden there. Then Brinda saw in her dreams that Jalandhar was naked and had an oily head. Who was riding on buffalo heading in South direction? He was wearing black flower necklace. All the wild animals were surrounding him. His city was drowning in the Ocean. Then Brinda woke up and started thinking about her dream. Then nothing motivated her to do anything. Then she with her servers went to the garden. There she saw a yogi looking man sitting on the garden which was Vishnu. Then she put her hand on his shoulder. Then suddenly all her fear vanished, and she felt good. Then she regarded the Yogi and gave her respect to him. Then two monkeys appeared in front of them, and after that they flew in the sky. In a little monkey came back with Jalandhar's head and other organs. Then after seeing that Brinda fainted and when she woke up she started saying all kinds of foul language to Vishnu. Then she started crying and begged Vishnu to make her husband alive again. Then Vishnu said Shiva killed Jalandhar, so it's impossible to make him alive again. But whenever someone takes refuge, then helping them is the rule of Sanatan religion, said Vishnu. So he made Jalandhar alive again. Then Jalandhar appeared before them and started hugging his wife and kissing her. They then made love with each other. While making love, Brinda notices that it is Vishnu.

Then she says one who uses other man's wife you are worthless. Now I know you say Brinda to Vishnu. She also says that you are a Mayabi (Illusionist), the two devils that you showed me the same will take your wife away. This yogi will be your friend, and monkeys will help you. You will suffer a lot, said Brinda to Vishnu. After saying all that she jumped inside the fired and it completely burned her was completely. The smoke from the fire dissolved in Goddess Parvati.

Killing of Jalandhar:

When Jalandhar disappeared, then Shiva became furious. Then Shiva started attacking Jalandhar with arrows. Jalandhar started cutting the arrows thrown towards him by Shiva. When Jalandhar couldn't cut the arrows anymore, then from Maya, he created Parvati and hanged on the wheels of his chariot. When Shiva saw that he became very sad and Rudra comes out of Shiva who was appearing very scary and dangerous for the devils. After seeing that Rudra figure of Shiva, no devils could stand in front of him. So they started running away from the battle. Even brave devils like Sumba and Nissumbha started running away. Shiva then says that you guys did all this to Parvati now all of you are running away. So killing the ones who are running away is sin. Therefore, I will not kill you two, but Parvati herself will kill you two. After that, Jalandhar becomes angry and starts attacking Shiva. Then Shiva made Sudarshan Chakra (Weapon) from his fingers and that cut of the head of Jalandhar. So with a loud noise, his head falls down at the ground and breaks into two pieces. The blood from the head covered the whole battlefield to make it red. By the order of Shiva, his blood and other body parts became a structure in Gaurav hell. By seeing Jalandhar die like that all the Gods, All devotees, Snakes, Human and other animals all became thrilled.

Ending delusion of Vishnu and creation of Amala, Malati, and Tulsi:

When Gods were quiet after celebrating Jalandhar's death. Shiva then says "hey Gods Jalandhar was part of me and the whole thing was a play that I had to conduct to teach everyone something about the world. Then the Gods told Shiva that Vishnu felt in love with Brinda. He has poured the ashes of Brinda after she gave her life by jumping in to the fire. Since you are the creator of everything, please advise Vishnu said the Gods to Shiva.

Then Shiva explained what Maya is to the Gods. He also said everything in the world is under the effect of Maya. So Vishnu also under the same effect of lust. Then Shiva said Maha Goddess Uma is the creator of three Veda and she is also the nature. They also know she is also a Gaura. That's why to cure Vishnu from effects of Maya, you should go to her, said Shiva to the Gods. Then all the Gods went to Goddess Uma to request her about Vishnu. There they started praising Goddess Uma, and then they heard the voice from the sky. The voice said I am present everywhere and I am Gaura in Sato goon, Laxmi in Rajo goon, and Knowledge as Sarswoti in Tamo goon. Therefore, all of you go to my energy are with three Goddess and they will help you. Then all the Gods went to the three Goddess Gauri, Laxmi, and Sarswoti. There they praised them all by singing their glory. After that all three Goddess appeared before them and gave them some seeds. And told the Gods by using these seeds you can have anything. Then the Gods took the seeds and poured where the ash of Brinda. Then from there Amala, Malati, and Tulsi grew out of it. Then Amala and Tulsi fell in love. By seeing this Vishnu went to Baikuntha and started meditating about Shiva like before.

Creation of Shankhachud:

Sanat Kumara tells Vyas Jee now you listen to different characters of Shiva, which also destroys one's sins. Vidhata had a son Name Marichi, and he had a son named Kashyap. That divine follower Kashyap was given thirteen ladies by Dakshya to get married. So Kashyap had thirteen wives. Out of those thirteen one was named Danu. Who was best in everything and was beautiful and talented. From her, Kashyap had lots of sons but one son named Biprachit. Who was very brave and hardworking? Biprachit had a son named Dambhaman. Who was very devoted to Vishnu? He didn't have any sons, so he got a spelling from Guru Sukracharya. So he performed a meditation at Puskar for one hundred thousand years. Then by seeing that Gods became scared and along with Brahmdev they went to Vishnu. Then Vishnu told them that don't be scared it's one of my devoted praising me. So I will fulfill his wish. Then all the Gods went back to their Loka.

Vishnu then arrived at Puskar to bless Dambhaman. Then as soon as Dambhaman asked Vishnu to bless him with a son that can defeat all the Gods, and others. Then Vishnu said as you wish and blessed him. So Vishnu then returned to his Loka. Then when the right time came Dambhaman wife became pregnant and gave birth to a son. Sudhama Krishna jee's friend came as a son. After birth his name was Shankhachud. By watching the childhood activities of Shankhachud, his parents were very pleased.

Wedding of Shankhachud:

Shankhachud also went to Puskar and did hardship meditation. Brahmdev became very pleased with him. So he appeared before Shankhachud to bless him. Then Brahmdev asked Shankhachud to tell him his wish. Then Shankhachud asked Brahmdev that Gods should not be able to win the battle against him. Brahmdev then blessed him. Brahmdev also told Shankhachud to go to Badrikashram and there Tulsi is meditating. You go there and get married with Tulsi. She is the daughter of Dharmaraj. After saying that, Brahmdev disappeared. Then Shankhachud arrived at Badrikashram and there Brahmdev himself performed the wedding of Shankhachud and Tulsi. Then they started living together as couple at different places of the world.

Kingdom of Shankhachud:

Then Sanatkumar says after wedding Tulsi Shankhachud came back to his home. Then he meditated and got and received what he wanted. Then Sukracharya also granted him a blessing with the post of Danabendra. The highest blessing received by the demons by Sukracharya. Then after that Shankhachud with many demon forces went to battle for Indra Puri. There they fought with Indra and other Gods. With their large force of demons, Gods lost the battle. So they went to different caves in Earth to hide. Then Shankhachud ruled all three Loka after capturing heaven from Indra. So he himself became Indra by refuging all other Gods like Sun, Moon, and Kuber, all were under his rules and regulations. Then one day all the Gods along with Brahmdev went to Vishnu to ask for help in Baikuntha. There.

Vishnu, after hearing the Gods, told them he knows about it. He also said that in the previous life Shankhachud was a dear friend of mine. He became demon because of curse from the previous life. But for now you don't worry about him, said Vishnu to the Gods and Brahmdev.

Gods Went to Shiva:

Sanatkumar says hey Vyas Jee, then Vishnu with Brahmdev and other Gods went to Shiva Lok to meet Shiva. At the Shiva Lok Shiva was surrounded by his followers Ganas. There Shiva along with Goddess Parvati was seated at the throne. Seeing Shiva like that made Vishnu thrilled and very pleased. Vishnu observed the dance and other rituals that was happening there very seriously. Then he started praising Shiva and told him that Shankhachud was giving lots of problems to the Gods, so please, Do something about him. Then Shiva said I know Shankhachud well. He took birth in demons because of the cruse of Radha back in the previous life. Then Shiva said don't worry I will kill Shankhachud to protect Gods from him. Then all the Gods became thrilled, and they went back.

Conversation of Shankhachud with Pushpadanta:

Then Maha Rudra Shiva then sends Pushpadanta as his messenger to Shankhachud. His town was near Mahendra, and Kuber's house. After reaching there the messenger told Shankhachud that "either you wrote everything that you took from Gods or else be ready to battle with Shiva". So what do you have to say asks the messenger to Shankhachud.

Then Shankhachud says I cannot return Gods their things or their rights. So I am ready to battle with Shiva, says Shankhachud. So tomorrow morning I will go towards Rudra Loka, says Shankhachud.

After hearing that Shiva became furious. So he called Bir Bhadra and other followers and told them to kill Shankhachud. Shiva himself along with his force started going towards Shankhachud. With Shiva all eight Bhairav, All eight Basu, Rudra, Second day Sun, Fire, Moon, Vishokarma, Ashwini Kumar, Kuber, Yam, Nalkubar, power of hundred Devi, Bhadra Kali, all had gone. Kali's tongue was spreading across four miles far while walking. She was holding the head of a devil. With her there were thirty million Yoginis and thirty million black magician women. As they were walking and during the night time, Shiva settled underneath a tree near Chandra Bhaga River.

Shankhachud Battle Journey:

After the messenger of Shiva, Pushpadanta left. Shankhachud goes to Tulsi and tells her he is going for a battle tomorrow morning. That night Tulsi and Shankhachud talked about different things, and they also made love to each other. In the morning Shankhachud made his son the king and asked his son to take care of his mother too. After that, he tries to please his wife Tulsi. Who was crying because her husband would battle? After that, Shankhachud called his commander of the soldier and told him to make a force ready to go to battle. So after that there were three hundred thousand soldiers ready to go to battle. Then Shankhachud leads the force of soldiers and heads to battle with Shiva. Then he settles the force at the bank of Pushpa Bhadra River. From there, he examines the force of Shiva.

Then king of Devils Shankhachud sends a messenger to Shiva, and he tells Shiva, that I the Shankhachud have arrived for a battle. So what do you want to do? Says the messenger to

Shiva. Then Shiva tells the messenger you go to your master and tell him. That you let go your anger towards from god, you return their countries to them. Don't hamper the cultural heritage because the result could be dangerous to you, says Shiva. You are the lineage of saint Kashyap says Shiva. Then that messenger says to Shiva "hey what you have said is true, but the devils are not to be blamed alone here. You are favoring the Gods over devils. You are a Lord of both the gods and devils" says the messenger. Then Shiva says "I am under the control of devotees and I have no shame to battle for good cause". Then that messenger returns to Shankhachud.

Then that messenger tells all the conversation he had with Shiva. After hearing the messenger, Shankhachud battles with the gods and Shiva. So he calls his soldiers and ask them to start the battle. So Shiva also told gods and his force to engage in the battle. Shiva himself gets ready for the battle. Then the battle started between Shiva's force with Shankhachud and his force. Then they started killing each other on the battlefield. Mahendra started battling with Bikchaya Parba. Dambha started battling with Vishnu, Kalasur battles with Kaal (death), Gokarna battles with Hutashan, Kaleyaa battles with Kuber, Malaka battles with Vishokarma. Shiva with his sons was sitting underneath the Bata tree. At the battlefield, all the soldiers were battling with the devils. They used many weapons in the battlefield. It covered the battlefield with blood of injured and dead soldiers.

Shankhachud Battle:

All the gods, being defeated by the devils, started running away from the battlefield. Some gods ran away and went to Shiva for protection. The Shiva became furious and got ready to battle himself. As soon as he entered the battlefield, he killed hundreds of devils. On the other side goddesses Kali also started killing devils and drinking their blood. She started eating hundreds of devils, thousands of elephant, an uncountable number of soldiers. Kumar also started killing thousands of devils with his bow and arrows. So remaining devil soldiers started running away from the battlefield. After that, Shankhachud came to battle himself. He started throwing arrows from the bow to everywhere. Soon the battlefield became dark because of it. The gods and Shiva followers couldn't understand the Maya (Illusion) of Shankhachud. Then Shankhachud attacked Kumar. Kumar also started battling with Shankhachud. Kumar destroyed the chariot of Shankhachud and he also destroyed all of his arms. Then Shankhachud attacked Kumar again made him fall on the ground. Goddesses Kali lifts Kumar and takes him to Shiva. Where Shiva heals Kumar to battle again. Bir Bhadra and Shankhachud were also battling with each other. Goddesses Kali started eating devils again.

Battle between Bhadra, kali and Shankhachud:

In the battlefield, Bhagwati started battling with the devils. Lots of devils became injured. Long tooth Chandi Devis started drinking devils' blood. All the devils started panicking. Then Shankhachud started battling with Bhadra Kali. Bhadra Kali showered arrows upon Shankhachud. Shankhachud somehow survive the arrows. Then Bhadra Kali used Narayan Asra

(Weapon) on Shankhachud. Then Shankhachud got off from his chariot and did Naman (Respect) to the Narayan Asra. Then Narayan Asra itself became quiet. Then **Bhadra Kali** used to Braham Asra to Shankhachud. But Shankhachud survives that, too. Then **Bhadra Kali** widens her mouth and started roaring loudly. From which devils got scared and started running away. Then Bhadra Kali used Pashupata Asra, but Shankhachud survives that too. Because his death was not supposed to be with that Asra (Weapon). After that Bhadra Kali killed one hundred thousand devils by stepping over them. Then Bhadra Kali ran after Shankhachud to eat him. Then Shankhachud used Rudra Asra to stop the Bhadra Kali. Then Shankhachud used different other weapon upon Bhadra Kali. Which Bhadra Kali destroyed all and eat them. Then Bhadra Kali punched Shankhachud so hard that he fell on the ground. Then Bhadra Kali picked him up and threw him up in the air towards the Sky. But somehow Shankhachud came down on earth and stood on his feet.

Then Bhadra Kali hears a voice from the Sky that only Shiva can kill Shankhachud. The Shiva riding his ride came to the battlefield. After seeing Shiva in the battlefield. Shankhachud comes down from his chariot and does Naman to Shiva. After that he rides his chariot again and picks bow and arrow to battle with Shiva. He battles with Shiva for one hundred years. They both used different Asra (Weapon) to attack each other. Then Goddesses Kali came and started eating lots and lots of devils alive. Bir Bhadra and Nandi also killed thousands of devils in the battlefield. Remaining devils started running away.

Shiva kills Shankhachud:

When Shankhachud sees that his force of soldiers is running away from the battlefield. Then he becomes furious and starts attacking Shiva with bow and arrows. Then he became invisible and start doing small damages to the gods. Gods didn't understand his Maya (Illusion). The Shiva destroyed all his Maya. After that Shiva picked up his Trident to kill the Shankhachud. The voice from the sky said as long as his wife is purely devoted to him. You can't kill Shankhachud. So after hearing the voice, Shiva decided not to use Trident over Shankhachud. The Shiva thought about Vishnu. The Vishnu appeared before Shiva. Shiva told him something. After that Vishnu appeared like an old beggar. He went to Shankhachud and begged him for Vishnu crown from him. So Shankhachud gave him the Vishnu crown. After that he went to Tulsi, Shankhachud wife. They're disguised as Shankhachud, Vishnu made love with Tulsi. After that Shiva attacked Shankhachud with a weapon which killed him right there. So after that it cleared all the Shankhachud sins after his death. After that from his dead body Shankha insect came out of his bones. Which makes the sound of Shankha. That sound which is very attractive to Vishnu.

Curse of Tulsi:

Vishnu, for goodwill of gods, disguised himself as Brahman asked for the crown of Shankhachud. After that he disguised as Shankhachud reached where Tulsi was. There Tulsi thinking it's her husband, did all things as a devoted wife. Then she asked him about the war. The Vishnu who disguised as Shankhachud says that Brahmdev made him compromise with the gods. Shiva also went back and so I also came back, said Vishnu.

The Vishnu made love with Tulsi. Somehow Tulsi realized that it wasn't her husband. So she was ready to curse. The Vishnu came in his real figure. Then Tulsi said, "You don't have sympathy. You ripped your most devoted devotee today. Your heart is like stone so you must become a stone", says Tulsi. After that she started crying loudly. The Vishnu thought about Shiva. So Shiva appears before them. Then Shiva tries to explain things to Tulsi that this is how world works. So he says, "I bless you for all your good work and devotion. You will become a holy River and a flower which is pure. Because since you cursed Vishnu, he will also be stone in Gandaki River. Where tiny insects will form disk on the stone. Then everyone will worship that stone, calling it Saligram. Those who wouldn't worship Sali River and the Saligram wouldn't know the difference between heaven and hell", says Shiva.

The Shiva disappeared from there. Then Tulsi also with Vishnu went to Baikuntha. The other part of Tulsi became River Gandaki and started flowing. Vishnu also became stone and stayed inside River Gandaki. Where tiny insects started craving the stone to make it a Saligram. Saligram are therefore holy stones.

Killing of Hiranyachya:

Once a time Shiva along with Goddess Parvati walked from Kailas to Kashi puri. Then he made Kashi his kingdom. He made Bhairav the security for Kashi. So started living there doing different Leela (Activities).

Shiva and Parvati used to mingle at Mandara Chal Mountain. There once Parvati closed all three eyes of Shiva with her hands. Which made the whole Universe dark. Then one scary dark blind person occurred before them, and he started dancing. Looking at him Parvati became curious and asked Shiva "who is this guy?" The Shiva smiling says "this blind person is your son. When you closed my eyes, then from my sweat he took birth. You created him. So it's your responsibility to protect him". Then Parvati does everything that was needed to protect that blind guy.

Then Hiranyachya a devil was praying to Shiva for a son. He was praying for a son for so many years. So Shiva appeared before him and said, "I have a blind child. Who is as brave as you? So pray for that child to be your son. Then I can grant him to you as your son". Then that devil prayed to Shiva and goddess Parvati to have the blind child as his son. So when Shiva and goddess Parvati were pleased with his prayer. The granted devil Hiranyachya a blind child as his son.

After having the son, Hiranyachya won all three Loka in battle. So he started ruling all three Loka. Then Gods started praising Vishnu. The Vishnu with his long tooth killed all the devils and also cuts off the head of Hiranyachya. Then he made his blinded son the king of three Loka. Then Vishnu lifted the Earth with his long tooth to bring it above from hell. After that, Gods started praising Vishnu.

Killing of Hiranyakasipu:

After Vishnu kills Hiranyachya, his brother Hiranyakasipu wanted to battle with Vishnu.

Then Hiranyakasipu went to Mandara Chal Mountain and in one of the cave there. He stands on one thump and starts doing hard meditation for years. Because of the power of meditation, Brahmdev appeared before him to bless him. Then he asked Brahmdev to bless him with no fear to death and no human should be able to kill him. Then Brahmdev agreed and blessed him.

Then Hiranyakasipu he started ruling all three Loka. He was the king of devils. Because of his rulings, everyone was suffering. So Brahmdev along with Indra and other Gods went to Vishnu. There they told Vishnu how Hiranyakasipu was making everyone suffer. Then Vishnu told them, "don't worry, I will kill him". After that Vishnu disguised as Narsimha figure went to the city of Hiranyakasipu. There he started killing all devils and was wondering around. Praladh, the son of Hiranyakasipu, started praising the Narsimha figure of Vishnu. Praladh also told his father to surrender to Narsimha, but he didn't agree. So battle begin between Narsimha and Hiranyakasipu. So during dawn time when it was neither night nor day, Narsimha cuts the body of Hiranyakasipu with his long nails. So Narsimha killed Hiranyakasipu, and after that he makes Praladh the king.

Story of Blinded Son:

One time the blinded son of Hiranyachya was sitting with his brothers. Then his brothers started pulling his leg. They said "why do you need a kingdom, what's the use of it? Your father Hiranyachya was foolish to ask for the blinded son as blessing from Shiva. You are not eligible to be king. How can someone else's child be the king? That will not happen instead we will rule the country", said them. After hearing all those things from his brother, the blinded son became very upset. Then at night time he left for jungle to do hard meditation. There he meditates, but we gained nothing from it. So he burns his body on the fire. By seeing that, Gods went to Brahmdev and asked him to save the blinded son. Then Brahmdev went to him to bless him. There Brahmdev asked the blinded son "what do you want in blessing"? Then the blinded son said, "I want my eyesight, I want my kingdom back, no one should be able to kill me, neither Vishnu nor Shiva". Then Brahmdev said "that is not possible, so ask for something else". The blinded son said "except Shiva no one will kill me". Brahmdev then blessed him.

After that he came back home. He got his Kingdom back. Praladh and his other brothers became his devotes. Then he ruled for ten million years. At the end he started getting into bad habits, so he left the rule of Vedas while ruling. He left his sons, Brahmans, Guru, and others. Then he went to Mandara Chal Mountain and liked the place. He then builds a palace for him there. He started living there while he carried all the bad practice while living there.

Then there his ministers told him that in same Mountain there is a dreadlock guy whose woman is beautiful. So they said, "You have to go with us to look at her". The blinded king told his ministers "you guys bring her here for me". Then those ministers went to the cave of dreadlock guy who was Shiva. There they try to make a fool of Shiva. Then they told Shiva that "their king wants his women, so hand her over to us". Then Shiva said "I am a yogi and supreme of everyone and doing fasting for Pashupata (Animals welfare). That my wife can deal things. So ask her about it" says Shiva.

Then those ministers went back and told everything to the blinded King. After hearing what they had to say, the blinded king became furious with Shiva. Then he battles with Shiva and goes to Puri with many of his soldiers. Then battle begin between blinded king and Shiva. In the battlefield, the blood started flowing everywhere. The Shiva told goddess Parvati, "Look how bad the condition of the world is you have to fight with your own self. Here I fasted for Pashupata, but here I have to do something else. So let's go to different jungle" said Shiva to goddess Parvati. After that Shiva left to go to another jungle. But goddess Parvati stayed there. She stayed there at Mandara chal waiting for Shiva. Some follower of Shiva stayed there to protect goddess Parvati.

After Shiva left, blinded king tries to enter the cave of Shiva. For five hundred and five days blinded king fought a battle with followers of Shiva. So deadly battle took place between blinded king and followers of Shiva. So many got killed and injured in the battle. After that all the Shakti (Energy) of gods came and stayed with goddess Parvati. They all surrounded her and started making different tunes of divinity. After hearing the tune, their forces of army started battling the blinded king more effectively. Also other goddess like Narayani, Brahmi, Gauri, Indreni, and others started battling the blinded kings with their weapons. Goddess Parvati also started battling along with other goddess against the blinded king. While battling one thousand years went by. After that Shiva also comes back to the cave. After seeing Shiva, the blinded king sends a messenger to Shiva. Asking for his wife. The Shiva being furious told the messenger to tell the blinded king "be ready for battle".

After that blinded king made demon named Mahabali the commander. Blinded king himself went to battle with Shiva. He broke the cave by hitting with Bajra (Weapon) and also attacked goddess Parvati with it. The soldiers of the blinded king also broke the cave of Shiva. Then Shiva ask Vishnu to put forward the ghost followers of Shiva to battle the enemy. In that battle one of the demon named Bidhas swallowed Brahmdev, Vishnu, Sun, Moon, and other all gods. They were all trapped inside his stomach. They left only one follower of Shiva outside, who was Virak. The Shiva started singing Sama Veda. Then he observed the light of brightness as big as Sun inside his body. In the meantime, Bidhas also swallowed Nandi. After that Shiva himself came to the battlefield. He then injured Bidhas with his bow and arrow. Then he made Bidhas throw up all the gods that he had swallowed. After that again deadly battle begins between Shiva and the blinded king. Sukracharya was making the dead demons alive again and again. Shiva then swallowed Sukracharya inside his body. After that gods started defeating the demons. Gods also captured the blinded king and started beating him along with other demons. After that the blinded king started praising Shiva. Which made Shiva thrilled. So he made the blinded king his follower as one who is close to Shiva. After that, the battle ended. So Shiva along with goddess Parvati went back to their cave.

Freedom of Sukracharya:

Sukracharya, who was inside the stomach of Shiva, tried different ways to come out of it? He looked for hole from where he can escape outside. But after searching all over, he was unsuccessful to escape out. So he started meditating Shiva from inside the stomach. After that with the wish of Shiva he came out from the sperm of Shiva. After coming out, he gave his respect and regards to Shiva. The Shiva told Sukracharya that the way you entered my stomach and came out. Because of it you will be named Sukracharya from now on, instead of Bhargava said Shiva?

How Sukracharya received Mrit Sanjivini Vidya:

Vyas Jee said "hey Sanat Kumara now let me tell you the story of how Sukracharya while being Bhargava received MritSanjiwini Vidya, listen carefully". Then he says once long ago Sukracharya went to Varanasi Kashi to meditate upon Vishwonath Kashi for a long time. In the jungle by the Ganga River he stayed there and meditate there. Then there he also made Shiva Linga. To whom he worshipped every day as a ritual. He also builds a well there for other devotees. He started saying different Shiva's name hundred thousand times, and he also performed Tandap every day while worshipping. Then for one thousand years he controlled his mind to concentrate on Shiva. Then from that Shiva Linga Shiva came out and asked Sukracharya for his wish. Then Bhargava started praising Shiva by singing his glory. Then being very pleased Shiva gave him MritSanjiwini Vidya as a blessing. Also told him that by this Vidya you can give life to the death and they will be alive again as before. This Vidya will give you whatever you wish, it will be complete. By my blessing now you will shine above the Sun as a star name Vimal said Shiva to Sukracharya. Whenever people will see you shinning in the sky that is when all the good work such as marriage and other rituals should take place. After saying that Shiva went back to the same Shiva Linga. This is how Bhargava received MritSanjiwini Vidya from Shiva, said Vyas Jee.

Varasor:

Vyas Jee then said hey Sanatkumar Jee you told a beautiful story about Shiva. Now tell us the story of how Varasor got the position as follower (Gana) of Shiva. After hearing Vyas Jee Sanatkumar says the son of Marachi was Kashyap Jee. The thirteen daughters of Dakshya was his wives. From the eldest wife Diti Devil were born. From other wives, Gods were born. From Diti Hiranyakaisyap and Hiranyayacha, two strong devils were born. Hiranyakaisyap had four sons Hanladh, Anuhadh, Sahadh, and Praladh. Praladh had a son named Birochan who was a devotee of Vishnu. Who also cut his head to give it to god Indra? Birochan had a son named Bali, who was also as generous as his father. Bali had given the whole land of Earth to god Baman. The son of Bali was Varasor. Who was very generous and great devotee of Shiva? He had won all three Loka and created a town in Earth named as Soritpur. Once Varasor at performed Tandav and pleased Shiva. Then Shiva asked him for his wish. Then Varasor asked

Shiva to settle in Soritpur with his followers. The Shiva started living in Soritpur with his followers.

Then one day Shiva created an event by the banks of the river that was flowing in Soritpur. There was dance and music. All the gods and angels also took part in the event. The Shiva invited goddesses Parvati from the Kailas. Then they decided that till goddess Parvati reaches there. Any women can make love with Shiva. The Usha daughter of Varasor to catch Shiva became like goddess Parvati. Right then goddess Parvati also arrived there. Goddess Parvati knew what Usha was feeling then. The goddess Parvati asked Usha, why did you look like me? Okay, never mind. "Now in this Kartik month you will go through periods and in Baisakh month you will see someone in your dreams and you will marry him", said goddess Parvati to Usha. After saying all that to Usha, goddess Parvati became ready to make love with Shiva. After that both Shiva and goddess Parvati became invisible.

Characteristic of Usha:

Sanat Kumara Ji says, "Hey Vyas Ji, one time Barasoor pleased Shiva. Then he requested Shiva, "Hey, the thousand hands that you have given me is no use for me anymore. Beside you, I have already won a battle with other gods like Kuber and Indra. Therefore, please battle with me. The moment enemy will cut off all my hands and as they drop on earth, then I will have full satisfaction", said Barasoor to Shiva. Ten Shiva being angry told Barasoor, "You egoistic, being from the family of Bali, you dare to challenge me in battle". "Now soon you will satisfy your ego", said Shiva to Barasoor. "Soon you will now battle with someone much stronger than you and he will cut off all your hands so they drop in earth", said Shiva. After saying that, Shiva disappeared. Barasoor being thrilled started offering fresh flowers to Shiva.

Barasoor used to think who beside Shiva could kill him. While Barasoor was thinking about it, death appeared before him. The also Usha daughter of Barasoor was also there. It was Baisakh month. Usha used to worship Vishnu every night. One night she was sleeping with her friends. Then the son of Krishna through Maya came into her dreams and made love to her. Then Usha felt guilty and left the body.

Then Chitralekha, daughter of Kushmandi Yogini, told Usha about her previous life story. After that, Usha started thinking about having that secret husband forever. Then Chitralekha draw a picture of Ram, Krishna, Praduymna, and Anirudh. Then Usha said to Chitralekha that it is Anirudh who abused her in her dreams. After that, Chitralekha described who Anirudh was and his whole family history to Usha. After hearing the stories about Anirudh, Usha started liking him even more. Then by Maya Chitralekha went to Puri and brought Anirudh with her to Usha. There Usha started making love with Anirudh. There were noise and guards came inside Usha's room. Then they found out about Anirudh and Usha. After that, Barasoor started worrying about his daughter Usha.

Battle of Barasoor and Usha's Wedding:

Then Barasoor entered the Pur where he found Anirudh with his daughter Usha. "You are guilty for all these, now be ready to battle", said Barasoor to Anirudh. Then Barasoor ordered his soldiers to capture Anirudh. So the soldiers brought Anirudh outside. There Anirudh killed all of those soldiers and again went back to Usha. Then Barasoor send his minister Kushmandi to battle with Anirudh. He defeated Kushmandi too. Then Barasoor himself came out to battle with Anirudh. Then he captured Anirudh and put him in a cage. Then he was about to kill Anirudh, right then the voice heard from the Sky, "It said hey Barasoor you are a devotee of Shiva, so Shiva is also the god for everyone. So don't kill him, otherwise you will make Shiva angry. Then Shiva will come to kill you", said the voice.

After that, Barasoor stayed silently. Then Anirudh started praising Goddess Durga, who came and freed Anirudh from the cage. After that Goddess Durga went towards Usha.

Description of Battle of Sri Krishna:

In Dwarika, after Anirudh disappeared, then the ladies in Dwarika started crying. Which made Sri Krishna very sad. After sometime Sri Krishna heard from Naradh Jee that Barasoor has kept Anirudh as a prisoner. Then Sri Krishna, with many solider, went to battle with Barasoor. To protect the devotee, Shiva also reached the battlefield. There Sri Krishna and Shiva started battling with each other. Also Praduymna battled with Kushmandi, Koop battled with Karna, Bara's son battled with Shamba, and Bara battled with Satyaki. In the battle Brahamsna (Weapon) was used. By the power of Shiva, Sri Krishna's soldiers were losing the battle. Then Sri Krishna used Sitala (Weapon). But Shiva easily defused it. By seeing that Sri Krishna was puzzled. Then everybody started praising Shiva. Then Sri Krishna told Shiva "I cut off all the hands of Barasoor, so please excuse yourself from this battle. Also give me permission to kill Barasoor," said Sri Krishna. Then Shiva said, "Are you sure? I have cursed Barasoor so you do please kill him", said Shiva. Then Sri Krishna cuts off all the hands of Barasoor, except for the two hands.

Then Barasoor took Sri Krishna to Anta Pur and there he wedded his daughter with the grandson of Sri Krishna. And also gave priceless stones as a dowry to Sri Krishna. Then Sri Krishna went back to Dwarika with his grandson and granddaughter in law. In Dwarika everybody celebrated for the victory of Sri Krishna.

Barasoor Being Garapati:

Then Barasoor was feeling very sorry for his foolishness. So he went to Shiva and started crying for what he did. Then he performed Tandap dance in front of Shiva. Then Shiva being very pleased asked him for his wish. Then he asked Shiva to give Sorit Pur kingdom to his Son in law and also to end his devil life. Then Shiva being very pleased made him a Garapati (Chief follower of Shiva).

Description of Killing Gajasoor:

When Devi killed Mahisasoor for the Gods, then his son Gajasoor did hard meditation to please Brahmdev. Then he won all three Loka in battle. Gajasoor then made all the Gods bow down to him and also made they leave heaven to settle at Mahindra Mountain. Then Gajasoor started using various weapons to destroy the Brahmins and meditators.

Then all the Gods including Indra went to Shiva. There, after hearing the complaints from God about Gajasoor, Shiva grabbed his Trishul and went to kill Gajasoor. Then Shiva was about to cut the throat of Gajasoor with Trishul. Gajasoor started praising Shiva. So Shiva became thrilled and ask him for his wish. Then Gajasoor told Shiva, "After killing me, then make my skin your blanket". Then Shiva blessed him. So then, Shiva made a Jyoti Linga in Kashi and named it Mirtunjaya. After killing Gajasoor, they thrilled all the Gods.

Killing of Nirhya:

When Sri Krishna killed the son of Diti, then Diti became very sad. So Nirhya came to console Diti and also told him that he would win all the Gods and make them his servers. So Nirhya thought Brahmins are the ones who are protecting religions. So he killed Brahmins. He then went to Kashi as he thought was the center for religions. There he started killing Brahmins. At day time he used to act as devoted, and at night he used to kill Brahmins. One day he was about to kill devotee of Shiva, but they protected the devoted with Shiva Mantra. So he couldn't kill him. Then Shiva appeared there and killed Nirhya.

Destruction of Devils Bindal and Utpal:

Sanat Kumara Ji says, "Hey Vyas Ji, there were two devils named Bindal and Utpal. Through hard meditation they had received a blessing that anyone would not kill them. They with their bravery won the whole Universe and also won Gods on battle."

Then all the Gods went to Brahmdev to complain about the two devils. Then Brahmdev told Gods "that Goddess Parvati will only kill these two devils. So now you guys meditate upon Shiva," said Brahmdev to Gods.

So Naradh ji went to two devils, Bindal and Utpal. There, as per the instruction of Shiva, he started describing the beauty of Goddess Parvati. After hearing the description from Naradh Ji about Goddess Parvati, the two devils planned to capture Goddess Parvati.

One day when Goddess Parvati was playing with her servers, the two devils appeared there disguised as followers of Shiva. Shiva recognized that they were the two devils, Bindal and Utpal. So Shiva showed with a signal that they are devils to Goddess Parvati.

Then Goddess Parvati threw the ball they were playing towards the two devils. As soon as ball touched them, they fell on the ground. Then all their body parts started disappearing, and they died. The ball then turned itself in to Shiva Linga.

That place is in India by Jaysthesowr known as Nandikeshowr. After that Brahmdev, Vishnu, Indra and other Gods all started praising Shiva.

Om Nama Shivaya,

Sat Rudra Sanhita:

Seventh Chapter:

Five Figure of Shiva:

Saunak ji says "Hey Shoot Ji now tells us the story of a different figure of Shiva, which is from eternal. Also by listening to this story will benefit all good men".

Then Shot Ji says, "Hey Muni (Saints), now you guys listen to the pure stories about description about different figure of Shiva. Sanatkumar Ji to Nandiswor asked the same question, now I will tell you all the same story as told by Nandiswor".

Once Sadhojat named incarnation of Shiva happened, on the nineteenth incarnation of a human being. The incarnation of Shiva occurred from a meditative state of Brahmdev through his head. Because of its formation, it was named Sadhojat. Brahmdev thinking incarnation is Shiva started meditating upon him. Then from that incarnation Sunandan, Nandan, Bishonandan, Anandan, four Kumar occurred. After seeing that, Sadhojat gave Brahmdev order to start creation.

After that creation, Rakta named twenty ideas developed. In that idea, Brahmdev became Red colored. When he meditated, the similar red colored and red-eyed son got created. Then Brahmdev naming that incarnation of Shiva as Kaam Dev. Then Brahmdev while praising him created another four sons named Viraj, Vivaha, Vishal, Vishobhawan. All of them also gave advice to Brahmdev, to create the World.

After that, Brahmdev had a son with large shoulders and very vibrant Kumar. Brahmdev, also acknowledging that incarnation as Shiva, started pronouncing Shiva Gayatri Mantra. Also lots of sons occurred from that Kumar too. After that, it stopped creating any more sons.

After that, Shiva named idea occurred. Brahmdev meditate on that idea for thousands of years dedicating towards Shiva. Because of meditation, black colored Kumar named Krishna was born.

Then Brahmdev worshipped that Kumar from which four other Kumar was born. They were Krishna, Krishna Shiva, Krishnasaya, and Krishnakanthadhari. They all were like Shiva. They also gave Brahmdev a Yog named Aghor to start the creation.

After that, Biswosorup idea occurred. While Brahmdev meditating on Biswosorup, Goddess Sarswoti got incarnated. At the same time with similar feature Shiva also incarnated as a Kumar Ish. Then to that incarnation of Brahmdev acknowledged and respected as Shiva. Then that Ish Shiva gave Brahmdev advice on what is "the right path". Then from that Ish four sons were born. They were Jati, Mundi, Shikhandi, and Arghamundi. They adapted Yog Marg. Then that incarnation of Shiva is known as Ishan.

This way Shiva has five names which are Ishan, Purush, Aghor, Kaam Samrakchyak, and Basru Samrakchyak. This way these five figures of Shiva became famous and are worshipped by all the devotees. Anyone who worships these five incarnations of Shiva and also listens to its glory will enjoy all that comes in life.

Describing Shiva's Idols:

Nandi says, to fulfill all requirements of the world, listen carefully about the different incarnation of Shiva. In those incarnations there are saying about eight idols of Shiva. We name them as Sarba, Bhava, Rudra, Ugra, Bhima, Pashupati, Ishan, and Mahadev. These eight idols of Shiva is in everything is in the Universe. He is a caretaker of Earth, Water, Fire, Air, Sky, Space, Sun, and Moon. So through all these things Shiva is present in everyone. Through Earth he takes cares of the entire world. Through water he makes everyone alive. Shiva also have a furious character in his idol Ugra. Another sky figured Bhima idol is also there. In Pashupati idol Shiva cuts the cord of all living beings. By Ishan idol of Shiva through the ray of Sun, he provides potion to the entire world. Eighth idol of Shiva, which is a soul, he then lives in everyone. So these are the eight idols of Shiva which are all over the world.

Ardanariswor Shiva:

When Brahmdev tried to create the world as per his thoughts, then it didn't happen. Then Brahmdev started meditating upon Shiva. Then Shiva along with Goddess Parvati appeared before Brahmdev. Then Shiva separated himself from Shakti and asked Brahmdev for his wish. Then, seeing Shakti being separated from Shiva, Brahmdev started praising Shakti. Brahmdev said, "Hey Shiva (Shakti) your husband is god of the gods too. Because of his will, they protected me. It is because of Shiva the whole creation took place. Hey Shakti, I continuously have created gods in my thoughts, but they are not incarnating. Now I want to create Maithuni creation, for that I also need women. Just by energy to create the world is not enough. So now, you provide me your energy because you are the energy that everyone has. So hey Shakti, now for creating the world you take birth as a daughter of Dakshya," said Brahmdev.

After hearing the request of Brahmdev, Shiva and Shakti blessed him. After that Shiva and Shakti again merged as one. After that for creation of human beings, women started playing an important role.

Nandikeshowr Incarnation:

Sanat Kumara says, "Hey Nandikeshowr, now I want to know from you, how you appeared from Shiva and became Nandikeshowr? How did you knew Shiva element?" asks Sanat Kumara. Then Nandikeshowr says, "Hey Sanat Kumara Ji. Once upon a time, Rishi Silad once did very hard meditation to have a son. Then Indra came in front of him and asked for his wish. Then Rishi Silad asked for an immortal son. Then Indra said that is not possible, but if you worship Shiva, then he can grant you that wish. So then Rishi Silad meditate on Shiva for thousands of years. Then Shiva with Goddess Parvati appeared before him. Then Rishi Silad asked for an immortal son as his wish, Shiva blessed him. After that Shiva and Goddess Parvati disappeared from there.

Rishi Silad told other Rishis about what happened. Then one day he was about to perform Yegya (Worshipping with holy fire ritual), as soon as they dig a hold to put fire. There was a baby with bright features smiling at him. I was born with three eyes and four arms with dreadlock hair. Rishi Silad became thrilled to find me as his son. Then I went to his Ashram with my father. There I was, a very normal boy. Then my father named me as Nandi. When I was a small boy, my father taught me the Vedas and its knowledge. Then one day Rishi named Mitravarun came to our Ashram. He was very pleased that at such a small age I knew all about Vedas. Then he saw my future, so he told my father that I would die within a year. After hearing that my father Rishi, Silad started crying. Then I told my father that don't worry, I will meditate upon Shiva, so he would not let me die. After that I went to a jungle to meditate.

Then at the Jungle I started meditating upon Shiva. After some time Shiva along with Goddess Parvati appeared before me. Then Shiva asked me for my wish. Then I told him I want to be immortal. So Shiva then hold both of my hands and told me you are my incarnation. So you need not fear death. Then he took out one of his necklace and put in on me. Then I became part of him. Then he took some water from his head and poured it over me. That water made a place called Panchanad, where Shiva became river Jaleshowr and started flowing on both sides of that holy place. Then Goddess Parvati asked Shiva to give me to her as her son. Then Shiva called all his followers and told them that from now on Nandi is my chief follower. After that we all along with Shiva and Goddess Parvati went to Kailas.

Bhairav Incarnation:

Once upon a time, Brahmdev was meditating at Sumeru Mountain. Then all the Gods came and started asking Brahmdev about the nondestructive element of the Universe. Then Brahmdev told the Gods that "he himself is the nondestructive, creator, and only God of the Gods. There is no one like me," said Brahmdev. After hearing Brahmdev, Vishnu asked Brahmdev, what is he saying? "By my wish you became the creator of the World, so why aren't you giving me the right credit?" Said Vishnu. Then there was an argument between Vishnu and Brahmdev. Then they called all four Vedas to decide who is great. Then all four Vedas said in one voice, the one who has all five elements inside him, from whom everything it creates, which is also known as pure element, and that one is Rudra, said the four Vedas.

After hearing what four Vedas had to said, Vishnu and Brahmdev said, "Hey Vedas, what you have said is because of lack of knowledge. The one who is always romancing with Goddess Parvati, and the one who puts ash all over his body, the one who rides a bull, and the one who wears Snake as a necklace, the one who wears tiger skins as clothes, the one with dreadlock hair, the one who inserts Moon on his dreadlock hair, the one who is always high with poison and other substances, the one who is always covered with Ganga. How can you say Shiva the pure element?" Asked Vishnu and Brahmdev. After that a divine light appeared before them, and from that light blue colored Shiva with a trident came out. Then Brahmdev said, "Hey Chandrasekhar, I know you well, you were born from my forehead, and at the time of birth you cried very much, that's why I named you Rudra", said Brahmdev. Then Brahmdev said, "So come under my surrender".

After hearing Brahmdev, Shiva became angry. So Shiva created Kal Bhairav out of his body and told him to rule the Brahmdev and the entire world. Shiva tells Bhairav that "You kill the ones who have committed sins. You are the guard of my Kashi Puri, so from now on punish all the ones who have committed sins, are in Kashi," said Shiva.

After hearing Shiva, Kal Bhairav from the nail of his fingers cuts off the head of Brahmdev. The forsaken Brahmdev started reading Satrudri to please Shiva.

Later on both Vishnu and Brahmdev both acknowledged that Shiva is actually the Universe and God of the Gods. So Shiva forgives them both.

Then Shiva told Bhairav, that "Now you carry the cut off head of Brahmdev, and start begging around the world, as an act of sin you have committed by cutting Brahmdev head. Then Shiva created a woman and told Bhairav that you can take this women anywhere and enjoy the world. But before this woman reaches Kashi, you better establish yourself as an idol in Kashi."

After that, by the wish of Shiva, Bhairav took Kapalik (Relating or belonging to a skull) fasting. After that he took the head of Brahmdev and start going to all Loka. Bhairav travelled all three Loka but even though that women never let Bhairav be alone. Once, while travelling, Bhairav reached Narayan's Loka. Then Vishnu along with other Gods stood up and gave them respect and regard to Bhairav. Then by doing Naman Vishnu started praising Bhairav with different glories of Shiva. Then Vishnu also told Goddess Laxmi that that are blessed today because the Shiva in the incarnation of Bhairav visited their Loka. "By being able to worship Bhairav will stop the human being from rebirth," said Vishnu to Goddess Laxmi. Then Vishnu asked Bhairav, "Hey, why are you travelling like this"? Then Bhairav said, "Hey Vishnu because of Shiva's advice I took this Kapalik fasting because of killing Brahmdev", said Bhairav. Then Goddess Laxmi gave Bhairav Sanorathi Vidya as for begging. Which Bhairav kept with him being thrilled? Then Bhairav went to different Loka for begging. Then one day Bhairav reached Kashi, as soon as he reached Kashi, then that Women vanished underneath the Patal (Hell). Then Brahmdev head dropped in the earth and that place became a holy place called **Kapalmochan** (Place to offer hair). Then Bhairav started dancing over that place. So there is a saying that person who offers his hair on Kashi on Tuesdays, then all his sins will be cleared.

Sarav Incarnation:

When Narsimha incarnation killed Hiranyakasipu, Shiva called Bir Bhadra to silence the anger of Narsimha. Then Bir Bhadra started counseling Narsimha Incarnation of Vishnu. Bir Bhadra said, "Hey Vishnu, you have completed your task by killing Hiranyakasipu. So please come out of Narsimha incarnation to do well for the world," said Bir Bhadra to Narsimha incarnation of Vishnu. Then Narsimha said, "You go away from here. Now I will finish this world. I am the destroyer, also I am the source of energy, and I am the Lord of all."

After hearing Narsimha incarnation of Vishnu, Bir Bhadra said, "How can you forget about Shiva, the destroyer of the world. You are lying to yourself. For your own good sake Shiva has sent me here to counsel you about the ignorance," said Bir Bhadra to Narsimha incarnation of Vishnu.

Then Bir Bhadra says, "Hey Hari, you are under Shiva. His energy killed even this devil Hiranyakasipu through you. At Dakshya Yegya I was the one who cut his head, also I was the one who cut your son Brahmdev head. Have you forgotten about it? All the energy in the world is all Shiva. So hey Narsimha, please leave this incarnation of Narsimha to come back to your original incarnation as Vishnu. Otherwise I will have to attack you to kill you," said Bir Bhadra to Narsimha.

When Narsimha heard what Bir Bhadra said, then he attacked Bir Bhadra. Then suddenly the energy of Shiva became active and visible everywhere. Then Bir Bhadra took Sarav incarnation and grabbed Narsimha with both hands. Then Narsimha couldn't move or do anything to protect himself. The Sarav incarnation of Bir Bhadra took Narsimha to Shiva and put him underneath Nandi and tied him. Then all the energy of Vishnu went to Bir Bhadra. So Sarav incarnation of Bir Bhadra grabbed the body of Narsimha to the top of Himalaya and left it there. Then Vishnu incarnated as himself and went back to Baikuntha. Then Shiva accepted that body of Narsimha on himself. After that, all, the Gods started praising Vishnu and Shiva.

Blessing to Bishwonar:

"Among many stories of Shiva, one of them is Shashi Shekhar taking incarnation in Bishwonar house. So listen to this story", said Nandi to Sanat Kumara.

Along the banks of Narmada River, there was a town called Narmapur, where Yogi Bishwonar used to live. He was literate in all divine books and stories. They married him to Brahmin women called Suchismati. She was very devoted to her husband. So she used to take good care of her husband, Bishwonar. So Bishwonar, being thrilled with his wife, told her to tell him her wish. He wanted to bless her for whatever she wants. Then his wife Suchismati asked him for a son like Shiva. Then Bishwonar said to his wife, "For that I have to take the permission of Shiva"." So I will start worshipping and meditating upon Shiva, so you don't worry about anything", said Bishwonar to his wife.

Then Bishwonar went to Kashi and start meditating upon Shiva at Marikarika Ghat in Kashi. After one year on the thirteenth month, as he finished his meditation, and was about to worship the Shiva Linga. He saw a beautiful boy next to the Shiva Linga. He fell in love with the boy because of his beauty. So he started praising the boy, thinking it is. So after that the boy said, "Bishwonar your wife's wish will come true." After hearing that from that boy, Bishwonar became thrilled, and he went back to his home.

Grihapati Incarnation:

After returning home, Bishwonar told his wife all the stories about what happened. Soon after that, his wife became pregnant. After some time a beautiful boy as good looking as moon was born. All the angles started dancing in joy. Also Atri, Pulaha, Bhardwaj, Angara, Dakshya, Balmiki, Vyas, Silda, Shankha, Katyayana, and other Muni were all there reading peace slogans from Veda. It was a great celebration at Bishwonar house. At Nawran they named the boy as Grihapati. All the great sage started praising the parents of the boy for their deed. Then the boy started growing with his parents. His father taught him a good culture from childhood. He taught him Veda and other holy books. When that boy was nine years old. Then Naradh Jee came to meet him. Then he told the boy's parents that when the boy reaches age twelve, he will have risk from fire. After saying that, Naradh Jee left.

After hearing what Naradh Jee had to say, the parents of the boy started crying. They started being anxious for their son. After seeing that condition of the parents, Grihapati asked his parents the reason for crying. When his parents told him what Naradh Jee had said, Grihapati told his parents that, "Don't worry about it. I will started reading Mahamritunjaya Mantra of Shiva to defeat death. So I will not die by the grace of Shiva after reading the Mantra for as long as I need to", said Grihapati. After hearing what Grihapati said, his parents told him, "Yes, if you read Mahamritunjaya Mantra continually then no harm will get you".

After that, Grihapati left to go to Kashi and start reading Mahamritunjaya Mantra. After reaching Kashi, Grihapati took a bath at Ganga Jee and went to Vishwonath temple to worship. There after seeing Vishwonath Jee he became very pleased and said to himself that he is very lucky that he got to worship Vishwonath Jee. So he thought what Naradh Jee had said made him lucky.

Then Grihapati established another Shiva Linga and started worshipping it every day. He used to water to the Shiva Linga one hundred eight times a day. And while worshipping he used to offer blue colored lotus flowered necklace to Shiva Linga every day. As per what Naradh Jee had said, at age twelve God Indra arrived there with Bajra in his hands.

Then Indra said to Grihapati "Tell me your wish?" Grihapati told Indra that he will not tell his wish to anyone but Shiva. Then Indra said, "I am the main god and I am the god of the gods, so tell me your wish so I will grant it to you", said Indra to Grihapati. Then Grihapati told Indra that he will only tell his wish to Shiva and no one else. Then they started having a debate. So Indra grabbed his Bajra, then from that electricity (Fire), Grihapati felt unconscious. Then Shiva along with Goddess Parvati appeared there and Shiva put his hands on Grihapati head. After that slowly Grihapati woke up and was thrilled to see Shiva and Goddess Parvati. Then Shiva told Grihapati that no one can kill him. Also Shiva told Grihapati that the Shiva Linga that he has made will have so much energy that no one can stand next to it. So he named the Shiva Linga as Agnishowr Mahadev. Shiva also told Grihapati that this Shiva Linga will protect devotees from fire and electricity. After that Shiva entered inside that Shiva Linga, which is known as Agnishowr Mahadev.

Yegyashowr Incarnation:

Now listen to the story about Yegyashowr incarnation of Shiva. When Gods and Devils started digging the Ocean, the poison came at the beginning. Then all the Gods rushed to Shiva to avoid the poison. Then Shiva drank all the poison, and the poison got stuck on his neck, which made his throat blue. So Shiva gained the name Neelkhantha because of blue throat. Then other angels, Laxmi, and also the potion came out of the Ocean. Because of the play of Vishnu, only the Gods got to drink the potion. Devils couldn't drink any potion. So because of that war broke out between Gods and devils. Because of fear of Rahu (Devil), Moon came surrendering himself to Shiva. So Shiva put the Moon on his head.

After drinking the potion, all the Gods became immortal. So devils lost the battle with Gods. So all the Gods became very proud that they defeated the devils. So they started celebrating it. Then Shiva taught the Gods lesson appeared before them as Yegyashowr. So he asked the Gods what they were up to. The Gods then said we are celebrating because we defeated devils.

Then Yegyashowr told Gods, "that there is nothing to be so proud." He said "If I put a stick here and if anyone of you can pick it up and throw it over, then I can understand you guys being proud. But if you can't move the stick, then there is nothing to be proud of," said Yegyashowr. Then all the Gods, including Vishnu, Indra and others tried to move that stick, but no one could. Right then there was a voice from the sky saying, "Hey Gods, the person in front of you is Shiva, and he always keeps everything in balance by destroying the fake proudness. After hearing that all the Gods started praising Shiva, who had incarnated as Yegyashowr.

Shiva's Ten Incarnation:

Among many incarnations of Shiva, Ten incarnation are the main incarnations. First one is Mahakal incarnation. The energy of Mahakal incarnation is Mahakali. Second incarnation of Shiva is named Tara, who provides happiness to its devotees. Third incarnation of Shiva is called

Bhuvaneshowr, which provides devotees with the desire whatever. The energy of Bhuvaneshowr incarnation is Bala- Bhuvaneshowri. We know fourth incarnation as Sodasi energy which lives in foreign. This energy provides devotees with happiness and peace. Fifth incarnation of Shiva is Bhairav. The energy of Bhairav incarnation is Bhairavi. This energy fulfills all desires of the devotees. Sixth is Chhinnamasta Incarnation. The seventh incarnation of Shiva is Dumrawan. Whose energy is Dhumravati, and it provides devotees with desire things. Shiva's eighth incarnation is Baglamukh whose energy is Banglamukhi. Shiva's ninth incarnation was Matanga whose energy is Matangi. Shiva's tenth incarnation is Kamal, whose energy is Bala-Bhuvaneshowri.

Establishment of Eleven Rudra:

At past when God Indra ran away from Amravati, then his father Kashyap who was a devotee of Shiva, became very sad. After consoling his son Indra, Kashyap went to Kashi Puri. After reaching Kashi, he took a bath at Ganga Jee. Then after properly worshipping Shiva, he started meditating on Shiva Linga made by him for many years. When Shiva became happy then Kashyap told his wish, which was he wanted to see his son free from devils destroying their pride. Also, Kashyap said he wants more son.

Then Shiva blessed him by saying Thatastu (Granted). Then Shiva took birth from Kashyap known as Sorvima. Then there was a big celebration for Shiva being born as Sorvima. Then following incarnations of Shiva took place.

They are as following, Kapali, Pingal, Vim, Birupachya, Bilohit, Shasta, Yegyapad, Apiburdaya, Shambhu, Chanda, and Bhava. All together this eleven incarnation of Shiva took place.

All these incarnations are door to store of happiness. All these eleven incarnations of Shiva have fought with devils to make Gods win every battle. Therefore, all these eleven incarnations of Shiva gives its devotees what we have desired.

Durbasa Character:

Maharishi Atri was the husband of Anushaya Jee. By the advice of Brahmdev Atri along with his wife meditation upon Shiva, to have a son as a wish. He did very hard meditation for years and years, by the Riccha Mountain by the river nearby Vrindavan. While meditating for a while, a fire ball started coming out of his body. That fire ball started destroying all three Loka. By seeing that all the Rishis, Gods rushed to Brahmdev. In front of Brahmdev they told their stories. After that, Brahmdev along with other Gods all went to Shiva. After reaching there, they all started praising Shiva. After that, they Shiva how the fire ball is destroying all three Loka.

After that Shiva, Vishnu and Brahmdev discuss the issue among themselves. Then all three of them went to Maharishi Atri to grant him his wish. Atri recognized all three s and started praising them. Then all three gods grant him the wish to have a son from each of them. After that, Atri and Anushaya had three sons. By the blessing of Brahmdev Moon was born as one, and by the blessing of Vishnu and Shiva Durbasa was born. Durbasa performed lots of characteristics in his life. King Ambrish tried to test Durbasa, which made Durbasa angry and he was about to curse King, Right then Sudarshan Chakra started following King Ambrish wherever he goes. So the voice from the Sky stopped the Sudarshan Chakra. That way Ambrish knew it was Shiva, so he started praising Durbasa and feed him good food.

Once the same Durbasa Kal (God of Death) was talking with Sri Ram and requested that no one should interfere with their time with each other. But Laxman came between them, and Sri Ram abandoned Laxman to be with Durbasa. Which made Durbasa thrilled.

Same way he also had tested Sri Krishna. Once by knowing that Brahmin are close to Sri Krishna. Durbasa appeared as a Brahmin in front of Sri Krishna. Sri Krishna also along with Radha took him on a ride on his own chariot by driving the chariot himself. Which made Durbasa very have and blessed Sri Krishna that his lineage will last forever.

Same way once Durbasa was taking a naked bath. Then Dropati gave her piece of her Sari (Women's Cloth) to Durbasa to cover himself. Which made Durbasa happy and blessed Dropati that her Sari may always increase. Which helped Dropati to keep Pandavas happy.

Hanuman Incarnation:

The time when Vishnu incarnated himself as Mohini, then Shiva felt so lust to see that incarnation of Vishnu. Because of that, his sperm flowed from him. Then Sapta (Seven) Rishi saved that sperm in a leaf. And planted in Gautama's daughter, Kesari. So after that Shiva appeared as Hanuman by taking birth from Kesari. He had a monkey like figure but was very brave from childhood. Hanuman once put Sun inside his mouth, thinking it was a flower. Later when all Gods prayed, he let Sun out.

All the Gods thinking he is the incarnation of Shiva, they all blessed Hanuman. After that he learned various teachings from Sun. Such as Arimadi Astasiddhi, Navanidhi Vidya and others. By the request by his mother, he became a friend with Sukrib. He also became Minister of Sukrib's kingdom. When Sri Ram became a friend with Sukrib. Then Hanuman went to Lanka to find Janaki (Sita). In Lanka he made damages all over by putting a fire there. Also, he found Janaki there which he came back and told Sri Ram. Then after that Hanuman along with Sri Ram and also the Monkey soldier force went to Lanka to battle. After that he made a Shiva Linga which is known as Rameshowr. After worshipping the Shiva Linga, Hanuman started making a bridge from there to Lanka. He gathered lots of and Mountains on the ocean to make the bridge. Then after reaching Lanka they started the battle with the demons. Hanuman killed lots and lots of demons on the battle. He also protected the force of Sri Ram. He also gathered Sanjivini plants to rescue Laxman who was unconscious due to injury from the battle.

Mahesh Incarnation:

Once Shiva and Goddess Parvati were making love. The Bhairav was the doorkeeper. When Goddess Parvati tried to come out of the door, then Bhairav looked at her with the wrong intention, and Bhairav didn't let her out of the door. So Goddess Parvati knew his intention, then she cursed Bhairav to live in earth being a human being.

Because of that curse, Bhairav came to Earth and became Betal. Because of the love of Bhairav Shiva and Goddess Parvati also came to Earth being Mahesh and Sharda. They made love at different places on Earth.

Brishavtar Incarnation:

When Gods and Demons started digging the Ocean for potion. Then when they found the potion, then they started fighting over for it. The few drops of the potion fell on the ground. From which beautiful looking few women appeared from it. By seeing those women, demons became lust and forgot about the potion. Instead, they took those women to Patal. Then Vishnu went after to rescue those women by killing Kati and other demons. When he reached Patal, he also became very lust to see those women. So he started making love to them and had so many kids from them. Who fought with Gods? By this act of Vishnu, all the Rishis (Saints) became worried. And so they went to Shiva to request him to bring Vishnu back. So Siva told the Rishis that he will bring back Vishnu, so not to worry about it.

Then Shiva appeared as a bull in Patal and as soon as he reached there, all the houses of Patal started falling down. The bull fought with sons of Vishnu, and he killed all of them. After that Vishnu came to fight with the Bull. Then Brishavtar the bull defeated Vishnu in the battle. So Vishnu meditate to see who this bull who defeated me in battle is. Then he could know that it was Shiva. So Vishnu apologize to Shiva for his mistakes. Then Shiva gave Vishnu Sudarshan Chakra and asked him to leave the Kaam Chakra in Patal. After that Siva went back to Kailas. Vishnu gave up his Kaam Chakra in Patal. He also said when women are covering their bodies then the peace will stay in the world, and when they lose clothes from their body, then peace will slowly disappear from Earth. When they have no clothes at all, then there will be no peace in the World. That's how he curse the world.

Characteristics of Piplad:

To kill Britasoor, Indra and other Gods made a weapon called Bajra. So they went to take advice from Brahmdev. Brahmdev told them if they make Bajra made from the bone of Rishi Dhadichi. Then Gods went to Rishi Dhadichi's Ashram to ask for his bone. Then Dhadichi send his wife Surbacha home and he himself gave up his body for Gods. So Gods made Bajra from his backbone and Indra killed Britasoor with that Bajra.

Surbacha when came out of the house then she didn't see any Gods or her husband. So by meditating see saw what happen to her husband. Then she curses Gods that they became animals and about to give her life by jumping on fire. Right then voice from the sky said, "Stop, don't give your life like that because there is a great Yogi inside you." Then Surbacha wrote Sri Ram on a stone and cut her stomach with that stone to take the baby out. After that, a very sharp looking baby was born. Then Surbacha thought it was Shiva, so she started praising him. Then she left the baby under the Pipal tree and told him to stay there and enjoy the World. After that she took Samadhi and gave up her life to be with her husband.

By knowing the boy was the incarnation of Shiva, Vishnu, Brahmdev and all other Gods came there and start celebrating. The Brahmdev named the baby Piplad. Then Piplad for the well-being of everyone in all three Loka meditate under the same Pipal tree for years and years.

This is how Piplad maintained religious order in the World. After many years, Piplad married King Arnyak's daughter Padma. Then he transferred his old aged body into young aged body. Then he made love with Padma and had ten sons. He also did lots of other good deeds for the world. He also told that from birth to age sixteen they will harm no one By Sani. Also, the Shiva devotees will never be harmed by Sani. By remembering Yogis Gadhi, Kaushik, and Piplad will make the difficulty produce by Sani be disappeared? After that if Sani tries to create problem, then Sani will dissolve into fire himself.

Story of Baisyanath Incarnation:

Once upon a time at Nandigram, a prostitute named Mahanada used to live there. She was very wealthy and was always covered with valuable ornaments. She used to meditate and repeat the name of Shiva most of the time. She always used to wear Rudrarakshya necklace and used to make three lines at her forehead with ashes. She used to keep Shiva's idol in front and used to dance. She also used to sing the glory of Shiva and Goddess Parvati. So Shiva wanted to test her, so he appeared as Baisya and went to her house. There Shiva was wearing a very attractive looking bracelet. So it attracted Mahananda to that bracelet. Then Shiva said, "You can have this bracelet, but there is a price to pay for it. So what will you offer for it?" Said Shiva who incarnated as Baisya.

Then Mahananda said, "I am a prostitute. So I will offer myself to you as your wife for three days and nights." Then Shiva liked the idea and while giving her the bracelet he says, "There is Sun and Moon here in this bracelet so witnessing them say the same thing three times and then touch my heart." So the Mahananda said three times the same thing by witnessing Sun and the Moon. After that, she touched Shiva's heart three times.

After that Shiva gave Mahananda Shiva Linga made of precious stones and told her to keep it safe. So she kept it in a safe place and then was ready to sleep with Shiva.

Then at midnight there was a voice from the place where she had kept the Shiva Linga it said, "There is a fire here and everything is burning." Then Mahananda went quickly and released all animals and birds that were kept on a cage. Later on the Shiva Linga which that Baisya gave got burned by the fire. So Baisya said now since that Shiva Linga which meant so much to they burn me. Now what will I do living without it, so he gave his life by jumping on the same fire. Then the prostitute Mahananda said I had promised him I would spend three days and three nights with him, but since he gave up his life, I can't keep my promise. So now she also gives up her life to keep her promise alive.

So she donated all her belongings to other people. So now she was ready to give her life. Right then Shiva appeared before her and said, "I wanted to test you, so I appeared before you as Baisya and took your test. So now I am thrilled with you", said Shiva. Then Mahananda said, "We all are your devotees and we would like to remain your devotee." Then Shiva took them all to his Dham (Holy Place).

Dijyashowr Incarnation:

Nandi says, "Now listen to Shiva's Dijyashowr incarnation story. Once there was a King Rishbharoop to whom Shiva had done favor. Because for him, Shiva took the incarnation of Dijyashowr. By the grace of Shiva, Rishbharoop won a Kingdom and became a King. He had married Chandrangaghadi's daughter named Kirtimalini. When he was in the jungle with his wife, Shiva and Goddess Parvati appeared before them as tigers. So the tiger took grab the wife and started pulling her and he was about to give up his wife and also his life. Right then Shiva appeared before them and told him he was only testing him. So Rishbharoop became thrilled. Whoever tells this story of Dijyashowr will receive Shiva's position.

Yetinath Hansaroop Incarnation:

Once upon a time, there were a couple living near the Arvoot Mountain. We named them Aahok as husband and Ahuka as wife. Both the husband and wife were the true devotee of Shiva. One day the husband had gone far to look for food for his wife. Then Shiva disguised as a Yogi came to their hut. Aahok the husband also came home right then. So the husband and wife feed the Yogi with whatever food they had. After that, the Yogi told the couple he wants to spend the night in their hut. Then Aahok said to the Yogi that their hut is too small to fit three people. Then the Yogi was about to leave, Ahuka said, "Don't leave, instead I will stay outside all night guarding the hut, while you and my husband can sleep inside." Then Aahok said, "No, I will stay outside and guard the hut, while you and our guest the Yogi can sleep inside the hut." So the Yogi and Ahuka slept inside the hut, while Aahok guard the hut from outside. At night the wild animals killed Aahok. In the morning when Yogi and Ahuka came outside, they saw his dead body. So the Yogi became very sad due to the incident. Then Ahuka told the Yogi, "Please don't be so sad, my husband died will do his religious duty. So now I will arrange for fire to burn his body, and I will also give up my life by going into the same fire. So you please go where you need to and don't feel sad about anything," Said Ahuka to the Yogi.

So Ahuka prepared fire for the funeral of her husband and was about to give up herself by going into the same fire. Then Shiva appeared in front of her from the Yogi. Shiva then said, "In your next life you guys will be King and Queen. And I will help you by being a Hansa (Duck) in your next life," said Shiva to Ahuka.

After that, by the blessing of Shiva, Aahok was born as prince of country named Nisadh. Later on he also became King of that country. Ahuka was born a princess of Bidarv named country, her name was Damayanti. Then Shiva the incarnation of Hansa and made the love connection between the two. So they got married again in the new life. Lived asking and Queen. Whoever listens to this story will lead in a devotional way.

Krishna Dashain Incarnation:

Shradadev had a child named King Navaga. He had two sons named Navak and Ambrish; they were both devotee of Vishnu. "Now you listen to the story of the grandfather of Ambrish. To whom Shiva himself had blessed him," said Nandi.

When Navak went to study Veda at Gurukul (School). Then his brothers divided the kingdom and took their shares. They saved nothing for Navak. So when Navak came back from Gurukul, then he asked his brothers for his share. Then his brothers told him that when they divided the kingdom, they didn't think about him, "So now you have to go to our father to ask for what they leave with him," said his brothers to Navak. Then Navak went to his father asking for his share, then his father told him that his brothers fooled him.

His father also told him to go to Angiras Brahman's Yegya and help him complete the Yegya by telling the rite Slokas (Sentences). "If you help him complete this Yegya, then he will give you all his property to go to heaven," said his father to Novak.

Then, as per his father's guidance, he goes to Angiras Brahman's Yegya. There he reads a few lines from Veda and the Yegya was complete. So Angiras Brahman gives all his wealth, which was on the Yegya to Navak, and goes to heaven.

Then Shiva appeared before Navak disguised as Yogi. Then Shiva said, "All this wealth is here at this Yegya is mine. So how can you take it?" Asked Shiva. Then Navak says, "Since the Brahman who did this Yegya gave all this to me, so how can it be yours? Asks Navak to Shiva, who disguised as Yogi. Then Yogi says, "Go ask your father about whose right is on this wealth, and whatever he decides is fine with me."

Then Navak goes to his father and tells the whole story about what happened. And asks his father, whose would be those wealth? Then his father says, "That Yogi no other than Shiva himself, so go back and apologize to him for your mistake. Actually, whatever is offered at Yegya, it's all Shiva's right," says his father to Navak.

Then Navak goes back and apologizes to Shiva. Also, start praising Shiva. Then Shiva blesses Navak and disappears from there.

Avadooteshowr Incarnation:

Once upon a time Shiva incarnated as Avdoot and was staying at Kailas. Then God Indra and Brihaspati came to meet Shiva. Indra asked the Avdoot if Shiva is inside, but the Avdoot answered nothing. So Indra kept asking for several times, but the Avdoot didn't answer at all. Then Indra became angry and said, "Do you want me to use this Bajra upon you and kill you?" But the Avdoot still didn't answer. Then Indra pulls his Bajra to hit the Avdoot, but his hands get stuck in the air. It didn't come down. Then Indra became furious and pours his anger towards the Avdoot. But the Avdoot didn't react at all. So Brihaspati then knows that it is Shiva who incarnated as Avdoot. So he praises Shiva. Then by praising Shiva, Brihaspati saves Indra. So from that day we know Brihaspati as Jiva (Chord of Life).

Vikchubarya Incarnation:

Once there was a King named Satyarath in Bidarv. He spends most of his time in life being Shiva's devotee. But at war his enemies killed him. At the time his wife was Pregnant. So she ran away towards the jungle to save herself and the unborn child. There, at the jungle, she rested under a huge tree. There she gave birth to a son. After that, she was very thirsty, so she went to look for water in a nearby pond. Three wild animals eat here. Her son was still underneath that tree. Then Shiva felt pity for the son of Satyarath. So by his wish a beggar woman arrives near the huge tree where the same baby was crying. After seeing such a young baby boy, she feels real pity for the baby. She then thinks whose baby it is? If she should take the baby or not? Then Shiva appeared before the beggar women and tells her, "You need not think too much, just take the baby and take care of him."

Then that beggar woman asks, "Hey Vikchu, who are you? Are you Shiva, who is doing this favor to me? At least tell me whose son is it, and how did he end up here?" Then Shiva, who incarnated as Vikchu says, "This boy is King Satyarath's son. He died in battle. Wild animals also killed his mother while looking for water. Therefore, you can take this boy with no doubts and raise him like he is one of yours," says Vikchu.

Then Shiva explains further and says, "His father Satyarath was Pandu in his previous life and was my Shiva's devotee. One day he was about to worship Shiva and his ministers came and told him that enemies have attacked his Kingdom. Then he thought maybe they are the enemy who disguised as his ministers. So he gets up and cuts off their heads. Later he didn't even worship and had dinner and went to bed. Therefore, in this life he is a King got killed by the enemies. Also his mother had cheated to kill he's step wife. So the wild animals also killed her." Said Shiva.

After telling the story, Shiva appeared on his real form in front of that beggar woman. Then that beggar women became thrilled and started praising Shiva. Then Shiva blessed the women and disappeared in the air. That beggar woman took the boy and raised him as he was also one of hers own. Then when hat boy became Young adult, then he worshipped Shiva for a whole year. Then he married a princess and became a King.

Sureshowr Incarnation:

Nandi says, "Now let me tell you the story of Upmanyou, who was the son of Byadrapadh. He was born in a poor family. His mother didn't have enough money to buy him a milk. So one day, his mother by crushing the rice and mixing it with the other liquid made milk out of it. But Upmanyou rejected to drink that saying it isn't a milk. So his mother cried and told him they need blessing from Shiva to have milk. Then Upmanyou told his mother that not to worry, Shiva will definitely bless them. After saying that, he went towards the Himalaya to meditate on Shiva.

There at the Himalaya, Upmanyou started repeating the Pancha Akshar Mantra (Om Nama Shivaya). After repeating the Mantra while meditating for some time, all three Loka felt the energy. Then Shiva along with Goddess Parvati disguised as God Indra and Goddess appeared before him. Then Indra said, "Hey boy, you need to repeat the Mantra to please God Indra, not Shiva. If you keep repeating the same Mantra, then I will send you do hell." Then Upmanyou says, "Even if Vishnu comes and tells me not to repeat this Mantra, then I will still not stop it. I want a blessing from Shiva and no one else," Says Upmanyou.

Then he picks up some ash and says, "For saying negative things about Shiva, I will destroy you with these ashes." Then he repeats a Mantra and throws the ash towards Indra and Goddess. Since it was Shiva and Goddess Parvati disguised as Indra and Goddess. So nothing happens to them. But then they appeared in their own image.

By seeing Shiva and Goddess Parvati, Upmanyou becomes thrilled. Then Shiva blesses Upmanyou. Then Upmanyou comes back home and tells the whole story to his mother, who becomes thrilled to hear it.

So later on, Upmanyou became very knowledgeable with holy books. He became worshiped character among people. So for Upmanyou Shiva had taken Sureshowr Indra incarnation.

Brahma Chari Incarnation:

When Sati Devi gave up her life in the same holy fire, her father, Dakshya organized which. Because of the insult she had to hear about Shiva. Then she took birth again as Parvati in King Himalaya's house. Then later by the advice of Narad Jee she started meditating to have Shiva as her husband. So testing the intention of Parvati Devi, Shiva sends Sapta Rishi to test her. Then Sapta Rishi tested Parvati Devi to know her intention. Then Sapta Rishi went to Shiva and told him that her intention is pure. Then Shiva himself took incarnation as Brahma Chari to test Parvati Devi. Parvati Devi with all respect and regard worshipped the Brahma Chari. Then Brahma Chari asked Parvati Devi the reason for such a hard meditation. Parvati Devi told him everything truthfully.

After hearing what Parvati Devi had to say, Brahma Chari said, "I couldn't understand your desire? Because Shiva has nothing besides an old bull. Also, he is the one who puts Bhasma all over his body and stays that way. Instead of Shiva, consider other Gods, said Brahma Chari."

After listening to Brahma Chari, Parvati Devi became angry with him. So she stood up to inside the hut. While standing up she told her friends to take the Brahma Chari outside the Ashram. She said, "Whoever talks bad about Shiva will commit a sin, also who hears the bad about Shiva also commits sin." As she was about to leave, then Shiva appeared in his form. Seeing Shiva there, Parvati Devi became very thrilled. And prayed to Shiva to accept her as his wife. Then Shiva said, I am yours and I will always serve you." After that Shiva went to King Himalaya's palace with big wedding procession and got married to Parvati Devi with traditional culture.

After hearing this story, they will wash away all the sins and life becomes peace and blissful. This story of Shiva is the eighty-fourth incarnation of Shiva.

Sunat-Natrka Incarnation:

Before marriage, Shiva promised Parvati Devi that he would marry her. After that, Parvati Devi became very glad and went home. Then her father King Himalaya arranged a big celebration to welcome her back home. At that celebration Shiva appeared in Sunat-Natrka incarnation. There he started dancing and doing different work, which attracted everyone. So Mainka gave him a gold tray full of ornaments as a gift. But he didn't take it. Instead, he asked for Parvati Devi. Which made Mainka and Himalaya both angry. Then Sunat-Natrka said bye to Parvati Devi and disappeared from there. Later on King Himalaya and Mainka knew that it was Shiva who had incarnated as Sunat-Natrka. So they thought they should have given Parvati Devi to him back then.

Hearing this story of Shiva will wash away all kinds of sins and lead a person to goodness.

Dijja Incarnation:

When Parvati Devi approached Shiva for marriage and when he agreed, then she went home, then Himalaya and Mainka agreed to wed Parvati with Shiva. After that, in Heaven Gods were scared that Himalaya will be powerful and he will change the situation of the Earth.

So all the Gods went their Guru Brihaspati to advise him to go to King Himalaya and tell him bad things about Shiva to cancel the wedding. But Guru Brihaspati refused to say anything bad about Shiva. Instead, he told them to do that themselves. But he would never do it. Then Guru Brihaspati told them to go visit Brahma Dev. then all the Gods went to Brahma Dev. There they told Brahma Dev the same thing. Brahma Dev also refuse to say anything bad about Shiva. Instead, he told the Gods to go to Kailas and pleased Shiva and ask him to do it.

After hearing that from Brahma Dev, all the Gods went to Kailas. There they started singing the glory of Shiva. Shiva being pleased ask them for their wish. So the Gods told him everything. Then Shiva agreed to say bad words about self to King Himalaya and Mainka. Then Shiva incarnated as Dijja and went to meet King Himalaya and Mainka. There he told them all the bad things he could about Shiva and asked them. So how can Parvati Devi be happy with him? Then he disappeared from there. Later King Himalaya and Mainka changed their mind about the wedding. This way Shiva by incarnating as Dijja favored to Gods.

Asawthama Incarnation:

Nandi says, "Hey Sanath Kumar, Guru Brihaspati had a son named Bhardwarka, and he had a son named Droara. Because of skill he learned from God Parshuram, he became Acharya of Pandus. Same Droara meditated to Shiva for a son. Shiva being very pleased with Droara blessed him with a brave and talented son. That son of Droara became the helper of Kauravas. All the Pandus had a difficult time defeating him. By the advice of Sri Krishna and by the blessing of Shiva, Arjun defused the powerful weapon that he discharged at them. He also discharged the same weapon on the son of Arjun, who was still at the womb. So by the blessing of Shiva, Sri Krishna destroyed the weapon with his Sudarshan Chakra. Sri Krishna laid down that powerful weapon in front of Asawthama after destroying it. Then Asawthama gave lots of truths to Sri Krishna and Pandus."

Kirat Incarnation:

While being in Jungle Arjun did hard meditation to please Shiva, by the advice of Vyas Jee. By doing that hard meditation, Arjun started glowing like bright light. Seeing self like that Arjun then knew about winning the battle with Kauravas.

While Arjun had gone to meditate his brothers, other Pandus became worried. Then Vyas Jee went to the Pandus and told them different stories from old days. Vyas Jee told them that human being has to face lots of difficulties in life. He told them that King Nal had to face the worst difficulties than what they are facing. He also told them that human beings face their own created problem through the life. Therefore, one should always worship Shiva.

When Arjun started glowing because of the meditation, then all the Gods started worrying. Then King of Gods, God Indra incarnated as Brahmin and appeared before Arjun. He then asked Arjun, why is he meditating like this? Then Arjun said that he is only following the advice of

Vyas Jee. Then God Indra appeared in his real image in front of Arjun and told him to follow the traditional way to meditate upon Shiva.

Arjun than stand on one foot and start meditating upon Shiva. He also starts repeating the Shiva Mantra. Then he started glowing more and more like a bright light. Even all the Gods became very surprised with Arjun's dedication. At the same time a devil named Muka send by Dryodhan, appeared there incarnated as wild Boar. With his Maya he started destroying the Mountains there. Arjun saw him and guessed that he might be someone send by his enemy. So while standing there Arjun pulled a bow and arrow and pointed towards the wild Boar. Same time Shiva to test Arjun's intention appeared there as Kirat. He appeared as King of small castes people. Kirat also pointed arrow on the wild Boar. So both Kirat and Arjun both released their arrow at the same time. Kirat's arrow hit the tail of the wild Boar, while Arjun's arrow hit him on the neck and came out of the other side. So that wild Boar died right there and at death he appeared in his own Devil form. So Arjun thought he was right to think it was an enemy.

Debate between Arjun and Kirat:

After the wild Boar died, Shiva sends his followers to get the arrow. Arjun also comes to get the arrow at the same time. Then they started debating about whose arrow it was. Arjun took both the arrow. Then Shiva's follower ask for the arrow. Arjun then said both arrows are mine and it print my name on it. Shiva's follower then said you are a liar devoted, if your name it prints your name on them, then show us the arrows. Arjun said, I will only show the arrow to your master. So somehow Shiva also came there as Kirat. After that they were ready to battle each other for the arrows. Then Shiva send a message to Arjun that leave the arrow, so there will be no battle. Arjun in reply said, if I give the arrow then they will call me a coward, so I will not let that happen.

After that, battle began between the two. Arjun worshipping Shiva started attacking Kirat and his followers with bow and arrow. Kirat also started attacking Arjun with bow and arrow. Arjun started attacking many arrows towards Kirat at once. But it was not affecting Kirat at all. Whereas Kirat was attacking Arjun only to tease him. Then Kirat came near Arjun and appeared in his form as Shiva. Arjun then started apologizing to Shiva. He also started singing glory of Shiva.

Shiva then became very pleased with Arjun and he said, I only came to test your intention. So I am very pleased to know your true intention. So now tell me your wish and I will fulfill it, said Shiva. Arjun than asked for Shiva's blessing to defeat any his enemy. Shiva then gave him his Pashupata weapon to Arjun and blessed him. After that, Shiva disappeared from there.

Kirat is the eighty-eighth incarnation. This story will fulfill all wishes of any human being.

Om Nama Shivaya

Koti Rudra Sanhita:

Astam Khanda

Eighth Chapter

Description of Twelve Jyotirlinga and Upalinga of Sada Shiva:

In Maharashtra there is Somnath, In Shreesail there is Malikarjun, In Ujjain there is Mahakal, In Omkar there is Amreshowr, In Himalaya there Kedareshowr, In Dakini there is Vimshankhar, In Kashi there is Vishwonath, By Gomati River there is Shree Trumbakeshowr, In Setubandha there is Rameshowr, In Bindya there is Omkareshowr, In Nepal there is Pashupatinath, In Sri Lanka there is Ghoormesh. These are Jyotirlinga. Any human who worship any of these twelve Jyotirlinga in the morning will wash away all his sins. There is no harm in eating the eatable used for worshipping at these Jyotirlingas. Eating the food used for worshipping these Jyotirlingas will wash away all sins of a human being. Anyone who worships any of these Jyotirlingas will not have to reborn after death. Even Vishnu and Brahmdev can't fully describe these Jyotirlingas. Now listen stories about Upalingas established from these Jyotirlingas.

In South India place called Milap there are Atrakesh named Upalinga established from Somnath. From Malikarjun Rudreshowr named Upalinga got established. This Linga is the one who gives happiness to everyone who lives in Bhrigu Kashya. By the bank of River Narmada there is Upalinga named Dugdesh, which is established from Mahakal Jyotirlinga. From Omkar Jyotirlinga, Kardameshowr Upalinga is in Bindhu. This Upalinga fulfill all desires of human beings. From Kedareshowr Jyotirlinga, it creates Bhuteshowr Upalinga which by the banks of River Yamuna. By worshipping at this, Upalinga will wash away all sins. From Vimshankhar Jyotirlinga, Vimeshowr Upalinga is created, and it is in Sandhya Mountain. Bhuteshowr is the Upalinga of Nageshowr Jyotirlinga, and it is by the banks of River Malika Sarswoti. From Ghushesh Jyotirlinga there is it creates Bygraesowr Upalinga. These Jyotirlingas and Upalingas will wash away all sins and fulfills all desires.

Meditation of Ansuya and Atri:

Shoot Jee says, "Hey Munis (Saints), in Brahmadev's town there is a Mountain. In that Mountain Brahmdev has established a Shiva Linga named Matagayanda. That Shiva Linga has the power to provide enough wealth to any human being. On the east side of it there is another Shiva Linga named Kodiha. Which fulfils all wishes of human beings. And it locates sin destroying Shree Pashupati on the banks of Godavari on the north side. West from there is wellness give Atrishowr Shiva Linga. Which is providing bliss to Sati Shree Ansuya Jee.

Brahmadev's son Atri Jee with his wife Ansuya did meditation there for ages and ages. Once, because of drought, there was a shortage of food everywhere. That year there was a lack of water and food. People started dying because of hunger. All the trees died, leaves died, flower didn't bloom, and fruit didn't grow. All the food and water became a shortage. So one day Ansuya told her husband, Atri, that she could no longer see the pain of people suffering because of lack of food and water. So she asked him to please think of some way to help those people. After hearing the request from his wife, Atri then started meditating upon Shiva. After seeing their Guru being in such a deep meditation, all of his disciples left his Ashram and ran away to save their lives. Only Ansuya was left to take care of Atri. Then Ansuya made a Shiva Linga there and started worshipping it every day. Ansuya started worshipping her husband and the Shiva Linga every day. Also, she used to take around and around them three times a day. Then Shiva with Dev Rishis came to Atri's Ashram because of their devotion. Then Ganga Jee and others also came there to see Shiva. Then everyone praised Ansuya for her devotion. Then Shiva started staying in that Shiva Linga made by Ansuya.

Glory of Atrishowr:

Many years went by and Atri finally came back from Samadhi (Deep meditation). As soon as he came out of meditation, he asked his wife for water. He said he is very thirsty and wants water. Then his wife Ansuya went to get the water from the river, but there was no water. So she couldn't get the water anywhere for her husband. Then Ganga Jee appeared before Ansuya and told her she is very pleased with her. So Ganga Jee asked Ansuya for her wish. Then Ansuya asked Ganga Jee to establish herself right there. Ganga Jee then told Ansuya to dig a hole. So Ansuya digs a hole where Ganga Jee establishes herself inside that hole. After that Ansuya fills her bucket with water from Ganga Jee, also requests Ganga Jee to stay there till she brings her husband there to worship Ganga Jee. After that, Ansuya reached home with a bucket of water. So her husband Atri drinks that water to quince his thirst. Then Ansuya tells the story about meeting Ganga Jee to Atri. After that both of them goes to meet and worship Ganga Jee. There they worshiped Ganga Jee and also sang glory of Ganga Jee. After that they took a bath at the Ganga Jee. That fulfilled the wish of Ganga Jee. Then Ganga Jee tells the couple that now she is about to leave.

Then Ansuya requests Ganga Jee that if it thrills you with my devotion, then please stay here forever. Start flowing from this Tapoban. Atri also made a request to Ganga Jee to stay there forever and help them in their meditation. Then Ganga Jee said to Ansuya that if you want me to stay here, then please give me the fruits you have kept aside for one year while worshipping your husband and Shiva. Then Ansuya happily gives the fruits of one year to Ganga Jee. After that she permanently settled there and started flowing from there.

After that Shiva also appeared before Atri and Ansuya. Then Atri requests Shiva to settle in that Tapoban with Goddess Parvati. So that there will be rain and food will grow around there. Which will benefit everyone there, including birds and other animals. Then Shiva blessed Atri and established himself there as Atrishowr Linga. Ganga Jee also settled there with the name Mandakini. Place where Ansuya had to dig the hole is still there were known as Mandakini. After Shiva and Ganga Jee settled there, then that place gained its greenery and water back. Also, all the Rishis who had left Tapoban came back.

Glory of Nandikeshowr:

Shoot Jee says, In Kalinchok Mountain there is it situates Neelkhantha Mahesower in Linga. By seeing he and taking the bath in the Lake there will wash away all sins. By the bank of Rewa River there are uncountable Shiva Linga. Rewa River is Shiva and all the Lingas there are Shiv. Artheswor Shiva Linga is also nearby there. On north side of Rewa River there is a town called Karniki. There a Brahmin with two sons and a wife used to live there. The Brahmin left his family to go to Kashi to die. He died in Kashi. The mother divided the property among the two sons. And wished to take her ashes to Kashi to flow on Ganga Jee. Then one of the son Subad took her mother's ashes to Kashi. While on the way he stayed at a Brahmin's house. Where he witnessed something that night.

There at the Brahmin's house there was a cow with babies. The Brahmin came late to pull milk from the cow. While trying to pull the milk baby cow kicked the Brahmin. Then Brahmin beats the baby cow. The cow tells the baby cow that next morning when he comes to get the milk from me, I will hit him with my thorn and kill him. The baby cow said you will commit a sin of killing a Brahmin, so don't do that. Then the cow said, I know how to wash away that sin. Next morning when the Brahmin came to get the milk, cow hit him hard with his thorn and killed the Brahmin. Then Brahmin's wife let go of the cow. The white cow turned black because of killing a Brahmin. After that, the cow went to banks of Narmada River. There is Nandikeshowr Shiva Linga there and there at the Narmada River the cow took a three dips in the River. After that, it washed away its sin. So cow turned back white. Then Subad had witnessed all these. After that he started walking towards Kashi to flow the ash of her mother at the Ganga Jee there. Then on the way he meets a beautiful lady. The lady suggests her, that day the Ganga Jee comes right there to Narmada River. So he could flow the ashes of his mother right there. So Subad flows his mother's ashes to Narmada River. So he saw his mother living for heaven from the water after his flow her ashes. On the way, his mother blesses him for his good deed.

Then Rishis asks Shoot Jee, "Why on Baisakh Sukla Saptami (In March) does Ganga Jee comes to Nandikeshowr?" Shoot Jee then says, Long time ago Brahmin's daughter named Rishika married and became a widow. She was the devotee of Nandikeshowr. One day she was meditating on Shiva, when a devil named Mayabi came there. He became lust with her beauty.

So he started creating problems for her while she was meditating. Then Shiva appeared there and killed that devil. After that Shiva ask, Rishika for her wish. Then Rishika said that he should always devote her mind to Shiva and also Shiva should stay there at Nandikeshowr Shiva Linga forever. Then Shiva granted her the two wishes. That day Ganga Jee, Vishnu also came and blessed Rishika. Since that day Nandikeshowr Shiva, Linga became very popular.

Glory of Mahabal Shiva:

In Ichyakumbas there was King named Mitrasha. He was a devotional and generous King. His wife was Damayanti, and she was also devotional towards her husband.

One day the King with his wife went for hunting. Then in that jungle he saw a devil named Karmatha creating problems for Mandap Jee. Then the King killed the devil with his bow and arrow. After that, the brother of that devil takes revenge with the King. So he appeared in King's palace as a cook. He told the King that he can cook anything and make it tasty. King then hires him as a cook for his palace.

Then one day on Guru Day. King invited Rishi Vasistha to his palace. Then he told that devil's brother to prepare the food for Rishi Vasistha. Then that devil prepared much food for Rishi Vasistha. Then to take revenge from the King, he mixes meat item on the food. He then serves that food to Rishi Vasistha. Rishi Vasistha as soon as he saw the food. Knew that meat is mixed with that food. So Rishi Vasistha becomes angry and curse the king. He curses that King become a devil. Afterwards Rishi Vasistha realizes that it wasn't actually a King's fault, but cook. So he tells the King since I have already cursed you, I can't take that back. But you will stay being devil for only twelve years. After that, Rishi Vasistha leaves. Then that King becomes the devil and start living in a jungle. There he used to eat a human being who would appear near him.

In that Jungle there was a Muni and his wife living in an Ashram. They were a young couple. That King who had turned devil hunted the Muni. He captured her and eat him. His wife made several requests to the King to let go of her husband. But the King didn't let go the Muni. Then he finished eating the Muni. Threw the bones. His wife collected all the bones and cursed the devil King that he would die while making love to his lover.

After that, twelve years went by and the devil became King again. So he went back to his palace. There he became King again. He also told his wife about the curse that Muni's wife spelled at him. Because of the curse, they couldn't come close to make love. They also didn't have any children, and they wanted to have children. So one day King went to jungle to hunt. There he witnessed a Brahmin killing, which then hunt him for his deeds as the devil. So he started visiting lots of Holy places to wash away his sins for killing a Brahmin. But he used to be scared all the time.

Then one day at one of the holy place he met Rishi Gautama. Who advise the King to go to Gokarna and takes the bath there. After that worship the Mahabal Shiva Linga there, which will wash away all his sins from the past. So it thrilled the King to hear that advice from Rishi Gautama. After that King went to Gokarna and took a bath there and worshipped Mahabal Shiva Linga. Which then washed all his sins.

Shoot Jee then continues and says, "Hey Rishis those were the Shiva Linga from North India. Now let me tell you about Shiva Linga from South. There is also another place called Gokarna where in that Jungle there another Shiva Linga is named Chandrabhal. That Shiva is brought and established by Rawan.

Beside that there is also a holy place known as Misrik. There Rishi Dadhichi had established Dhadhichisowr Shiva Linga. There devotees feel peace with in them. There on Naimishara there is Rishiseyshowr Shiva Linga established by Rishis. By only seeing that Shiva Linga, it will wash away all the sins. In Devparyag there is Laliteshowr Shiva Linga. In Nepal there is Pashupatinath who destroys all the sins and also fulfills all the wish of a devotee.

Reason for Linga Incarnation:

Shoot Jee says, "Hey Rishi Munis, a long time ago, In Bharat there was a jungle named Daruk. Near that jungle there was a Shivalaya (Shiva's temple). In that temple there was a Rishi who used to worship Shiva three times a day. In the morning, afternoon, and in the evening. He used to meditate and sing the glory of Shiva while worshipping. When he was completely devoted in meditating Shiva. Then there at that jungle, lots of Rishis gathered to conduct Hawan (Holy fire ritual). Then Shiva wanted to test the intention of those Rishis. So Shiva incarnated as a low caste male. Then he shows off his pins (Linga) went to the Ashram of the Rishis. There the Rishi's wife saw him coming their way with showing off his pin (Linga). So the wives of the Rishis started hiding. But he kept showing his pin, started playing with his hands. After that, the wives of the Rishis started being attracted to that pin (Linga). So they came out and started touching and playing with it. Some of them even made love with it. Then the Rishis came towards the Ashram and saw their wives with a stranger who is showing off his pin (Linga). Then Rishis asks their wives who is this guy and what is he doing here? But they didn't answer. Then Rishis ask that guy, who he was several times. But Shiva didn't answer at all. Then Rishi curse Shiva that his pin be dropped to the ground. So after that, his pin dropped on the ground. There at the ground it started jumping up and down and start troubling all the people.

Then Rishis went to Brahmdev to take his advice. There the Rishis told the whole story to Brahmdev. Then Brahmdev told them it was Shiva to whom they had cursed. So now do meditation of Jagdamba, Goddess Parvati, to please her. So she can silence that Linga, said Brahmdev to the Rishis. Then Rishis started meditating and singing glory of Goddess Parvati. So Goddess Parvati became happy and was ready to help them. Then Goddess Parvati also took the shape of a female sexual organ. The Rishis then pushed that Linga inside the sexual organ of Goddess Parvati with all tradition as explained by Brahmdev. After that, they worshipped that Shiva Linga.

That Shiva Linga in the world is known as Hatkeshowr Shiva Linga.

Release of Andhakasoor:

Once upon a time, there was a devil known as Andhakasoor. He was very brave devil. He had imprisoned all human beings under his control. All the human beings of the world were suffering because of him.

Even Gods were suffering because of him. So all the Gods went to Shiva. There they started praising and singing the glory of Shiva. So Shiva being very thrilled ask them about their problem. Then Gods told Shiva about Andhakasoor and how his activities are making them suffer. Then Shiva told them to take their soldiers to battle with Andhakasoor. Shiva also told them he will be behind them to support them. Then all the Gods with their soldiers went to the palace of Andhakasoor. Andhakasoor saw the Gods with their soldiers, so he also came out to battle. So battle began between Gods and Andhakasoor. Gods defeated Andhakasoor in the battle. So Andhakasoor went inside his palace to hide. Then Shiva with his trident kills Andhakasoor. Before dying Andhakasoor tells Shiva that it is a great opportunity to see the face of Shiva because after that one becomes the purest devotee of Shiva. So he says that he is very fortunate to die from trident of Shiva. Then Shiva being very pleased with him, ask him for his wish. Then Andhakasoor asks Shiva that he be his pure devotee and also that Shiva should establish himself right there. Then Shiva grants him his wish. So he becomes Shiva's pure devotee and Shiva also establishes himself there as Shiva Linga.

Story of Batuk's Glory:

Once upon a time there was a Rishi named Dhadichi. Who was very devoted to Shiva and also had knowledge of all four Vedas. He had a son named Sudarshan. Sudarshan was also devotee of Shiva like his father. But his wife named Tukula was not so patience. She had kept her husband under her control. From her Sudarshan had four sons. One day Sudarshan's father Dhadichi had to go to a visit his relatives in a village. So he made his son Sudarshan in charge of worshipping Shiva in his absence. So Sudarshan started worshipping the Shiva while his father had gone to the village. So one day on Shivaratri, Sudarshan was worshipping Shiva. Then suddenly he had to go to his room. There in his room, his wife Tukula made him make love to her. After that, without taking a shower, Sudarshan went back to worship Shiva.

Then Shiva knowing what Sudarshan did, cursed him it will vanish all his Knowledge about Shiva. So it happens. All his knowledge vanished. So he started shouting on roads like a madman. He became mad.

After some ages his father Dhadichi came back from the village and found out what happened to his son Sudarshan. Then he thought his son had done a terrible job. So he started thinking what to do, to find the solution. So he then meditates upon Goddess Parvati. He praises her and starts singing glory of Goddess Parvati. Then Goddess Parvati appears right there in front of Rishi Dhadichi. The Goddess Parvati, knowing what Dhadichi wanted, took Sudarshan on the feet of Shiva. And she said "Hey this Sudarshan is my son, so please forgive him and give the sixteen letter Shiva Gayatri Mantra to him," said Goddess Parvati to Shiva. Then Shiva gives Sudarshan a sixteen letter Shiva Gayatri Mantra. And tells him to worship Shiva with that Mantra twice a day.

After that Shiva also blessed the four sons of Sudarshan saying they are as good as Batuk Bhairav. Shiva also said that whoever worships the Batuk, then I will feel like they have worshipped me. After that, Sudarshan became famous in the world as Batuk. So on any occasion worshipping Batuk is always beneficial.

Establishment of Somnath:

Moon had married twenty-seven daughters of Dakshya. But among them all he used to only give his attention to his wife Rohini only. Other twenty six of his wives felt neglected. So they went to complain to their father, Dakshya. Then Dakshya came and counsel Moon. He told Moon that he should give attention to all his wives. Otherwise he will have to go to hell for loving one only. After that, Dakshya returned to his own place. But Moon didn't care what Dakshya had said. So he still gave his attention to Rohini only. Then again, his other twenty-six wives went to complain to their father Dakshya again. This time Dakshya became furious with Moon, and he cursed him. Dakshya cursed Moon that he would glow less and less every day and will disappear in darkness.

Then Moon told God Indra and other Gods about the curse. Then they all went to Brahmdev to ask for advice. Then Brahmdev told Gods that Moon had once taken Guru Brihaspati's wife Tara out. Then when he returned Tara back, she was pregnant. So Brahmdev had to make her pregnancy disappear, to heal the relationship between Tara and Guru Brihaspati. So because of that act he is now suffering, said Brahmdev. Brahmdev then advice Gods to go to place called Pravas and pronounce Mirtunjaya Mantra one hundred million times, also keep repeating the Mantra Om Nama Shivaya.

So the Gods along with Moon went to Pravas. There they did what Brahmdev had advised them to do. Then Shiva appeared before them. So Shiva then asks Moon what does he wants? Then Moon says, "Oh, please make me free of a curse." Then Shiva says, "I can't take your curse away, but you only will fade away for the first fifteen days and second fifteen days will start glowing brighter and brighter." Moon then becomes thrilled. So all the Gods worship and praising Shiva. They also request Shiva along with Goddess Parvati to settle there as Somnath Shiva Linga. Then Shiva grants them their wish and establishes self with Goddess Parvati as Somnath Shiva Linga. They also made holy pond there naming it Chandra Kund. Taking a single deep in that pond washes all the sins.

Establishment of Malikarjun Shiva Linga:

Kumar Kartikya, when roaming on Earth as per the advice of Shiva, met Naradh Jee on the way. Naradh Jee, being very mean, said, "Your father send you to Earth to suffer, whereas for Ganesha he is getting married." Then Kumar Kartikya becomes furious and goes to his parents, Shiva and Goddess Parvati. There he says nothing and starts heading towards Kaunj Mountain. Shiva and Goddess Parvati tried to counsel him, but Kumar Kartikya didn't listen to them. After a while Goddess Parvati misses her son, Kumar Kartikya. So Shiva and Goddess Parvati went to Kaunj Mountain to bring Kumar Kartikya back home. But as soon as Kumar Kartikya heard that his parents are there to take him, he went even far away from there. So Shiva settled there at Kaunj Mountain. Then Shiva establish himself as Malikarjun Shiva Linga there.

Establishment of Mahakalleshowr Shiva Linga:

There used to be a Brahmin living in a town called Avanti. He used to worship Shiva in Shiva Linga with the traditional way. He also was well off with property and wealth. In Earth he witnessed all kinds of happiness and at the end receive Shiva at death. That Brahmin had four sons. They were Devpriya, Meghapriya, Sukrit, and Dharmabhahu. They were all devoted to Shiva like their father. Near their house, there was a Mountain named Ratnamalla. In that mountain, a demon named Dusar used to live. He had meditated and had a blessing from Brahmdev. So he won two Loka Swarga (Heaven) Lok and Mirtyu (Earth) Lok and in a battle and started ruling on them.

So one day he arrives at Avanti. There he asks four of his demon soldiers to find Shiva devotees and tell them to change their views. Also, he tells them that "if they don't agree then punish them." So the four demons started terrorizing everyone in that village. They killed some people, and others ran towards the four Brahmins for protection. They're all the people ask the four Brahmins to refuge them and protect them. Then the four Brahmins said that they don't have any weapon or any other things to protect them from those demons. All they have is Shiva and they are taking refuge in him. After that, the four demons arrives there. Then everyone except for the four Brahmins runs away. Then four Brahmins as usual starts worshipping Shiva. The four demons come to attack them but land tears apart and Shiva emerges from it. Then Shiva kills all of those demons.

After witnessing that all the Gods and Rishis became thrilled. So they started throwing flowers from the sky towards Shiva. Shiva then asks the four Brahmins for their wish. Then the four Brahmins says, "we want to establish in us and also if you could establish yourself here forever," says the four Brahmins. After that Shiva along with Goddess Parvati establish themselves in Shiva Linga known as Mahakalleshowr Shiva Linga.

Devotees who worships Mahakalleshowr Shiva Linga will wash away all problems and fulfils all wishes.

Glory of Mahakal:

Shoot Jee says, "Now listen to the story of Mahakalleshowr Shiva. It is a great story and you should all pay attention to it."

There was King named Chandra Sen in Ujjain. The King had a friend named Maribhadra. Maribhadra was a devotee of Shiv Shiva. Once Maribhadra was impressed with the King. So he gave the King Kaustuv Mari. Thant Mari (Stone) was as bright as Sun. So the King started wearing that Mari with his necklace. So the King started looking dazzling because of the Mari. The other Kings started feeling jealous of it and also tried to attack the King to get the Mari.

Then Kings allover united and came to attack Chandra Sen for the Mari. Chandra Sen took refuge in Mahakalleshowr Shiva Linga temple. There the King started worshipping Shiva. Right then there a widow with her five-year-old son also came there. They watch King worshipping the Shiva. After that, they went back to their home.

After reaching home, that five-year boy worships Shiva similarly like that of King. So he goes to the River, there he picks up a nice stone. Starts worshipping that stone thinking its Shiva. So in his mind he offered Shiva incense, fire, fruits, etc. Then his mother called him for food. But he couldn't hear her, as he was deeply devoted in meditating Shiva. Then his mother came looking for him. When she sees him in meditative state worshipping Shiva. Then his mother grabbed the boy in the shoulders and started scolding him. She also threw away the stone from there. While pulling the boy, he falls on the ground and becomes unconscious. Seeing that her mother also becomes unconscious. After sometime the boy wakes up and finds himself inside the temple of Mahakalleshowr Shiva Linga.

Realizing that he was inside the Mahakalleshowr Temple next to the Shiva Linga. So he bows down to Shiva Linga several times. After that thinking about Shiva, he ran towards his home. At home it surprised him to see everything was great. His small hut turned into a big house with everything new inside. He also saw his mother sleeping on a bed made with ornaments. Then he wakes his mother up and tells her the whole story about how Shiva became happy with them. So all those nice things happen to them. His mother also becomes thrilled by seeing everything around.

The King when finished his worship to Shiva, then heard the news about the five-year-old boy. The King then with all his ministers went to the boy's house. There he witnessed the blessing of Shiva to the boy, so he became thrilled. The King then celebrated all night by the boy's house. The next day everyone in Ujjain heard about the news of the boy. Then all the other Kings who came to attack the King Chandra Sen, knew that Mahakalleshowr Shiva Linga blessed him. So he was friends with King Chandra Sen. so they all came to the boy's house and witnessed the blessing of Shiva to the boy. So they extended their friendship with King Chandra Sen.

Then there Shree Hanuman Jee appeared. So all the Kings there started praising Hanuman Jee. They also worshiped Hanuman Jee. After that, Hanuman Jee grabs the boy and hugs and kiss him. After that he tells everyone, "This boy had seen King Chandra Sen worshipping Shiva, so he also in mind worshipped Shiva similarly. As a result, Shiva who is the father of the whole Universe blessed him. In his family after eighth generation, a Maha yogi will be born. His name will be Nanda and Sri Krishna will be born in his family. And it will know this boy as Shrikat," said Hanuman Jee. After saying all that, Hanuman Jee vanished from there. After that, King Chandra Sen respected and gave his best to all the other Kings who were there to kill him. So all of those Kings became a very good friend with King Chandra Sen. After that they all returned to their respected homes. After that Chandra Sen and Shrikat worshipped Shiva traditionally for the rest of their life. After death they both went to Baikuntha. This story about achieving Moksha which takes so many lives happen in a single life for the Chandra Sen and Shrikat. Hearing this story will wash away all suffering and Shiva's blessing always be with him.

Glory of Omkareshowr:

Shoot Jee says, "Hey Rishis, now listen to the story of Omkareshowr Shiva Linga. Please pay attention as it is a great story." Once upon a time, Narad Jee worshiped Shiva named Gokarna. After that he went to Brinda chal. There all the Rishis and saints worshipped and sang the glory of Narad Jee. So he was very pleased. Then Brinda thought he is the superior Mountain and became jealous of Narad Jee. So he came and sat right in front of Narad Jee. Narad Jee then knew what Brinda had on his mind. So he said, "I know Brinda that you are one of the superior Mountain. But in front of Sumeru Mountain you are nothing," said Narad Jee.

After hearing that from Narad Jee, Brinda chal make furious and started degrading self. Then he thought about worshipping Shiva to be superior. So he builds a Shiva Linga and started worshipping it for six months. Then Shiva was very pleased with Brinda Chal. So Shiva appeared before Brinda Chal. And asked him for his wish.

Then Brinda Chal respected and regarded Shiva. After that he asked Shiva to bless him with superior thoughts. Then Shiva blessed him. Also the other Rishis present there at that time asked Shiva to settle there. Then Shiva also agreed to settle there for the benefit of the world.

So in this area, they situate Omkareshowr and Parmeshowr. They both are the same Shiva. Both of Shiva will grant a wish to heaven and Moksha.

Glory of Sri Kedareshowr:

Shoot Jee says, "Hey Rishis, now listen to the story where Vishnu did hard meditation at Badrika Ashram. Shiva, being very pleased with Vishnu, also came in Shiva Linga figure. Then Shiva and Vishnu spent a lot of time there. Then one day Shiva ask Vishnu for his wish. Then Vishnu said, "Hey, please settle here for the goodness of the world. Then Shiva grant him that wish by establishing self as Kedarnath Shiva Linga. So whoever goes to Kedarnath and worships Kedarnath Shiva Linga, then all his wishes will be fulfilled.

Once Pandavas saw Shiva in a Buffalo incarnation. So they came close to him. Then the buffalo started running, Pandus grabbed the tail of the buffalo. They also said, "Oh Shiva, we know it's you so please don't run away. Then that buffalo convert itself into Shiva Linga. After that they solved all the problems of Pandavas. So by worshipping Kedarnath Shiva Linga, all wishes of a person will become true.

Establishment of Bhimeshwor Shiva Linga:

Shoot Jee says, "Hey Rishis, One day someone went to Bhim the demon, and told him that the King there is planning to kill him. Then that demon Bhim went to the king with the sword in his hand. Then he tries to threaten the King. King then in his mind worships Shiva. Also, he tells that demon Bhim that he is worshipping Shiva, so he isn't scared of him. Then that demon Bhim talks bad about Shiva and smashes his swords on the Shiva Linga there. Then Shiva appeared from the Shiva Linga and starts fighting with that demon Bhim. The Shiva followers also starts fighting with other demons. By that battle Earth, Jungle Mountain all became scared. Then Shiva produces a fire, and that fire kills that demon Bhim.

After that in that place lots of herbal plants grew. Those plants can cure any disease. Then all the Rishis started requesting Shiva to settle there for the goodness of the world. After that Shiva established himself in a Shiva Linga there. Which known as Bhim Shankar Shiva Linga. This Shiva Linga takes away the pain and grants wishes of the devotees.

Glory of Shree Bishwoshwor Shiva Linga:

Shoot Jee says, "Hey Rishis now listen to the story of Shiva Linga in Kashi known as Vishwonath Shiva Linga. At one time Goddess Parvati had asked Shiva about Vishwonath Shiva Linga. I will tell you the same story", says Shoot Jee. Shiva says to Goddess Parvati, that Kashi is the place to provide Moksha to all living being. That Dham is also the living space of Shiva. Enlighten one's comes to Kashi to describe different incarnations of Shiva. No matter what other holy place one goes to, but Kashi is the place that will provide Moksha to the ones who die in Kashi. It doesn't matter what race, or gender, or sinful the person may be, if he dies in Kashi, then he will have Moksha. The secret of Kashi is note one to heaven.

There are all together three types of Karma. First is one is born with certain Karma which is known as Sanchit Karma. Second is Karma done on present life? So the combine Karma which is a mix of those two is called Prarapda Karma. So all these Karma can be cleared in Kashi only. Person living in Kashi will die in Kashi in his next life. There by taking bath, by facing the Ganga on the East, by standing on the South, will wash away all kinds of negative Karma. Only by doing good deeds, one gets to live in Kashi. Fully known to Vishnu or Brahmdev either. Rishis goes life after life meditating to have Moksha, and by dying at Kashi anyone can get Moksha. After receiving Moksha, a person doesn't have to be reborn and die. Also, anyone does anything sinful within a certain territory of Kashi will go to hell for thousands of years. Also, doing noble work for other while being in certain areas of Kashi will take one to heaven. Only by doing good deeds, one gets to live in Kashi.

Glory of Maha Rishi Gautama:

Shoot Jee says, "Hey Rishis, once upon a time, Maha Rishi Gautama did a meditation for ten thousand years to be enlighten in South India's Brahma Mountain. There was a drought for almost a year. So all the living beings were dying because of lack of water. So Maha Rishi Gautama meditate upon Varun Dev. Six months after the meditation Varun Dev appeared before Maha Rishi Gautama. Then Varun Deva asked Maha Rishi Gautama for his wish. Then Maha Rishi Gautama said, "All the living beings are suffering for lack of water so please provide rain for all beings." Then Varun Dev said, "It is not up to me to provide rain. Without the permission of Shiva, I can't provide rain. Then Varun Deva said, "Let me know your other wish." Maha Rishi Gautama said, "I don't have any other wish but the water for everyone." Then Varun Dev said, "Dig a hole in the ground and I will fill it with water which will never end." then quickly Maha Rishi Gautama dig a hole in the ground, which Varun Deva filled it with water. After that, all the living beings in that area could get the water from there. That place also became a holy place because of the deeds of Maha Rishi Gautama.

They blame Maha Rishi Gautama for Killing a Cow:

Shoot Jee says, "Hey Munis, followers of Maha Rishi Gautama used to bring water from the same pond Maha Rishi Gautama created which. One day when the followers of Maha Rishi Gautama went to get the water from the pond. The wives of other Rishis were also there, to get the water from the same pond. So those wives told followers of Maha Rishi Gautama that they could take the water only after they are done. Then those followers left without getting the water. So by seeing this Ahilya Jee wife of Maha Rishi went and get the water herself. From that day she started getting the water for her husband, Maha Rishi Gautama every day. So someday the wives of other Rishis said bad things about Ahilya Jee. They also went home and told their husband that Ahilya Jee doesn't let them take water from the pond and she shows off saying that it is my husband who build this pond.

By believing in their wives, the other Rishis became furious with Maha Rishi Gautama. So they started worshipping Ganesha to take away Maha Rishi Gautama and his followers away from there. So after worshipping and meditating upon Ganesha. Ganesha appeared before them. When Ganesha asked them for their wish, the Rishis said that they want Maha Rishi Gautama to move away from that place. Then Ganesha said, "Maha Rishi Gautama is innocent, so to punish him would not be right. It would not do any good to any of you. So let me know some other wish," said Ganesha. But the Rishis didn't give up their wish, so they said that's all we want. Then Ganesha said whatever you guys wish and vanished from there. So the Rishis became happy that their wish will become true.

After granting the wish of the Rishis. Ganesha to make that wish come true incarnated as a cow. And started roaming near the Ashram of Maha Rishi Gautama. So Gautama with a light stick hit that cow to make him go away. But the cow collapsed and died right there. So then those other Rishis blamed Maha Rishi Gautama of killing a cow. Then they started saying that Maha Rishi Gautama and his followers can't stay there anymore. Maha Rishi Gautama with his wife and his followers moved further away from that place.

Fifteen days after that, Maha Rishi Gautama came to those other Rishis and asked for ways to wash away his sins. Then those other Rishis said either you meditate and call Ganga Jee here and take a bath on it. Then worship Shiva Linga, made from earth ten million times, that will wash away your sins.

Then after that Maha Rishi Gautama came back, and he went around the Brahma Giri Mountain. After that he made a Shiva Linga from Earth and started worshipping it. His wife Ahilya Jee also worshipped along with him.

Establishment and Glory of Trayambakeshowr:

Shoot Jee says, "Hey Rishis, So Maha Rishi Gautam and his wife started worshipping Shiva in Linga figure made from Earth material. By their devotion Shiva along with his followers appeared there, in front of Maha Rishi Gautama and his wife. Then at first Maha Rishi Gautama worshiped Shiva and asked him to wash away his sins of killing the cow. Then Shiva told Maha Rishi Gautama that it was the Maya created by those other Rishis. So he has committed no sins. Then Maha Rishi Gautama said, "Hey because of those rishis, I got to see you, so I am thankful for it." After hearing that, Shiva became thrilled and ask Maha Rishi Gautama for his wish. Then Maha Rishi Gautama asked Shiva to make Ganga Jee appear and start flowing from there. So that by taking bath in Ganga Jee it will wash all the sins of others.

Then Shiva gave Ganga Jal to Maha Rishi Gautama, and from it Ganga Jee appeared in front of them. Maha Rishi Gautama then started praising Ganga Jee. He said, "He Ganga Devi, you wash all the sins I have committed and save me from going to hell."

Then Shiva tells Ganga Jee to wash all the sins of Maha Rishi Gautama and his family. Then Ganga Jee says to Shiva that she will wash away all the sins of Maha Rishi Gautama and his family, then only she will come back to Shiva. Then Shiva told Ganga Jee, that she has to stay on earth till the twenty eighth generation of humankind in Kali Yug to wash away their sins. Then Ganga Jee says to Shiva that he also has to settle near there for her to stay on earth for so long.

Then Shiva told Ganga Jee, that there is no difference between the two. But if she wants, he would settle there. So Shiva settled themselves known as Trayambakeshowr Shiva Linga. Ganga Jee also settled there with the name Gautami Ganga.

When Maha Rishi Gautama requested Ganga Jee to appear her in Ganga (Water) form. Then in Brahma Giri water started flowing from a branch of Dupri (Gular) tree. Then in that Ganga water Maha Rishi Gautama and his followers took a bath. Then those other Rishis also came to bathe there, but Ganga Jee disappeared from there. Then Maha Rishi Gautama became curious and said to Ganga Jee, "Hey Goddess Ganga, whoever comes here to take a bath in here should be able to. Discriminating no one for their good or bad deed."

The voice came from sky and it said, "Hey Muni, they are the ones who destroy other people's progress. They are a sinner."

Then again, a voice came from the sky and said, "Hey Gautama, you are right. But it must punish them for their deeds. So they must apologize to you and make one hundred round of Brahma Giri Mountain," said the voice. Those other Rishis also heard the voice, so they rushed to Maha Rishi Gautama and apologized for their deeds and made one hundred round of Brahma Giri Mountain. Then they could see Ganga Jee and take a bath on it.

Glory of Baidyanatheshowr:

Shoot Jee says, "Hey Munis, a long time ago Rawan did hardship meditation to please Shiva. But Shiva didn't care. Then Rawan dig a hole and put a holy fire there in summer and started doing hard meditation on Shiva. He also meditated on cold winter days. But that didn't impress Shiva. So he started cutting his heads one by one and started putting in that fire. When he was about to cut his tenth head, then Shiva appeared before him. Then Shiva let Rawan have all his heads back. Also, Shiva made Rawan brave.

Then Rawan asked Shiva if he could take him to Lanka as his wish. Then Shiva told Rawan that he could take his Shiva Linga to Lanka. The Rawan became thrilled. Shiva also told Rawan that it put that Shiva Linga on the ground anywhere while taking it to Lanka. Then that Shiva Linga will stay wherever it touches the ground, and it will not move from there. Rawan agreed and took that Shiva Linga with him to Lanka. On the way, Rawan had to pee. So he let one of the boy to hold the Shiva Linga till he pees. So the boy hold the Shiva Linga for one hour and later because of its heaviness put it on the ground and ran away from there. When Rawan came back, he saw the Shiva Linga on the ground. Which is known as Baidyanatheshowr Shiva Linga. So he couldn't take it to Lanka. Then he went to Lanka without the Shiva Linga. So Rawan since he was blessed to be brave. He thought about attacking all three Loka and start ruling. Then Narad Jee came to Rawan and started praising him for his bravery. Then Narad Jee gave the idea to Rawan to show his bravery on Shiva himself. Then Rawan thought about carrying the Kailas with Shiva in it and bring it to Lanka.

So Rawan with all his armies went to Kailas, and they started trying to life Kailas Mountain. Then Kailas Mountain started shaking. So Shiva told Rawan that someone is coming soon to kill him. The Rawan didn't think Shiva was serious. So he again had to leave empty hand back to Lanka.

Establishment and Glory of Nageshowr:

Shoot Jee says, "Hey Rishis, a long time ago, there was a demon named Daruk and his wife name was Daruka. That couple used to live in the jungle provided by Goddess Devi. That jungle was in the north India by the ocean. People living there were suffering because of the demon couple. So one day all the people went to the Rishi named Aurva and told him their complaint against the demon couple. Then Rishi told those people not to worry and go home. If those demons came again to kill anyone of you or tried to disturb a Brahmin Yegya, then they will be killed for their act.

After that, Rishi Aurva started meditating for the goodness of the world. After knowing that Rishi Aurva had cursed those demons, Gods came to battle with those two demons. Then Daruka, because of the blessing from a previous life, lifted that town and put it safely on the Ocean. Then all the demons started living there peacefully. One Daruka was on the beach and saw a lot of men and women on a boat heading towards them. Then Daruka ordered her other demon friends to capture the boat and make all of those people prisoner. Then they made those people prisoner and put them in jail. In that, a prostitute named Supriya was also there. Then in that prison she started worshipping Shiva. So other prisoners also did the same as that was their only option. After six months of worshipping Shiva, one of the demon saw her worshipping Shiva.

Then that demon asks who she was worshipping. But Supriya didn't answer, and mentally she surrendered herself to Shiva. That demon then threatened to kill her if she said nothing. Then Shiva appeared there and killed all those demons. Then that jungle became demon free. Shiva also said that from now on only people who follow Veda will live here. When people living here will sacrifice Veda and follow non-Vedic religion, then demons will enter here again.

After Daruk died, the Daruka started praising Goddess Durga by singing her glory. The Goddess Durga appeared before Daruka. And told her that "Now because of Shiva, no one with non-Vedic religion can stay here. So you go away for and when Sri Krishna comes to earth and one thousand years after he leaves earth. One thousand years after that there will be no Vedic rules followed here. Then you along with other demons can return here to create fear for those people," said Goddess Durga. After that, she vanishes.

"There is also another story about Nageshowr Shiva Linga, that I will tell you guys," said Shoot Jee. There was a king named Birsen, he was a devotee of Shiva. So Shiva had given him the stick with fish on it. Because of this stick you along with your solider will reach Nageshowr Shiva Linga. There by worshipping Nageshowr Shiva Linga he would receive a special weapon. By which he can then win many demons. So the king won many battles with different demons.

So by the blessing of Nageshowr Shiva Linga, King Birsen became successful in winning all the battle against many demons.

Glory of Rameshowr:

Shoot Jee says, "Hey Munis, When Ram Chandra Jee went to jungle by obeying his father's order. Then there Rawan captured Sita Jee and took her to Lanka. Which Hanuman Jee found out by going to Lanka? When Sri Ram went to get Sita with his force of army, then there was an Ocean on the way. Then Sri Ram couldn't think of anyway of crossing that Ocean to go to Lanka. Then Sri Ram made Shiva Linga from earth and started worshipping it. He worshipped the Shiva Linga to win the battle against Rawan. Then Shiva appeared from that Shiva Linga and blessed Sri Ram. Sri Ram told his wish to win the battle against Rawan to Shiva. Shiva then blessed Sri Ram that he would be the one who would win that battle. After that Sri Ram asked Shiva to settle in that Shiva Linga, so he can do well for the world. Shiva then blessed Sri Ram and settled in that Shiva Linga. So the name of that Shiva Linga became Rameshowr. This Rameshowr Shiva Linga provides Moksha to the devotee of Shiva. Whoever takes the water from Kashi, to Shiva in Rameshowr and worships will be pure devotee.

Story of Sudeha and Sudharma:

Shoot Jee says, "Hey Munis, now you listen to the description of Ghusmesh Shiva Linga."

In South India, there is Mountain named Dev. Near that mountain, a Brahmin named Sudharma used to live there. That Brahmin was from Bhardwaj Gotra (Belonging to one of the seven Sapta Rishi). He had a beautiful wife named Sudeha. Sudeha was a devotee of Shiva and didn't have any children. She always used to dream about having children. So she used to complain to her husband about not having any children. Her husband used to counsel her by saying having children will only take them away by Maya. So he used to say they are better with no children. One day Sudeha went out with her friends and she had quarreled with them. Then her friends teased her by saying she has no children and all their wealth will be gone to the King after they die. That made Sudeha very upset. So she again complained to her husband about not having any children. She proposed her husband to marry another woman for children. But her husband refuse to do that.

So one day Sudeha asked her husband to marry her sister. But Sudharma again refused it at the beginning. But later on he had to agree. So he married Gushma, the sister of Sudeha. Sudeha taught her sister to worship the Shiva Linga and later on to flow the Shiva Linga on the river. That way Gushma worshipped one hundred thousand Shiva Linga and flowed them in the river. After that Shiva became very thrilled and grant her the wish to have children. Within a year, Gushma gave birth to a beautiful boy. After that, Sudharma also started spending more time with Gushma. That started making Sudeha jealous of her sister.

Establishment of Ghusmesh Shiva Linga:

Shoot Jee says, "Hey Rishis, slowly Gushma's son started growing and became a young adult. Then Sudharma arranged a wedding for his son with a Brahmin girl. After the wedding, Gushma took the son- and daughter-in-law to her sister Sudeha to bless them. Gushma told her daughter-in-law that Sudeha is her real mother-in-law. So always give good care of Sudeha. But the jealousy of Sudeha against her sister Gushma was still there. So one day Sudeha killed Gushma's son by cutting his head and threw the dead body on the same Pond where Gushma used to worship Shiva. Next day, when they couldn't find the son, they started crying. Then Sudharma also arrives there and tells Gushma that she shouldn't abandon worshipping Shiva in those difficult times. So Gushma goes to the Pond to worship Shiva, there she sees her son standing near the Pond. His son told her that even after dying he came back to life because of her worship to Shiva. Then after that Gushma again starts worshipping Shiva. Shiva then appears from the Shiva Linga. Then Shiva told Gushma that her sister Sudeha had killed her son, so now he would punish her for her deed. Then Gushma tells Shiva that she doesn't want any punishment for her sister Sudeha, instead she wants the punishment for herself. She tells Shiva that she doesn't want any bad towards her sister, even though she treated her badly. That makes Shiva thrilled, and he asks for Gushma's wish. Then Gushma asks Shiva to stay in that Shiva Linga to bless the world. Then Shiva establishes himself in that Shiva Linga and stays there. Whoever worships the Ghusmesh Shiva Linga will have all their wished be fulfill.

Vishnu receives Sudarshan Chakra:

Shoot Jee says, "Hey Brahmins, Once upon a time demons were powerful then Gods. Because of demons activities all the human kind were suffering. Those demons were out there to wipe out the Vedic believes and religion. They were destroying all Brahmins will by giving them troubles. They used to bring lots of women to Brahmins, so Brahmins would forget their duties to perform. That way Demons were becoming stronger than Gods. So all the Gods went to Vishnu and prayed him to kill the demons. Then Vishnu told the Gods that, "Don't worry, I will now worship Shiva and everything will be fine," said Vishnu to Gods.

After that Vishnu went to Kailas, and there he establishes fire in Agni Kund (Holy fire burning place) and started meditating upon Shiva. He meditated for so long, but Shiva wasn't happy with it. So after that Vishnu started saying one thousand names of Shiva and also started worshipping the Shiva Linga made from Earth. He used to pronounce each Shiva Mantra and put one Lotus flower on the Shiva Linga. That way every day he used to worship Shiva Linga with one thousand lotus flower.

One day Shiva hides one of the lotus flower. So when Vishnu counted the flower, one was missing. So he looked for that flower everywhere but couldn't find it. Then he took one of his eye and worshiped with it. That made Shiva very thrilled, and he appeared before Vishnu. And ask for his wish. Then Vishnu told Shiva that he needs something to kill the demons. Shiva then gives him a shiny and sharp Chakra. Which is known as Sudarshan Chakra. With that, Vishnu could kill those Demons and establish peace on Earth.

Benefit of Pronouncing Shiva's Name (Shiva Shashra Nam):

Shoot Jee says, "Vishnu himself told that pronouncing one thousand eight names of Shiva is beneficial. By worshipping Shiva while pronouncing one thousand eight names of Shiva, Vishnu received Sudarshan Chakra as a blessing. Whoever pronounce the one thousand eight names of Shiva while worshipping will be free of any kind of fear.

Stories of Devotees of Shiva:

Brahma Dev said to Narad, "Hey Narad all the people in the world who worshipped Shiva, were fulfilled with their desires. All the Rishis, Gods, have worshipped Shiva and had their desires been fulfilled. Sri Ram was also a great devotee of Shiva.

Rules to Follow While Fasting on Shivaratri:

Rishis asks Shoot Jee, "Which days are important to fast for Shiva, so he will be pleased?"

Shoot Jee then says," Hey Rishis, once Parvati also asked the same question to Shiva. Shiva then says there are lots of fasting that one can perform to please me. Veda describes ten fasting days to please Shiva. Which I will explain it to you, so listen carefully."

On Astami (Eighth) day of every month one should fast during the day and at night one release the fasting by consuming food. On dark Astami one should not break the fasting even at night. Ekadasi of Krishna month one should fast and worship Shiva during the day and release the fasting at night by having pure meal. On the third day of Krishna month one should fast all day and also can't eat night. On the third day of Sukla month one can have a pure meal at night. All these fasting are done by devotee of Shiva.

Shivaratri fasting is superior then all other fasting. The blessing of doing fasting on Shivaratri is greater than other fasting. So now listen to the rules to follow while fasting on Shivaratri. Early in the morning one should freshen up and should visit a Shiva temple. At the temple, one should worship Shiva as per Veda. Then one should pray to Shiva saying "Hey Lord I am fasting today on Shivaratri so there should be no obstacles, so my desire to worship should be fulfilled. No problem of any kind should occur while I am fasting. No one should be able to destroy my fasting. So protect me from all obstacles, from anyone while I am fasting. So one should say all these things before worshipping Shiva. At night collect all necessary items to worship Shiva and be at the temple. It must be genuine Shiva Linga. After reaching the temple, one should shower and wear clean clothes. Then sit facing east and start worshipping the Shiva Linga. At night worship Shiva Linga four times.

Then one should spell Shiva Mantra one hundred eight times while offering water to the Shiva Linga. Also, one has to pick up everything that was offered to the Shiva Linga. Then after that one should offer sesame seeds one hundred eight times while spelling Mantra given by Guru. Then by saying eight names of Shiva which are Bhamba, Sarva, Rudra, Pashupati, Ugra, Mahan, Bhim, and Ishan should be repeated accordingly and offer Lotus flower. After that light up incense and light a Diya, and offer fruits to the Shiva Linga. Then one should say Om Nama Shivaya one hundred eight times. Then offer pure water to the Shiva Linga. Then one should promise to feed the Brahmins. Then offer all fruits to Shiva Linga. After that, one should finish worshipping as per Veda.

One should follow the procedure as done on first worshipping also on second worshipping. On second worshipping, one should spell the Mantra two hundred sixteen times while offering water. One must repeat the Mantra twice and offer water each time. Bel and other fruits should be offered to the Shiva Linga. One must also offer pudding on the second worshipping. On third worshipping it is the same process as first worshipping but should offer wheat and flower should be offered. Also, light incense and Kapur. After that, one should promise to feed the Brahmins.

On fourth worshipping, one should invite Shiva. Then worship with Mas, Kagun, and Mung, seven components, and Shankha flower. Then offer seasonal fruit and then other food items. The Mantra spelling should be twice more than before. Then promise to feed the Brahmins and sing the glory of Shiva till sunrise. Then take a shower and worship Shiva Linga. Then at night one must feed the number of Brahmins that was promised during the worshipping. Then one must say to Shiva that one should always remain being the devotee of Shiva. One should also say to Shiva, that I have done worshipping to you please accept my worshipping. Then distribute the fruits and other food items to all.

So by worshipping like that, one will receive Shiva's blessing at the end. Shoot Jee also says, while telling all these processes to Parvati, Vishnu also heard the procedure. So Vishnu then for the benefit of all said the procedure to other Gods and human beings.

How to End Shivaratri Fasting:

Shoot Jee says, "Now let me tell you about how to end Shivaratri fasting. The day before one should only have one meal and on Shivaratri one should fast all day.

One should at night make a Mandala named Tilak. One must create Linga in the middle of the Mandala. Then offer cloth, fruit, and money to the follower of Shiva. Gold or Silver Kalash (Pot) should be placed in the middle of the Mandala. Then one should make an idol of Shiva and Parvati. The idol of Shiva should be on the right side and Parvati on the left side of the Kalash. Then one should select the Brahmin to do the rituals. Then as per the instruction of the Brahmin one should stay awake all night and invite and worship Shiva. One should also sing Shiva's glory all night long.

The next morning after a shower, one should worship Shiva with pure mind as per the instruction by the Brahmin. Then after that decorate Shiva with cloth and ornament, and donate a cow. Then after that provide money to the Brahmin for his service. After that, one should pray to Shiva. While praying one should say thank you for making the worship successful. One should also ask for blessing of Shiva. After that, one should apologize for any mistake that happened while worshipping Shiva. This is how one should conclude the worshipping on Shivaratri.

Nisad (Degraded) Character:

Shoot Jee says, "Hey Rishis, once upon a time, a Bheel used to live in the jungle with his family. His name was Gurudruha. He used to steal from nearby villages at night and hunt wild animals during the day. So one day on Shivaratri his family didn't have any food to eat. So they asked Gurudruha to bring some food for them. Then that Bheel went to the jungle with his bow and arrow to hunt the wild animals.

That day, all day, he didn't find any animals to kill. So at night time he climbed a tree nearby the river to wait for animals. It was Bel tree. After waiting for a while, a deer came to drink the water from the river. So he targeted the deer with his arrow and bow. Right then the leaf from the Bel tree fall with water on it and it drop on the Shiva Linga which was underneath the ground. So first phase of worshipping Shiva Linga on Shivaratri occurred. By doing that, all the sins of that Bheel Gurudruha destroyed.

After that deer saw the bow and arrow pointed towards her and was frightened. So deer requested Gurudruha not to kill her right away. She will go home and arrange her children to her sister, and she would come back. So the Bheel let her go. Then after waiting for some time another deer came. Same story got repeated so that deer also went home to arrange things for her family and would come back later. So he let her go too. Then after some time another deer came to drink water there in the river. So Bheel pointed a bow and arrow towards the deer. That deer also told the same story. So he let her go to. While doing that two more time Bel leaf and water drop right on the Shiva Linga. So the procedure to worship Shiva Linga on Shivaratri was complete without the knowledge to Bheel. Then Shiva appeared from the Shiva Linga. Then Bheel lied down on ground to regard Shiva. Shiva then asked Bheel for his wish. Bheel said that he wants to be a devotee of Shiva forever. Then Shiva grant him his wish. Shiva also told Gurudruha that he would go to a city where he will have a good friendship with Sri Ram. After a long time by the blessing of Sri Ram that Bheel received Moksha.

Om Nama Shivaya

Uma Sanhita

Naam Khanda

Chapter: 9

Conversation between Sri Krishna and Upmanyou:

Rishis says, "Hey Shoot Jee, you are really a devotee of Shiva. So do us the favor and tell us about Uma Sanhita. The stories where Shiva and Parvati did all kinds of things, which excites us and makes us more knowledgeable."

Then Shoot Jee says, "Hey Rishis, now listen to the stories of Shiva which gives both Moksha and pleasure from worldly affairs. Vyas raised same question Jee to Sanath Kumar. So I will tell you the same story."

Sanath Kumar said to Vyas Jee. "Sri Krishna went to Kailas to pray to Shiva to have a son. But when he reached Kailas, he saw Upmanyou meditating at Kailas. Then Sri Krishna gave his regards to Upmanyou and asked him a question. Hey Upmanyou you are a real devotee of Shiva and I came here to meditate upon Shiva to have a son. So tell me a story of Shiva which will ignite devotion in me and so I could meditate with full devotion. Then Upmanyou says once I was meditating and saw Shiva. There was Brahma and other Gods who was serving Shiva. They were all there with their family. Then there I saw different weapons around Shiva. One of them was a sharp trident which could dry up the ocean. With same trident Shiva had killed demon named Lavarasoor. Then there was a sword which was also very sharp. The same sword Shiva gave to Parshuram Jee. So with same sword Parshuram Jee cut off the heads of so many Chettri on Earth. There I also saw Sudarshan Chakra. That Chakra had thousand faces. That Chakra was as bright as one hundred Suns. There also was a bow and arrow named Pinak. Same time I also saw Brahma. Brahma was sitting on the right side of Shiva. Likewise, Vishnu was sitting on the left of Shiva. Similarly Swyambho, Manu, Vrighu, and other Rishis were also there along with Indra and other Gods. In front of Shiva, Nandi was there holding a trident. Ghosts and others were also there, giving their service to Shiva. All of them were singing glory of Shiva.

Then Shiva became pleased and told me, "Hey Brahmin I am pleased with you so ask for any wish that you want to have." Then I said, "If you are pleased with me then I want the knowledge of past, present and future. I want the knowledge to understand everything that is happening all over the world. I also want to remain as your devotee forever, said Upmanyou. Then Shiva blessed me and told me to stay close to Chirsagar (Ocean). Also Shiva told me he will always remain within me and whenever I think of him, he will reappear before me. After saying all these, Shiva disappeared from there. So hey Krishna, by the grace of Shiva I have all the knowledge of all three Loka. Shiva is the one who is an Universe and he is the first being who is everywhere. By the grace of Shiva, everything is possible. Therefore, now meditate with full devotion towards Shiva to have the son", said Upmanyou to Sri Krishna.

Description of Shiva's Devotees:

Shri Krishna says, "Hey Upmanyou Jee, now tell me about all the devotees of Shiva, who have receive Siddhi (Enlightenments) by being a devotee of Shiva."

Then Upmanyou says, "Hey Shri Krishna, Hiranyakasipu meditated ages and ages. As a blessing, he ruled one of the town of Indra for one million years. He also was in charge of Indra for one million years. Likewise, by devoting to Shiva, Satmukh demon had one thousand children by the blessing of Shiva. By the blessing of Shiva, Eklavya became the great saint to advice and educate other saints. Even Vyas Jee could write four Vedas, eighteen Purans, eighteen sub Purans, and other holy books.

Once, because of the anger of Shiva, all the water on Earth dried. Then, by the request from Gods, Shiva took water from his head and filled it all over the Earth. Also, king Chitrasen being a devotee of Shiva won all battles against the enemies. By seeing king Chitrasen, Shrikat also became a devotee of Shiva.

By doing fasting every Monday, Chitrangada's wife saved him from death in the river. Even prostitute like Chanchala by doing devotion in Gokarna could destroy all sins committed. The devotion of Shiva destroyed sins of Mahakal. Everyone knows about a devotee named Durbasa. Brahma Dev and Prajapati could manage the World by being a devotee of Shiva. By the blessing of Shiva, saint Sandilaya became worship able. So everyone became successful by being a devotee of Shiva. So Shree Krishna, you also start being a devotee of Shiva and receive the son you want," said Upmanyou to Shree Krishna.

Greatness of Shiva:

Upmanyou said to Krishna, "Hey Krishna, you will soon be able to see Shiva by doing his meditation. You will receive brave sons by worshipping and meditating upon Shiva. I will give you a Shiva Mantra (Spelling), which you can read by being very sincere. By doing so, you will see Shiva. Only by reading this Mantra one will fulfill all wishes. It will award Moksha and Baikuntha. Nama Shivaya is that five letter Mantra and by pronouncing Om before it. While telling the glory of this Mantra, eight days and two hours went by. Only on the ninth day Sri Krishna receives the Mantra from Upmanyou.

Then Sri Krishna standing upon one thumb of his hand started reading the Mantra for fifteen months, meditating upon Shiva. On the sixteenth month Shiva with Parvati appeared next to Sri Krishna. Then Sri Krishna started singing glories of Shiva. Then Shiva asked Sri Krishna for his wishes. So Sri Krishna asked for eight wishes, which are:

1. My mind should always be devoted towards religion.
2. In the entire world, let me have the most pleasure.
3. Let me live by your side always.
4. Let me be your true devotee.
5. Let me have ten brave sons.
6. In battle let me win the ego centric enemies.
7. Let me be the favorable one among all saints.
8. Let me always be on your devotion service.

After hearing the eight wishes of Sri Krishna, Shiva granted him the wishes by saying Thatasthu. Also Parvati told Sri Krishna that she is also very pleased with him, so I will also grant you some wishes that you still have. Then Sri Krishna said let me always serve the Brahmins and let me always respect my parents. Then Parvati also granted him his wish by saying Thatasthu. After that, Shiva and Parvati disappeared from there. Sri Krishna then went to Upmanyou. And told him that Shiva and Parvati were very pleased with me, so they granted me my wishes. Then Upmanyou told Sri Krishna that Shiva gets pleased easily and he grants wishes like no other in the entire Universe. Shiva's play is limitless.

After receiving eight wishes, Sri Krishna went back to Dwarika. Also Sri Ram Chandra after worshipping Shiva could make a bridge on Ocean and also received uncommon weapons from Shiva. Which helped him to kill Rawan. Also Parshuram Jee by the blessing of Shiva could kill the person who stole Kaamdhenu Cow. He also killed Chettri twenty one time to wipe out them from Earth.

Description of Shiva's Maya:

Vyas Jee asks Sanath Kumar Jee, "Tell me about a unique act of Shiva." After hearing such a desire of Vyas Jee, Sanath Kumar Jee said, "Hey Vyas Jee, Shiva is a soul of the Universe. Shiva's eight divinity's character, one human character, and five birds character are present. So fourteen types of characteristics are designed by Shiva. Brahma, Vishnu, Indra, Snake, Gods, Demons, and others, on everyone Shiva is situated. All life are subject to Shiva's Maya. Kaam Dev could control all Vishnu, Brahma, Indra and others through Maya of lust by the help of Shiva. Indra had misbehaved with Ahilya, and the Maya of Shiva did it. Lord Vishnu became lust and started having sex with different women by the Maya of Shiva. Moon had taken his Guru's wife and disappeared to have sex. Later he was forgiven by Shiva. Once Mitra and Varun were lusted after because of the beauty of Urvashi and dropped semen From which Kumbach Rishi and Vasistha Rishi were born. These happened because of the Maya of Shiva. Before Brahma, also became lust by seeing his own daughter. By seeing Sardati Gautam, Rishi also became lust and dropped his semen. From which Droracharya was born.

Also, Bishomitra Rishi became lust after seeing Menaka and start making love with her. From which Shakuntala was born. Bishomitra had complained that Vasistha Rishi didn't make him a Brahma Rishi, but because of Shiva Vasistha later made Bishomitra Brahma Rishi. Dev Guru Brihaspati also had sex with his brother's wife after becoming lust. So Bhardwaj was born. So these are only some Maya I could describe you, but no one can fully understand them except Shiva," said Sanath Kumar Jee.

Descriptions of Sinners:

Vyas Jee said, "Hey Muni, now you tell me about people who go to hell."

Then Sanath Kumar Jee says, "Hey Vyas Jee, there are twelve types of sins that are committed by body, mind, and words. To wish for other people's wife, to wish for other's property, to wish ill or bad for others, and be irreligious. These are the four sins the mind commits that.

Similarly, talking to women who have periods, to tell lies, speaking harshly, to talk badly about others, are four sins committed while speaking.

To eat forbidden food, illegally working, to be violent, and to steal are four sins committed by the body.

Likewise, people who earn money by stealing from others, also people who steal Brahmin's money or property, also tearing or firing Shiva Grantha, also throwing it, are all sinners. Also, people who doesn't enjoy Shiva's worshipping, also people who doesn't want to hear Shiva's stories, also people who doesn't bow to Shiva Linga, also people who doesn't sing Shiva's glory, and also people who don't respect Shiva and Guru will all go to hell as sinners. People who want to hear a glory of God without worshipping Guru, also people who service Guru without feeling and devotion, also people who doesn't care for people who are suffering and are in need, will all also are sinners and will go to hell.

Brahmin killer, People who drink alcohol, sleeping in Guru's bed, sleeping with Guru's wife are all sinners. People who steal land devoted for cow's cottage, temple, land donated to Brahmin, are also sinners. They are equal sin as killing a Brahmin. People who read Veda and other holy books and stop devoting to Shiva, are all sinners too. People who earn a living by cheating others are also sinners.

Also, people who are eligible but the elders who don't arrange a wedding for them are also sinners. People who mistreat their own brother and sister in-laws are also sinners. Also, people who sleeps with unmarried women and also people sleeping with women who drinks alcohols are also sinners.

Likewise, there are unique types of sinners who commit original sins. It is not possible to describe all the sins. But people who surround themselves with sinners are also sinners.

Description of Hells:

Sanath Kumar Jee says, "Hey Vyas Jee, all the human beings who sinned in their life while being alive, will go to hell. It will take all the human beings who have sinned Yama Loka (Hell), after death. It will be very hard and difficult for sinners on the way to hell. There will be lots of difficulties on the way. So sinners have to bear all the difficulties while death angels take them to hell. So depending upon if the person is a sinner or not, I will send them either to hell or heaven. There are all together twenty-eight types of hell and they are as following.

Ghora Koti, Suchara Koti, Atighora, Mahaghora, Ghorrupa, Talatal, Chandakolahala, Bhayanaka, Kalratri, Bhayotara, Chanda, machined, Vimakoti, Padmakoti, Visarnaieka, Karala, Chandanaika, Prachandakoti, Bikarala, Bajra, Trikon, Panchakosh, Sudirgha Akhiladirt, Sam, Sim sab Lav, Ugrakoti, Narag, Visarakoti. These are the names of twenty-eight types of hell.

The greatness of Donating Food:

When one lives his life pleasantly, then God takes them to Yama Pur without taking them to hell. People who donate Brahmin shoes will go to Yam Pur on a horse. People who donate a Brahmin with Umbrella, bed, and other things will also easily go to Yam Pur. It will take people who build the temple and home for the homeless to Yam Pur in a plane. People who bring awareness in others will also be taken to Yam Pur easily. People who massage Brahmin's feet will also easily go to Yam Pur. People who donate gold and jewelry to Brahmin will also easily go to Yam Pur.

Food donation is the best donation that one does for Brahmins or other hungry people. Food gives energy to the body, so that body can do different activities. If there is no food, then nothing can be developed. So donating food is the best type of donation. People who eat after donating food will have a healthy body. So the body can do religious and good work. The human body is the vehicle for economy and religion. So keeping the human body healthy, we must do food donations. Humans should feed the hungry beggar by donating little food every day. Also, one should feed the guest that comes in our homes. By doing so, one will have space in heaven. Donating food is the best donation that one could do to benefit oneself.

The greatness of Donating, Water, and Meditation:

All living beings are part of water. If there is no water, then the World will be dry and it can't sustain itself. Therefore, donating water is the best donation in the World. People who build a pond, well for others, will have their sins destroyed. People who build water storage for others and if that water is worshipped or offered to the Gods, then their entire family will benefit from it. People who built ponds that is full of water even in winter then that is equal to donating one thousand cows. So donating water is the best donation of all.

Similarly, planting trees along the road is also very beneficial to the one. So planting trees where there are no trees is beneficial for all. People who plant trees will benefit the entire family. Flowers that grow in those trees will be worshipped by God, and also fruits will be offered to the ancestors. And people can sit under the tree to rest. So planting a tree is the best thing we can offer to all.

Truth is the best meditation in the world. Everything in the World is part of the truth. There is no holy thing other than the truth. Therefore, people should always speak the truth.

For the benefit of self-meditation is very important. Through meditation, one receives everything in life. Some kind of meditation has to be done to receive heaven, or Brahma Loka, and Shiva Loka. By doing meditation, one can get rid of big sins like killing Brahmin. Even with one of Brahmin's truthful meditations entire world can benefit. Through meditation, Brahma Dev creates the World, also through meditation Vishnu takes care of the World. Meditation fulfills all desires and gives happiness and peace. Therefore, on Bartamanda (Thread ceremony) the Mantra (Holly spelling) is given to the boy. Which he reads daily to fulfill all his wishes.

The greatness of Holy Books:

Brahmin who studies Veda and other Puran (Holy Books) and teaches other Brahmin about it will benefit from it. Brahmins study Puran and teach other people about heaven and how to avoid hell by doing the right things. Those Brahmins will also benefit from doing so, and they are called the expert of Puran.

People who teach Puran to others are the same as Brahma, Vishnu, and Mahesh. Because they help people to gain the right knowledge and also those people will not go to hell. Donating things to Puran expert people will benefit people. Donating land which is fertile to Puran expert will save the person's ten generations of a family from going to hell. For such a person coming generation will also not go to hell because they won't commit any sins.

The person who teaches Puran in Vishnu's temple will live in Surya (Sun) Loka. People who wish for liberation should listen to stories from Shiva Mahapuran every day. If every day is not possible, then they should at least listen to Shiva Mahapuran once a month. People who listen to stories of Puran will have their sin destroyed. So one should listen to any Puran in their lifetime.

Description of Donation:

Donating gold, land, cow all are beneficial for both the giver and receiver. Donating Cow, land, education, and Tula are all great for giver and receiver. Donating cow, food, cloth, umbrella, shoes, etc. is beneficial for the giver.

Ten great donations are gold, Teel, elephant, girl, servant, house, chariot, precious stone, cow, and food. By donating these things, people will not have emotional suffering. King Raghu had donated Earth and receive the grace of God. A person who decorates a cow with cloth and ornament and donates will receive liberation from life. This type of donation is very precious. By measuring the weight of self and donating valuables of the same weight will destroy all sins committed by the person. Donating Tula to true Brahmin will receive the respect of god Indra and will also receive space in heaven.

Description of Hell (Patal):

Shree Sanath Kumar Jee says, "Hey Vyas Jee, now you listen to me about the description of the Universe. This Earth is above the water. It is held by the Shesh Nag (Snake) on his head. This Shesh Nag is known by other names also and is very talented. All the female Nag serves him. They also know Shesh Nag as Sakarsar Rudra. Even Gods don't know how much energy he has.

Underneath the Earth, there are seven Loka known as Atal, Bital, Sutal, Rasatal, Talatal, Atital, and Patal. These Loa are ten thousand times wide and twenty thousand times tall. There is a garden made of precious jewels and stones. Snakes live there. They're always bright because of priceless stones. There are also clean lakes. Where different Lotus flower is growing. In the air and on the side of the lakes bees are dancing. Snake Ladies and Goddess are showering in the lake. To live in that area, man, snake, devils have to perform deep meditation. Then only one is allowed there.

Ways to get out of Hells:

Vyas Jee says, "Sinful people suffer in hell for their sins. There is a good deal of hell where sinful people suffer. Once you go to hell and suffer for your sins, then you take birth again on Earth to repeat the same Karma as before. After repeating the same sinful Karma you will again go to hell. So similarly, people who don't commit sinful acts go to Heaven and enjoy. After that, they again take birth on Earth and do the same Karma as before. So they will go to heaven again for not committing any sinful acts. So people from hell will always commit sinful acts after taking birth, and people from heaven don't commit sinful acts after taking birth.

The only way to get released from the hell and heaven cycle is by pronouncing the name of Lord Shiva. By pronouncing the name of Shiva with good intention, one doesn't have to go to hell or heaven. One becomes liberated from birth and death.

Description of seven lights:

Sanath Kumar Jee says to Vyas Jee, "Now let me tell you about the lands near the seven lights. Jambu, Plakchu, Salmali, Kush, Kaunch, Sarak, and Puskar are the seven lights. All around them are seven oceans. Sumeru Mountain is between all of them. This Mountain is sixty-four miles wide and three hundred thirty-six miles high. On its west side is a Mountain name Indrakut. It spreads all these mountains to forty thousand miles.

Bharat Barsha, which is forty thousand miles. Where there is Purush and the west side of Meru is located. On the south is Ramayak Mountain. Next to it is Hiranya Mountain. On the south is the country name Kuru.

Jambu light is in south Bharat. It is on the south of the Ocean and the west of the Mountains. We know this light as Karma Bhumi (Land). People living here will go to hell for sinful acts and will go to heaven for righteous acts. Will go to its original place known as Param Dham for the right knowledge they receive. Being on the south side of it, one can have whatever one wishes for in life. Which is only possible in this Jambu light. There are nine parts to the Jambu light, which are, Indradhumna, Kaseru, Tamrabarna, Gavasimna, Nagdeep, Saumya, Gandarva, Barun, and Bharatkhanda. On the east side of it is Kirat, Demons on the west, on the north is Yeon, and on the south are Sages living. In this area, there are four castes which are Brahmin, Chettris, Baisya, and Sudra. All of them do their part of the work.

Puskar light is surrounded by the ocean, which comprises honey. It is double the size of Jambu light. Here there is a mountain name Manas. In this light people don't age, they don't suffer from any disease, nor do they become sad. People here will have the age of ten thousand years or they are immortal. Brahma dev also lives in this light. God and demons both worship Brahmdev. People here receive their food and water automatically. It makes the land here up of gold. Besides this, there is no other Loka for human beings.

Describing Horoscope, Graha Mandal, and Loka:

All the places where the ray of Sun and Moon is reflected in those places are known as Earth (Bhoolok). Seven hundred twenty thousand Km above Earth is Surya Mandal (Sun). Seven hundred twenty thousand Km above Sun is Chandra Mandal (Moon). Seventy-two thousand Km above Moon is Graha Mandal (Nine Planets). Seven hundred twenty thousand Km above Nine Planets is Sapta Rishi Mandal (Seven Saints). Seven hundred twenty thousand Km above Sapta Rishi Mandal is Dhurba Mandal. Below Dhurba Mandal there are three Loka known as Bhuloka, Bhuabraloka, Sorloka, Between Dhurba Loka and these three Loka there are Kalpa Niwasi Rishis. Above Dhurba Mandal is Maha Loka. In Maha Loka Brahmadev's sons Sanak, Sananda and other sons live. One million four hundred forty thousand Km above Maha Loka is Sukra Loka. Seven hundred twenty thousand km above Sukra Mandal is Budha Mandal. One million four hundred forty thousand Km above Budha Mandal is Mangal Mandal. One million four hundred forty thousand Km far from Mangal Mandal is Brihaspati Mandal, and one million four hundred forty thousand Km above Brihaspati Mandal is Sani Mandal. All these planets move as per their horoscope. One Million four hundred forty thousand Km above the Planets are Sapta Rishi Mandal and Nine hundred thirty-six million above Sapta Rishi Mandal is Dhurba Mandal.

Tapo Loka is One billion eight hundred seventy-two million Km above Jana Loka. Six times further than Tapo Loka is Satya Loka. They create this Universe with five elements: Earth, fire, water, air, and sky. So lord is in everyone. When Shiva meets Shakti, then it creates the

Universe. Similarly, when Shakti meets Shiva, then it destroys the Universe. Above all, these are Shiva Loka. Where lord Shiva lives. The way to all the Loka is only by gaining knowledge.

Moksha through meditation:

Vyas Jee asks, Sanath Kumar Jee, "Please describe which Loka does devotee of Shiva reach.

Sanath Kumar Jee says, "Hey Vyas Jee, to receive the blessing of Shiva meditating is the best way. Without meditating, Shiva Loka can't be gained. By meditating, only devotees of Shiva receive Shiva Loka. Meditation is the primary vehicle to achieve Shiva Loka. All the Gods and goddesses do meditation. Even Vishnu and Shiva meditates. They also divide meditation into three parts: Satwik, Rajas, and Tamas. Demons or sinners meditate to purify themselves is Tamas meditation. The meditation which is done with no desire is Satwik meditation. To achieve a desire when meditation is done, then it is known as Rajas meditation. Meditation which is done to achieve liberation is Tamas meditation. To do well for society and also be a devotee of Shiva is the best meditation.

Good-looking women, alcohol, a nice dress, ornaments, perfume, a pleasant house, and other things are all enjoyment only. Being carried away in desire for these things, Human being gets trap in painful situations. To bear as a Brahmin is rare in the Universe. Being Brahmin, one must help self to realize the Universe within through knowledge.

Bharat region is a Karma and Success Bhumi (Land). By being born here only one can do excellent work in the World. Then only he/she receives to enjoy heaven and other joy. It is hard to meditate when one becomes old. So it's better to start early to meditate and worship. Only by pronouncing Shiva's name, one can be free from fear. One will also break the cycle of birth and death by keeping pronouncing the name of Shiva.

Formation of body and responsibilities inside the womb:

Vyas Jee says, "Hey Sanath Kumar Jee, now please kindly tell me about the formation of the body and what they go through in the womb. Please describe to me the process."

Sanath Kumar Jee says, "The food we eat is converted into juice and distributed throughout the body through veins. It takes the waste from the food out by body parts as dirt, sweat, urine, stool, cough, etc. It connects all the veins to the heart. Through the heart, they pump all the juices all over the body. The same juice with the help of a Soul becomes a skin and forms a body. There will be a circulation of blood inside the body. After that hair, flesh, bone, nails, and other parts of the body are formed."

The food a male eats will convert itself into juice and becomes a sperm, and through the penis, it goes to the uterus of a female. There it mixes with the female's sperm and it froze and becomes a body. It will be small on the first day, and on the fifth day, it becomes like a bubble. On the seventh day, it becomes flesh. In two months, shoulders, neck, backbone, stomach, chest, and other parts are formed. In the third month joints, it forms fingers. In the fifth month, it forms a face. In the sixth month nose, ear, hair, it forms teeth. In the seventh month, it forms the anal and other body parts. So after that, the body inside the womb will eat whatever food the mother eats and develop itself. There is no pain like the one inside the womb. The fetus stays next to all kinds of waste inside the body. Also, after death, the blood vapors itself to go mix with clouds and by the heat of the Sun, the clouds convert themselves into rain. That rain gets collected through fresh fruits and vegetables. By consuming that fruit and vegetable, the juice from it becomes sperm and takes life again. It also brings the culture of the previous life to the next life when taking birth again. So human life is precious and one should try to get Moksha. Also, heaven and hell are experienced while one is in a cloud state.

Impurities of the body and sorrow:

Sanath Kumar Jee says, "Hey Vyas Jee, this body comprises blood and sperm. It stays close to dirt while in the womb. That's why it always stays impure. No matter how hard one tries, it will not be pure. It remains impure.

While being in the world, the body engages itself in the dirt. Even though the body never feels Vairagya (Disinclination). Even if the body meditates for hundreds of years, that body cannot let go of the negativity from the self. Only by purifying the feeling inside and praising the Lord with pure feeling. If one dies while doing so, then in the next life he will have pure thoughts and feelings.

By gaining the knowledge and also having Vairagya (Disinclination) towards the material world. Also, by establishing peace on the mind, the one who attains the supreme truth will be free of life and death.

The sinners will not hear the things that are for their good. Similarly, they will not see the things that are good for them. Because of the sin, Karma controls their mind. So they enjoy all the sorrow of the world, thinking it's a pleasure. They usually lust in life. Thinking it's genuine pleasure. So for the sinners, Lord Shiva has told these stories on Shiva Mahapuran to erase all negative Karma and get Moksha.

Knowledge about death:

Vyas Jee says, "Hey Sanath Kumar Jee, now tell us the knowledge about death."

Then Sanath Kumar Jee says, "Vyas Jee, once Lord Shiva told Parvati about the death cycle. I will tell you exactly as what Lord Shiva had said, so listen carefully."

Lord Shiva says, "Hey Devi Parvati, death is close when the person becomes yellow and redness from face disappears. That person will die within six months. The person who can't listen to the arguments of others that person also dies within six months. The person who doesn't see Sun and the Moon but sees everything dark will also die within six months.

The person whose right-hand jeeps vibrating for a week will die within a month. The person who starts feeling cold and feels dry head will also die within a month. The person whose nose is running but feels dry at throat and head will also die within six months. Similarly, if the tongue gets swollen and teeth are always wet, then that person will also die within six months. The person who doesn't see his image in a mirror or water but sees something else will also die within six months.

The person who doesn't see his head in the mirror or water also doesn't see his shadow, will die within six months. The person who doesn't see the brightness of the sun will die within fifteen days. The person who doesn't see the bright stars in the sky will also die within one month.

Way to escape death:

Parvati says to Lord Shiva, "Hey Nath, could you also please explain the ways to escape death."

Lord Shiva says to Parvati, "Hey Devi, since you asked me the way to escape death. I will explain it to you for the sake of human beings."

"Hey Devi, the five elements Earth, Water, Fire, Wind, and Sky make up a human body. Among the five elements, Sky is the biggest, it is where everything vanishes. Then Parvati again asks lord Shiva, ,"Hey Lord, please explain to me how one can win death and escape from it."

Then Lord Shiva says, "Hey Devi, you know that they make the body with five elements, and later after death it will go back to those five elements. From the sky the wind gets created from wind fire is created and from fire, water is created and from water, it forms Earth. So these are five qualities. Water has four, a fire has three, the wind has two, and the sky has one quality. Qualities are only hearing, seeing, feeling, taste, and smell." Lord Shiva says, "Hey Parvati Yogis, try to win over these five qualities, some win and some who rarely win in next life or so. The Yogis who try to achieve the supreme truth will feel the bliss in life. People who don't know the supreme truth will only suffer from the death cycle. But after knowing the supreme truth, they also escape from the fear of death. After they will receive Mukti and will not return to death and birth cycle.

Lord Shiva says, "Hey Parvati, these Naad (Brahma) are unlimited, which can't be described in words. From this unlimited Naad, nine words got created. The nine words are Ghosh, Kansya, Shringha, Ghanta, Bira, Bansaj, Dandubhi, Shankha, and Megh. Yogis pronounce these words accurately and become Mukta (Free) from the death cycle. Without proper knowledge, one can't win death to receive Mukti. One should know who I is? It is that brightness that is far from darkness. While living and knowing that I, will ultimately lead to Mukti."

Lord Shiva and definition of death:

Parvati says, "Hey Lord Shiva, How do Yogis win the air, and receive the title, please explain it to me."

Lord Shiva says, "Hey Devi, the air inside the body and outside the body are both capable of bringing brightness. All the knowledge, science is all done with the help of air. Therefore, the person who wins over the air will control everyone. Yogis can store air inside their body and when they become perfect, then he becomes an unlimited source of energy.

Pranayama is the process where one breathes in the air while pronouncing Gayatri Mantra.

Lord Shiva says, "Hey Devi, now I will also tell you about the enlightened yourself by concentrating on heat between your eyebrows. So Yogis go to the Mountains and there they meditate, concentrating on the heat between their eyebrows. They will completely focus on the heat of the fire between their eyebrows. After that, they will close their eyes with their finger for about an hour. After some time and practice, the Yogi will start seeing the light of divinity in their mind. When the Yogi sees the bright light with a pure heart, then Yogi becomes enlightened. When that Yogi reaches the fourth stage of Yog, then it is called Turiya Awastha.

After that, Yogi will have no attachment to the world and worldly affairs.

When the Yogi sits in a Yogic position and starts breathing slowly, then after some time the liquid will drop from the top of his head. After drinking that liquid Yogi becomes free from hunger, thirst, and death.

Description of Shadow Man:

Lord Shiva says, "Hey Devi, any person with the white cloth facing his back to the Sun and Moon, stares at his own shadow, and worship it with incense and Diya (Light), will also be enlightened. While staring at his own shadow, if he pronounces Om Nama Bhagbhate Rudra ya,

then even the sins of killing a Brahmin will go away.

If anyone sees his reflection in the mirror or water without the head, then he will die within six months. If any person sees his shadow white, then his divine service is increasing. If one sees a red shadow, then one will be in relationship issues. If one sees a yellow shadow, then enemies are alert. If one sees only the nose in shadow, then one will die of hunger. If one doesn't see his hip then the wife could die and if one doesn't see the legs then separation occurs. If one pronounces the nine letters Mantra while looking at owns shadow for a year, then one becomes enlightened in many aspects.

Hey Devi, now let me tell you about the Khechari Vidya (Knowledge) which is in the head of Brahmins. It divides this Khechari Knowledge among Hasya, Ahasya, Nischala, Sanatani, Bindu, and Bhagalini. Even the Veda praises these Khechari Vidya. By knowing the Bhagalini Vidya Yogis fulfill their wishes. By Yog, all the Siddhis can be achieved. By practice, only the knowledge can be gained and by knowledge alone Moksha is possible.

After listening to this story from Sanath Kumar, Jee Vyas became very uplifted and wrote the scriptures. After that Vyas Jee went to write the scriptures and Sanath Kumar Jee also went back to heaven.

Description About Creation of the Universe:

Shoot Jee says to other Rishis, "Hey Rishis, today let me tell you about the creation of the Universe. First Male, Lord himself, as Brahmdev created the Universe. Where the creator is Brahmdev, the caretaker is Vishnu, and the destroyer is Shiva. Brahma dev first created the water.

Narayan (Vishnu) lives in water. It created a universal egg on the water. God, Hiranyagarva divided that egg into two parts. From which one part became the Sky and the other part Earth. It created all ten directions of the Sky. After that Marichi, Atri, Angira, Polsatya, Pulaha, Ritu, Vashistha, and other great Rishis were created. From the anger of Brahmdev, it created Rudra.

Then Rig, Yejur, Sam, and other Veda were created. From the head of Brahmdev Devine were born, from thigh, human was born, and from under the thigh, demons were born. Then the population didn't grow, so again humans were divided between males and females. After which it introduced Maithuni culture to grow the population. Likewise, Brahmdev created everything in the Universe.

When Brahmdev created the Universe, Prajapati got married to Satrupa. Satrupa had meditated four hundred years to have a divine husband. From them, two sons were born. They were Priyabrat and Uttanpad. From Uttanpad, Dhurba was born who saw and found God. From Dhurba Pusti and Dhanya, two sons were born. From Pusti Chakchos named son was born. From Chakchos Varun named son was born.

From Puruki six sons were born. From Angaki Wayn named boy was born. Wayn was a sinner. Rishis killed him for his sins. Later by the request of his mother Sunita Rishis create King Prithu from the right hand of Wayn, who is an incarnation of Vishnu. Prithu did a great Yegya for the benefit of Earth.

King Prithu had two sons Haryesho and Bishowjit. Both the sons became very popular in the world. Then Shikhandi gave birth to Mari. He was married to Brichu's daughter Birbarahini. From Birbarahini Dakshya Prajapati was born. Dakshya Prajapati produced four legs animals. He was married to Birani and started a Maithuni (Marriage) culture. After that Dakshya Prajapati with Birani gave birth to Harasyo and one thousand other sons. All of those sons by the advice of Naradh Jee became Vairagya. After hearing all his sons became Vairagya then Dakshya Prajapati gave birth to Sabalshro and one thousand more sons. They also became Vairagya by the advice of Naradh Jee. After hearing that Dakshya Prajapati cursed Naradh Jee that he could never stay still.

After that Dakshya Prajapati and his wife gave birth to one thousand daughters. Dakshya Prajapati then gave his daughters to Dharma, Kashyap Rishi, Angarika Rishi, Krishashrwa, and other daughters to Chandrama (Moon). Then they were known as Nagstrya as the wives of Chandrama (Moon). From them all the Gods and devils were born.

Dharma has ten wives they were Arundhati, Basu, Yami, Lamba, Bhanu, Maruti, Sankalpa, Maharuta, Sandhya and Bishwa. Different types of children were born from them.

From Bishwa Bishwodeva was born. From Sandhya Sadhya was born, Maharuta Mahurtaj was born. From Sankalpa only one son Satyabakta Sankalpa was born. From Maruti Marutiyan was born. From Bhanu Bhara Bhanu was born. From Lamba Ghosh was born. From Yami Nav was born. From Basu Astabasu and from Arundhati Prithivi was born.

From Basu Aya, Dhurba, Som, Dhar, Anil, Dhar, Pratusya, and Pravas these eight sons were born. From Dhurba Kal named son was born. From Som Barcha named God was born. From Dhar Drabini and Drabya named two sons were born. From Mohanohar Raman, Shishir, Pran and other sons were born. From Shiba named wife Anil had a son named Purojab. Anil then had two sons, one of them was Agni Putra Kumar Kartikya Swami. From Kartikya Sarab, Bishakh, Taigomya named three sons were born. From Basuprabha Bishokarma was born.

Then Raibat, Agya, Bhav, Vim, Bam, Ugra, Brisakapi, Ajaikpad, Ahibhdhanya, Bahurup, and Mahan all together became eleven Rudra. The population of Rudra is in billions but these eleven Rudra became the Swami (Care taker) of the world.

Description of Kashyap Generation:

Shoot Jee says to Sanakadi and other Rishis that he is going to tell about the generation of Kashyap Rishi. Kashyap Rishi had Aditi, Diti, Sursa, Arista, Ila, Danu, Suravi, Binita, Tamra, Krodhbasa, Kadru, Swabharnu, and other wives. In first human form, twelve gods were born named Trushita, from Rishi Kashyap and Aditi. They were born for the benefit of humankind. After that, Rishi Kashyap and Dakshya Kanya gave birth to Indra and Vishnu. Aryama, Dhata, Twasta, Pusha, Bibasana, Sabita, Mitravarun, Atabhag, and others were born from Aditi.

Shoot Jee then says, "Now listen about Som generation. Som had twenty-seven wives. They had thirty-eight children. Arastanemika had sixteen sons and one daughter.

From Swadh Pritu were born. From Sati, Angira was born. All of them were born at the end of Shashra Yug. Rishi Kashyap with Diti gave birth to two sons named Hiranyakashipu and Hiranyayacha. They both became very popular and strong. From Bripachitika Singhika named daughter was born. Hiranyakashipu had four sons named Anuhad, Halad, Shalad, and Prahad. Kukari, Sakuni, Mahanad, Bikrant, and Kal were all Rishis and brave. They were all sons of Diti.

From Danu, brave hundred sons were born. Sursa had a daughter named Parba. Puloma had two daughters. They married those two daughters to Marichi Rishi. From those two wives, Marichi Rishi produces sixty thousand demons. Biprachit with Singhika had many sons. From Binita Garud and Arun, two sons were born. Garud was best among birds. From Sursha brilliant snakes were born. From those thousand snakes Basuki, Takchak, Eraot, Mahapackshya, Kabal, and shorter became Prime Kings. They all used to roam the sky. From Ila Pada, Karkotak, Dhanjaya, Mahanil, Mahakarna, Dhritarastra, Balahak, Kuhar, Pushpadanta, Durmukh, Sumukh, Bahatar, Kher, Rama, Pari and other sons were born. Likewise, Krodhbasa gave birth to Marudgarn. From

Krodhbasa also Andaj, animals, birds were also born. From Barahi Pasu (Animal) was born. From Anusiya fifty brave sons were born. From Suravi, Ranga and Janga were born. From Ila, Bahar, and Brikchya (Tree) was born. From Shashra Rishis, demons, Angels, and Munis were born. From Arista, evil humans and nasty snakes were born.

Then Shoot Jee says, Brahma Dev then gave half of the kingdom to Prithu. Brahma Dev made Som the king of Brahman, Trees, Nakshytra, Horoscope, and Ghosts. He made Varun the king of water. They made Vishnu king of Aditya. Paok became king of Basu, and Dakshya became king of Prajapati. Indra became king of Marudgarn. Praladh became king of it. Baibasot became king of Yam and dead humans. Lord Shiva became king of all the humans, fasting, Mantras, Cow, Yechya, Demons, Ghost, and others. That is how Brahmdev made different kings for unique elements.

Birth of Vyas Jee:

Shoot Jee says, "Hey Rishis, one day Sri Parasar Jee was traveling to different Tirtha Sthal (Holy lands), so he reached the edge of Yamuna River. There he asked the fisher to carry him on the other side of Yamuna on his boat. But the fisher was eating his lunch, so he asked his daughter to take Sri Parasar Jee across the Yamuna River. So his daughter took Parasar Jee across the Yamuna River. While crossing the River Parasar, Jee held the hands of that girl. So the girl said, "You are a great sage and I am an ordinary low caste girl. How can we do this? Then Parasar Jee took his hands off from her. But Kaamdev (Lust) had already grabbed his attention, so after reaching across the Yamuna River, he again grabbed her hands. Then the girl says if you want to have sex with me then it must be at night time. Then Parasar Jee created a night atmosphere with his Maya. Then they made love on the sands of the Yamuna River.

Afterward, the girl says to Parasar Jee, "You are going to leave and what will happen to me?"

Parasar Jee then says, "Since you pleased me by letting me fulfill my desire, so I will bless you with whatever you want in your life. You will now be famous with the name Satyawati. Then Satyawati says, "Hey Rishi, my act should not be known to anyone. I also want to give birth to your son with no one knowing about it." Then Parasar Jee blessed her and said, "You will have a child who has an element of Vishnu and he will be born very soon. You will always look pretty from now onwards. You will give birth to a son after I leave. And he will start walking as soon as he is born. He will immediately leave you to do meditation. After that, you will again become Kumari (Virgin) and you will go back across the Yamuna River." After saying all that, Parasar Jee left.

After some time, Satyawati gave birth to a son. After that boy walked and told his mother that he is going to leave to do meditation. But whenever she wishes, he will come in front of her. After that, Vyas Jee said goodbye to his mother and left to do meditation. After that, Satyawati came across the Yamuna River and told her father that Parasar Jee blessed her to be a beautiful lady for the rest of her life. Also, she told him that Parasar Jee changed her name to Satyawati.

Also, the boy, Vyas Jee, finished his meditation. While in the Ashram, he divided the Veda into different parts. After that, he became famous as VedVyas Jee. After that, VedVyas Jee meditates upon a Shiva Linga to know all the knowledge about Religion, Finance, Lust, and Moksha.

Madhyameshowr Shiva Linga in Kashi is where he started meditating.

Vyas Jee then started meditating upon Madhyameshowr Shiva Linga every day. He used to shower in Ganga Jee every morning and then meditate in front of the Madhyameshowr Shiva Linga in Kashi. Then one day Lord Shiva appeared in the child's image and blessed Vyas Jee that from now on Lord Shiva will stay in his throat. By which he will write history, Veda, Puran, and other books. They also blessed him with the knowledge of the past, present, and future.

After the blessing of Lord Shiva, Shree VedVyas Jee wrote Brahma Purana, Padma Purana, Vishnu Purana, Shiva Purana, Bhagwat Puran, Naradh Puran, Markanday Puran, Agni Purana, Linga Puran, and other Purans. All together he wrote Four Vedas and eighteen Purans. Hearing this story swipes all the sins committed by anyone.

Description of Maha Kali and killing of Madhu Kaitav:

Rishis asked Shoot Jee, to tell them the story about Jagat Mata (Universal Mother) Uma Devi. Then Shoot Jee says, "Hey Rishis you are all great to ask me to tell you about Uma Devi. So now listen to the story about Uma Devi."

Once there was a king named Virath. His son was Surath. Surath was an intelligent and brave warrior too. Once nine kings get together and attacked Surath, so by defeat he went to Jungle. There he reached the Ashram of Rishi Megatithi. Also at the same time, one rich merchant also arrived at the same Ashram. They threw the Merchant out of his house by his own children. So he was very depressed with life and came to that Ashram. So the Surath and the Merchant both went inside the Ashram and gave their respect to Rishi Megatithi and told him everything about their stories. After that, they both asked Rishi Megatithi to explain how to survive or get rid of the power of Maya.

Then Rishi Megatithi told Surath and the Merchant that the Maya which attracts everyone towards her is actually a Maha Devi who handles creation caretaker and destroyer. After hearing that Surath and the merchant asked Rishi Megatithi to please explain more about this Maha Devi.

Then Rishi Megatithi told Surath and the merchant that when there were nothing and they destroyed everything. Vishnu went into a deep sleep. After some time two devils named Madhu and Kaitav came out of Vishnu's two ears. Also at the same time, a lotus flower came out of his naval. On the lotus flower was Brahmdev. Then those two devils Madhu and Kaitav attacked Brahmdev. Brahma dev then started singing the glory of Maha Devi, who is also the creator of Vishnu. Then being pleased with Brahmdev Maha Devi came out from Vishnu's eyes and mouth. Right then, Vishnu woke up and killed those two devils by rubbing them in his thighs.

Rishi Megatithi says, a long time ago there was a demon named Rambhasoor. He had a son named Mahish. He defeated all gods and took over the kingdom of Indra. Then all the gods went to Brahmdev. **Brahma** dev then took them to Lord Shiva, where Vishnu was also there. Then all the gods complain about how Mahish is troubling everyone. Lord Shiva and Vishnu became furious with **Mahish**. Then all the gods turned red, and from that energy, a beautiful Devi got created. Then all the gods started praising her and gave her valuable ornaments and jewelry. After that Devi made a sound that disturbed the whole Earth.

After hearing the sound demon Mahisasoor came looking for the Devi. He came with millions of soldiers. Then Devi alone on one side and Mahisasoor along with his millions of soldiers on the other side. Devi started killing all the soldiers of Mahisasoor. Then Mahisasoor converts himself into huge Buffalo and breaking the Mountains. After that, he converts himself into Lion. Then Devi cut off his head and pushed his body into Earth that he could never get up. After that, all the gods including Indra came and started praising the Devi.

Death of Dhromlochana, Chanda Munda, Ratktabij, and Sumbha Nishumbha:

Rishi Megatithi says, once there was Sumbha and Nishumbha two brother demons. They had captured all the areas of Earth and also heaven. They were giving lots of trouble to gods and saints. So all the gods went to Parvati Jee and begged her to help them by killing Sumbha and Nishumbha. Then Devi came out of Parvati Jee, and she told the gods don't worry, she will kill Sumbha and Nishumbha for them.

Then that Devi by Maya converted herself into a beautiful looking girl. So the soldiers of Sumbha and Nishumbha saw her. So they informed Sumbha and Nishumbha that there is this beautiful lady on the top of a hill. She is the most beautiful lady, so Sumbha and Nishumbha should have her as their wife. Then Sumbha and Nishumbha send a messenger to that Devi.

That messenger told Devi that since Sumbha and Nishumbha ruled the world and heaven and they have all the luxury, so she should marry them. Then Devi told the messenger she is only going to marry a person who can defeat her. The messenger went back to Sumbha and Nishumbha and told them her message. Sumbha and Nishumbha then became furious and they send a small group of soldiers to bring the Devi. When the soldiers reach the Devi made a sound, they all burned into ashes. Then Sumbha Nishumbha sends Dhromlochana Chanda Munda and Ratktabij to bring the Devi. But Devi killed all of them.

Then Sumbha and Nishumbha themselves came with millions of soldiers to defeat the Devi. Then a fight began between them. Devi killed all their soldiers. Then Sumbha came to fight with the Devi. Devi cuts off his head. After that, Nishumbha came to fight with the Devi. Devi kills him with the Trishul. So both Sumbha and Nishumbha also died. Then all the gods came and started praising the Devi. That incarnation of Devi is known as Chandika.

Creation of Uma:

Shoot Jee says, "Hey Rishis, once Devi had rescued gods from demons by defeating demons. After the victory, gods started praising each other. They forgot about the Devi. Then Devi converted herself into a bright ray of light. Then all the gods became scared of the bright ray of light. So they went to Indra. Indra then send god Pawan to know what that bright ray of light is. God, Pawan then reaches to where the bright light was and asked the light who is it? Then light says in reply who are you to ask me? Then God Pawan told the light that he is the Pran (Breath) of all living beings. Then the light says here is a stick and pick that stick with all your energy. Then god Pawan tried to pick up a stick from the ground, but he couldn't even move it. He tried with all his energy, but he still couldn't move that stick. Then he goes back to Indra and told him that that bright ray of light defeated him. Then Indra sends other gods one after another. But the bright light defeated them all. Then Indra himself goes to where the bright light was. Then Indra thoughts about surrendering the self to the bright ray of light. Then Goddess Uma appeared from the light. Goddess Uma then told the gods that they need to sing the glory of the Goddess. Then all the gods told Goddess Uma that they will from now on sing the glory of the Goddess Uma. Then gods also told Goddess Uma that to bless them so they would never forget the glory of Goddess Uma. The Goddess Uma blessed the gods. After that all the gods started singing the glory of Goddess Uma.

Description of Sri Vidya of Sati:

Shoot Jee says, to Saunak Jee and other Rishis, that there used to be a brave male. He had a son named Durgam. Durgam by pleasing Brahmdev got all four Vedas for himself. Brahma dev also blessed him that not even gods could defeat him. After that, Durgam started giving lots of trouble to the gods and other human beings. Since he had all the four Vedas, religion and culture started vanishing. Brahmins forgot their Brahmin's rules and regulation. By seeing all these, all the gods went to Devi to ask her for her help. All the gods told Devi that Durgam has created lots of problems for them and also he is keeping all four Vedas with him. Then Gods asked the Devi to bring back the Vedas from Durgam by killing him. Then Devi blessed the gods and told them not to worry. She will kill Durgam and bring back the Vedas for them. After that tears came out of Devi's eyes and those tears brought greenery and water to Earth.

After that, Durgam came to Dev Nagari to attack Devi with millions of soldiers. Then Devi appeared at the battlefield. Then ten other Devis got created from Devi's body. The name of those ten Devis is as following. Kali, Tara, Chhinnamasta, Sri Vidya, Bhuvaneshowri, Bhairavi, Bagola, Dhuma, Tripura, and Matangi. All of those Devis killed the soldiers of Durgam. Then at the end Devis kill all the soldier and Durgam as well. Then all the gods became very happy and started praising the Devi. They also named her Durga for killing Durgam. They also named Devi with Saatchi, and Sakambhari for incarnating in the original figure to protect the gods and also for greenery around the world. After that Devi told the gods that she will appear again to protect the gods if that is required. Whenever demons come and trouble you, I will appear to protect you said the Devi to the gods. So Shoot Jee says to Saunak Jee and other Rishis that all three Saatchi, Sakambhari, and Durga is all one Devi.

Description of Kriya Yog:

Shoot Jee says, "Hey Rishis now I will tell you about Kriya Yog which was told by Sanath Kumar Jee to Vyas Jee."

Sanath Kumar Jee says, "Hey Vyas Jee, Devi's Gyan Yog (Knowledge), Kriya Yog, and Bhakti Yog (Devotion) all gives blessings as well as Moksha. Kriya Yog is the primary vehicle of the Yog. Any person who makes Devi's temple with stone, mud, and wood his entire family will be blessed. The person who makes the temple will release all sins committed. As long as the stone and woods on those temples remain, his family will benefit from the blessing of Devi. By establishing Devi's temple, it gives more pleasure than creating three Loka. Any person who builds a temple and puts Shiva Linga in the middle will receive unlimited blessings.

When there is a solar or lunar eclipse pronouncing Vishnu's one thousand names benefits the doer, also if someone pronounces Lord Shiva's one thousand name then blessings will be a hundred times more. The person who meditates with Uma Devi with the name Durga, that person will be awarded as a Gan (Guard) of Goddess Durga. Goddess Durga will bless the person who cleans the temple. Goddess Durga will bless the person who meditates Goddess Durga with her Mantra on the eighth and ninth day of the month. The person who offers a gold, silver, flower to Devi they will go to heaven.

After worshipping Devi, one should apologize to her for any mistakes. By eating the eatables offered to Devi one's all sin will wash away. The person who fasts for Devi on Chaitra Shukla will receive Moksha. One should regularly fast for Devi on the days as described in the scriptures. King Surath had fasted on those days for Devi, so he got back his lost kingdom. A person who regularly worships Devi with all his wishes will be full filed. Especially women should fast for Devi on required days to have the blessing of the Devi for the entire family.

So this is how the Uma Sanhita is finished. In this chapter, they mention different stories of Devi. These stories will award Moksha.

Om Nama Shivaya

Dasham Khanda

Chapter ten

Kailas Sanhita

Conversation of Sri Vyas Jee with Saunak Jee:

Once Rishis from Himalayas went to Kashi. So they came to Kashi and showered at Ganga Jee and after that they worshiped Vishwonath Jee. At the same time Shoot Jee also appeared at Kashi. So the Rishis gave their respect to Shoot Jee. After that Rishis started saying since you are the best disciple of Vyas Jee who wrote all the Puran and Veda. So please tell us a story that would give us bliss from hearing it.

Then Shoot Jee says, "Hey Rishis, you all are very lucky because today I will tell you a story about Vyas Jee. Who told this story to Rishis of Naumisarari long time ago. So please listen carefully.

Rishis were doing Yegya. Then Vyas Jee also arrived there. Vyas Jee asked Rishis, what is this one thousand years long Yegya for? Then Rishis said to know Veda and meaning of Omkar. Then Vyas Jee said Puran are in Veda Ved in Omkar and Omkar in Brahma (Shiva).

Goddess Parvati Asks Lord Shiva About Prarav:

Vyas Jee says, "Hey Rishis knowing Prarav (OM) is knowing Shiva. Only by the grace of Lord Shiva one will understand it. Now let me tell you the story about a conversation between Lord Shiva and Goddess Parvati. One day Parvati asked Lord Shiva to teach her Bisudha Tatwa (Pure Element). Then Lord Shiva took Goddess Parvati to Kailas and gave her the knowledge of Bisudha Tatwa (Pure Element). Then Goddess Parvati asked Lord Shiva why did he start the Mantra with Prarav (OM)? She told Lord Shiva please tell me how did it occur and so on.

Describing Prarav:

Lord Shiva says, "Hey Devi, the meaning of Prarav, that you are asking is the Main Mantra of all the Mantras. It is a root Mantra of all the Mantras. It is far from all three Guna (Tamo, Rajo, and Sato). It is Shiva, and only selected ones will know that. From Brahma to all living creatures, Prarav is the life among all. From its Rajo Guna Brahma from Sato Guna Vishnu and from its Tamo Guna, it creates Shiva.

Sanyasi Rule:

Lord Shiva says, "Hey Devi, now let me describe the rules of Sanyasi. First meditate the Guru by waking early in the morning. Then dedicate the day to the lord for everything that you do that day. Then meditate on the six Chakras (Energy Centers). After that do Pranayama. After that, meditate upon Shiva. Spell the Mantra one hundred eight times. While going inside the worshipping room clean your hands and feet. Then put the right foot inside first.

Sanyasi Mandal Rule:

Lord Shiva says, "First clean the floor. Then put a square cloth and divide it into thirteen parts. Make center the energy point and imagine everything white. Then Yellow and then decorate it with red. In the center write Prarav (OM).Then worship the Sun.

Lord Shiva says, "Hey Devi, Lord Shiva has eight popular names: Shiva, Mahesower, Rudra, Pitamaha, Sansar, Kapardi, and Sarvagya. But lord Shiva is most popular with the names Shiva, Shankar, Mahadev. Shiva devotee usually pronounce the name Shiva. These name Shiva is far from twenty-three major elements, and also far from nature the twenty-fifth Purus (Male) is Shiva.

We know the same Shiva as Omkar in Veda. That Lord can be known through Veda and nature is under his control. Indestructible Maya is his nature. By the grace of the same Lord, only one can receive Moksha from Maya. He despairs sadness that's why his name is Rudra.

Vyas Jee says, "When Lord Shiva told these things to Goddess Parvati, then Goddess Parvati became thrilled and pleasant. She then with all rules worshiped Lord Shiva. Then Goddess Parvati became even happier. Hey Rishis, I told you a secret story on how to worship Lord Shiva.

Bamdev:

Rishis says to Shoot Jee, "Hey Guru Shoot Jee, please tell us about Bamdev and what was in his mind." Then Shoot Jee says, "Hey Rishis, once there was a Muni named Bamdev. He went to meditate as soon as he was born. He knew all Veda, Purans and knowledge of all elements. He used to know future of human and demons. He used to purify Earth wherever he used to go by spreading the knowledge of Lord Shiva. Then once he met Sri Skandha Jee and gained the knowledge that to the meaning of Prarav (OM), is actually knowing Shiva.

Description Of Shiva:

Bamdev Jee asks Kartikya Kumar, "Hey Lord, what are the six knowledge? I want to know full knowledge of Lord Shiva. So please explain to me about these six knowledge. After hearing Bamdev Jee, Kartikya Kumar says, "Six meaning Akar, Ukar, Mahar, Bindu, Naad and we know these five as Omkar in Veda. It is the crucial knowledge of this Mantra, and it is Shiva.

Worshiping The Idol:

Kumar Kartikeya says, "The owner of everything including the sky is Lord Shiva. It creates Mahesower from Sada Shiv Shiva. The one being unlimited being the king of Vayu (Air), his name has Maya, one who is everything.

It creates Rudra from Mahesower and is of eleven. Who are the Swami of all warm elements. He carries Shakti (Energy) on his left side and at the end act as a destroyer. The same Lord Shiva is doing all the acts that are happening in the world. Shiva is the only energy.

Shiva Element:

Shoot Jee says, "When Skandha Guru gave advice to Bamdev Jee, then he had a doubt about it. Then he asked there are male and female which are Shiva. But in the same world there are transgender too and why is that?

When Skandha Jee heard the question, then he smiled. He then said about this secret knowledge Lord Shiva once told Goddess Parvati about it. I was drinking milk from my mother's breast, but I was listening carefully. There is only one Shiva who is in all.

Description of Creation:

Bamdev says, "Hey Nath, now my doubts are gone." Then Sanak Jee again says, "There are no dualities in Shiva Naad (Vein). It is unlimited and indestructible. Therefore, there is only one Shiva, which Sat Chita Nanda (Pure Bliss). Who is Sarvagya and who the creator of all three Gods. He is the one who created Sky, Air, Fire, Water, and Earth, they call these the five elements. After hearing these, Bamdev was very pleased, and he thanked Sanak Jee.

Rules to Make Disciples:

Saunak Jee says, "Hey shoot Jee, Bamdev Jee is great because of him we got to hear this story." Shoot Jee then says, "Hey Rishis, now I will tell you about the conversation between Saunak Jee and Bamdev Jee.

Bamdev Jee asks Saunak Jee, "Hey Muni, now give me the knowledge that is required by Jiva (Living beings) to achieve Mukti (Moksha)."

Saunak Jee says, "Hey Bamdev Jee, during Baisakh, Shrawan, Ashwini, Kartik, and Magh months on full Moon day, give respect to guru. Then by pronouncing Prarav (OM) Mantra invite the Guru then clean his feet. Then think Guru is Shiva. Then Guru gives Ham Sa So Hum Mantra. Then think you are Shiva. Then Guru gives disciple Mantra with meaning in twenty-two words :

Description of Yog Knowledge:

Saunak Jee says, "Guru must teach their disciple in such a way. 1. I am Brahma 2. That is you 3. Soul is Brahma 4. Universe is guarded by the Lord 5. I am life 6. Soul is the knowledge 7. The one who is here 8. He is far 9. He is your soul, knower, and potion 10. I am the one 11. I am also the Main Brahma 12. One who is far knows everything, Guru, Self-bliss is also me 13. I am the one in everyone's heart 14 Life of element and Earth is also me 15. Life of Air and Sky is also me 16. One who knows everything is also me 17. Life of all three Guna is also me 18. Everything is Brahma 19. I am Moksha for all 20. The one is me and So Hum is also me 21 Meditate like this.

Rules For Yog Knowledge:

Skandha Jee tells Bamdev Jee about rules to follow while showering. First one should wash his clothes, hands, leg then rub clean mud three times. Then take twelve dips in the water. Then by pronouncing Omkar do Pranayama sixteen times. Then clean the body with mud and then water. Look at the Sun and remember Guru's advice. Then Dip three more times in the water, thinking about Lord Shiva.

Yogis Death:

Bamdev Jee asks Skandha Jee, "Hey Nath, I have heard that Yogis are not burned on fire after death, instead they are buried and make a Samadhi. What is the reason for that?"

Skandha Jee says, "It is a secret. Once Bhrigu Jee asked Lord Shiva the same question. I will tell you exactly what Lord Shiva told Bhrigu Jee. You must only reveal this to devotees of Shiva. Only Yogis with patience will achieve the state of Samadhi. He then becomes one with Shiva.

The Yogis who are impatience should listen to the Mantra from Guru and start meditating on Lord Shiva. By doing so, Yogi will gain the knowledge of all three elements. Yogi should always pronounce Prarav (OM). When Yogi becomes old, then he should only meditate on Lord Shiva. So at the end Yogi will go to Pure Soul Lok.

Eleventh Day Ritual:

Skandha Jee says, "Now I will tell you about the ritual of the eleventh day of death of a Yogi. Take a clean mud and make square bed (Bedi) and on the East and West side make five Mandap (Holy Stage). Then worship five Gods on those Mandap. Then meditate upon the figure of the five Gods. Lord Shiva has accepted five idols. So worship that five figures and offer pure water to it. Also chant the Mantra (Gayatri Mantra) and light up incense. Then circle it. Then pray that the soul goes to Lord Shiva. Then finish the process by distributing the Prasad (Eatables) to Kanyas (Girls) or feed it to cows, or put it in a river. But don't throw anywhere. If one can't do eleventh day ritual, then feed the hungry near Lord Shiva's temple.

Twelve Day's Ritual:

Skandha Jee says, "The one should wake up early and take a shower. Then invite six Brahmins. After that prepare food for the Brahmins. Then invited Brahmins should be seated next to Lord Shiva's idol. Then worship as per the Brahmins advice for the twelve day's ritual. Then give respect to Brahmins wash their hand and feet. Then feed them food. After that give them Dasina (Money) and see them off to door. Also at the door ask them if you can go back. After that feed other guests and Brahmins. One should eat at the last."

Skandha Jee then gave his regards to his parents and left for Kailas. Then Bamdev also performed everything, as advised by Skandha Jee.

Shoot then says, "Hey Rishis, you should also always chant the Mantra of OM. Then meditate upon Lord Shiva. After saying all these Shoot Jee also left to go to Badri Ashram.

Om Nama Shivaya

Vaiviya Sanhita:

Ekadash Khanda

Eleventh Chapter:

Story of knowledge:

Once there was Yegya being held at the junction of Ganga and Yamuna Rivers. the Rishis were doing the Yegya. At the same time Shoot Jee arrived there. When the Rishis saw Shoot Jee there then they asked him to tell the story of Lord.

After hearing the Rishis, Shoot Jee first meditate upon Lord Ganesha and Lord Shiva. Then Goddess Parvati and his Guru Vyas Jee. Then he started saying, "Hey Munis, I will now tell you what Purans actually are. Once what Basu Dev has said is now known as Puran. There are four Ved and eighteen Purans. So all together there are eighteen knowledge of wisdom and its creator is Lord Shiva. Lord Shiva first created Brahmdev and gave these eighteen wisdom of knowledge to Brahmdev. After that to protect the Universe Lord Shiva gave energy to Vishnu. After receiving eighteen wisdom of knowledge Brahmdev created eighteen Purans. Then from four face of Brahmdev four Ved was created. But it was hard for ordinary person to understand. Then Lord Shiva send Vishnu on Earth incarnated as Vyas Jee to classify the Ved and Purans. Vyas Jee divided the Ved into four parts. After that he was known as Ved Vyas. One should always learn the Ved and Purans from the expert. One will have hard time to understand if one tries to study them on their own. The eighteen Purans are as follows Brahma, Padma, Vishnu, Shiva, Bhagbhate, Bhavisya, Naradh, Markanday, Agni, Brahmabiarbat, Linga, Baraha, Baman, Kurma, Matsya, Garud, Brahmanda, and Skandha. Among these the fourth one The Shiva Maha Puran is the one which fulfils all the wish of the listener. Also to achieve Moksha one should listen to Shiva Maha Puran.

Rishis Asking Question To Brahmdev:

Shoot Jee says, "Hey Rishis, after so many Kalpa (One day of Brahmdev), at the start of Brahe Kalpa. All the Rishis started debating who is the Brahma? They all were confused not knowing who the Brahma was. So they all went to Brahmdev and asked him who is this Brahma who is immortal? Then Brahmdev meditated upon Lord Shiva.

Story of Naimisarariko:

Brahmdev says to Rishis, "Hey Rishis, and the one who is far from mind and words, the one who created Brahma, Vishnu, Rudra, as well as all senses. Also the one who is worshipped by Brahmins. The one who is more bright and powerful than Sun, Moon, Current, and Fire. It is no other than Lord Shiva. One can never understand Lord Shiva completely. There is no one to compare with him. He is the one who creates everything and at the end also destroys it. Only the devotee of Lord Shiva can see him.

Brahmdev then says, "I will release this Chakra and wherever it lands you do ten thousand years long Yegya there." After that Brahmdev releases a Chakra and it landed while crashing at the stone. That Place where it landed is known as Naimisarariko.

Arrival of Vayu (Air):

Shoot Jee says, "Those Rishis performed the Yegya at same place Naimisarariko. They completed the Yegya after ten thousand years. Then inspired by Brahmdev Vayu Dev arrived there at the Yegya. After seeing Vayu Dev all the Rishis gave their respect to Vayu Dev. They provided a special place for Vayu Dev to sit. Then Vayu Dev asked the Rishis, "Hey Rishis did you had any problem conducting this Yegya? Did you finish the Yegya? Did everything went well at the Yegya?

After hearing Vayu Dev, Rishis said, "We did this Yegya to gain knowledge about our doubts. By the grace of Brahmdev we started this Yegya. He gave us the Shiva Mantra to pronounce at the Yegya. He also had told that you would come. So you being here this completes the ten thousand years long Yegya.

Description of Shiva's Devotion:

Rishis asked Vayu Dev, "Vayu Dev how did Brahmdev gave you the knowledge of Lord Shiva." Then Vayu Dev says, "Hey Rishis, when twenty first Kalpa named Soytrup, then Brahmdev did hard meditate to please Lord Shiva, to create the Universe. Lord Shiva being pleased with

Brahmdev, he appeared before Brahmdev. Then Lord Shiva gave Brahmdev a Brahma Gyan (Knowledge). Lord Shiva said, the knowledge I gained about Pashupati Gyan, it is a joy giving knowledge. Only knowledge can replace ignorance of human being. Only by knowledge one can swipe his pain and suffering. Nature is Maya and one who maintains relation with Maya is Purus. Both are controlled by Lord Shiva. Maya is the energy of the Lord. Lord Shiva himself created Maya. Because of Karma one falls under the influence of Maya. When one's mind is purified then one receives Moksha. The same soul due to ignorance goes to heaven and hell.

Then Rishis asked, "Hey Vayu Dev, who is the master of this Pashupati?" Then Vayu Dev says, "Lord Shiva is the master of Pashupati. That Lord is present everywhere. He is in all and he is also the doer. People with ignorance won't see him because their third eye is covered with Maya. The same Lord Shiva is the creator care taker and destroyer of the world. The whole Universe is his different organs. He is the one who created Brahmdev and created the whole Universe and also will destroy it. By gaining the knowledge of Lord Shiva only one can free himself from world affair. Only by gaining the knowledge of Lord Shiva one achieves Moksha.

Age of All Three Gods:

Rishis asks Vayu Dev, "Please tell us about the age of all three Gods."

Vayu Dev then says, "Hey Rishis there are four Yug. Satya Yug, Tretya Yug, Duarpa Yug, and Kali Yug. When combined all four Yug then it became one Maha Yug. When One thousand Maha Yug is gone than that's one Kalpa. In one Kalpa there are fourteen Manu. With eight thousand years that is one Yug of Brahmdev. Thousand Yug like that makes one Sawan. So thirty thousand Swan is the age of Brahmdev. Likewise Brahmdev whole life is one day of Vishnu. Vishnu's whole life is one day of Rudra. Likewise when Rudra whole life is Lord Shiva's one day.

Lord Shiva's five hundred forty thousand years completion is what creates the Universe, then taking care of the Universe and at the end destroying it. But Lord Shiva is immortal and never dies.

Description of Armageddon:

Vayu Dev says, "First of all energy of Param Brahma is established. Later on the same energy will be known as Maya. Nature is created from same energy of Maya. From nature the whole world is created. This world is govern by five energies. Lord Shiva is the creator, take career, and destroyer of this world.

At night Mahesower enjoys his time with Mahesowri. When the day breaks then same Mahesower becomes Purus in Nature. Because of Mahesower and Mahesowri humans are created.

The first Purus Puru, will create intelligence as well as problems in the world. Because of all the problems Rudra, Brahmdev, and Vishnu is created. These three God's responsibilities are to create, take care, and to destroy it. All three Gods are controlled by Lord Shiva. All three gods got created from each other. Anyone who doubts among the three Gods will suffer.

Then Rishis asked Vayu Dev, to explain them Kalpa and Manbantar.

Then Vayu Dev says, "Hey Rishis, at the time of creation Lord first created Brahmdev. There are fourteen Manbantar in Brahmadev's one day. When first Kalpa is finished then Armageddon happens. At that time wind will destruct Earth. There will be no greenery and mountains. Everything will be covered by water. When Vishnu notices that world is being destroyed by water then he goes and sleeps inside that water. When creation is about to take place then all the Siddha Gurus will start praising Vishnu to wake him up. When Vishnu wakes up then he realizes it's all water. Then he incarnates as Bore and carries the Earth in his tooth to Patal. There he takes all the water from the Earth. After that everyone praises Vishnu.

Description of Creation:

Vayu Dev says, "Hey Rishis, after that Brahmdev wanted to create the world. Then he started meditating and felt the feeling of love. After that intelligence, along with senses and soul was created. Like this soul of creation was created. On the second creation birds were created. On the third creation Brahmdev created Gods. On the fourth creation Brahmdev created human beings. Brahmdev created nature with five elements. At first Brahmadev's first human son was born. As soon as he was born he went to meditate. Then tears that came from anger gave birth to demons. Then from Brahmadev's mouth Lord Shiva was born. Then Lord Shiva created eleven Rudras from his body. Who became famous with the name eleven Rudras. From Brahmadev's east mouth Gayatri Mantra was created. From Brahmadev's west mouth Ved was created. Then all of them became busy with their responsibilities. So they started Karma and got into the cycle of birth and death."

Then Rishis asked Vayu Dev, that Lord Shiva is the creator of everything, so how come he took birth as Brahmadev's son?

Then Vayu Dev says, "Hey Rishis, Lord Shiva created all three Gods to create, to take care, and to destroy the world. But the three Gods started becoming jealous of each other. Then all three Gods started meditating to please Lord Shiva. Then by the grace of Lord Shiva they all received their higher positions. In some Kalpa Brahmdev gives birth to Vishnu and in other Kalpa Vishnu gives birth to Brahmdev and Rudra. So this process of giving birth to each other is been going on. By the grace of Lord Shiva, Vishnu ad Brahmdev both are equally strong and powerful. But because of jealousy Vishnu and Brahmdev got into fight. Even Lord Shiva watched them fight each other. After seeing lord Shiva there Brahmdev and Vishnu stop fighting. They gave their respect to Lord Shiva and started praising Lord Shiva. After that Lord Shiva helped them to release their anger. After that Lord Shiva vanished from there.

Creation of Rudra:

Vayu Dev says, "In every Kalpa Brahmdev creates an egg to start the creation, but every time it was not creating. Seeing this Brahmdev becomes sad. Then Lord Shiva allows Rudra to born as a son of Brahmdev to start the creation of the world. Then Brahmdev requests Rudra to help him start the creation. After that Rudra creates another eleven Rudras from his body. After that Lord Shiva gives Brahmdev permission to start the creation. Lord Shiva becomes free of creation.

Creation of Shiv-Shiva:

Vayu Dev says, "Hey Rishis, by the grace of Lord Shiva, Brahmdev created different creation. But with so much effort also the population wasn't growing. Then Brahmdev decided to start the creation with Maithun culture (Marriage).

Thinking about Maithun culture Brahmdev started meditating. He did very difficult meditation and in that meditation he thought about pleasing Lord Shiva. Then Brahmdev start meditating upon Lord Shiva with Shakti. After doing meditation for quite some time, Lord Shiva incarnated in front of Brahmdev. Lord Shiva was half male and other half as female. This incarnation is known as Ardanariswor. Half Lord Shiva and other half Goddess Parvati.

Then Brahmdev started singing the glory of Lord Shiva and Goddess Parvati. He praised them. Then he asked for blessing from Goddess Parvati to start the Maithuni culture.

Creation of Maithuni Culture:

Vayu Dev says, "Hey Rishis, when Brahmdev praised Lord Shiva in different ways, then Lord Shiva became happy with Brahmdev. Then Lord Shiva says, "Hey Brahma I know why you did such a difficult meditation for, so I will grant you your wish. After that Lord Shiva created a female from his body. Brahmdev then started praising that female energy. After that the female energy asked Brahmdev what he wants. Then Brahmdev says, to increase the population of the creation I want to start Maithuni culture. It can only be done when there is female energy present. So if you could please become the daughter of Dakshya who would be known as Dakshya Putri.

Then that female energy from her eye shadow created another female who became Dakshya Putri. From her the Maithuni culture was started.

Staying at Mandarachal:

Once Mandarachal Mountain had did very difficult meditation to ask Lord Shiva and Goddess Parvati to stay over at Mandarachal. So Lord Shiva being very pleased started living at

Mandarachal with Goddess Parvati. At that time the population of human beings also rapidly increased. Then Sumbha and Nissumbha two demons also took birth. Then they did meditate upon Brahmdev. Brahmdev blessed them to be very powerful and brave. Then they started capturing all Loka. They used to trouble Gods and other Rishis all the time. So Brahmdev went to Lord Shiva and asked him to make Goddess Uma (Parvati) angry. So due to effect of that anger Sumbha and Nishumbha the demons would die.

Then Lord Shiva decided to tease Goddess Uma. So Lord Shiva made fun of female character. That made Goddess Uma very angry. So she started asking Lord Shiva different questions. She wanted to know why he wasn't happy with her. Then Lord Shiva said to Goddess Uma that he was only teasing her to make her angry. So that because of the effect of that anger Sumbha and Nishumbha would die. Then Lord Shiva told Goddess Uma that she is the mother of the whole world and he is the father. So there is no need to doubt. then Goddess Uma started meditating upon Brahmdev. So Brahmdev appeared before Goddess Uma. When Brahmdev asked Goddess Uma what she wants then she told Brahmdev that she wants to be Gauri. After that Goddess Uma again started doing difficult meditation to be Gauri.

Creation of Kali:

Then Uma Devi prayed to Lord Shiva and circled Lord Shiva. Then she went to her father's house. After that she went to the same place where she had meditated before. Then she started doing very difficult meditation. Then after some time a huge dangerous Lion came there, he was thinking about attacking Uma Devi. Uma Devi then looked at the Lion and she washed away all his sins. then that Lion became devotee of Uma Devi. Lion then started protecting Uma Devi from other wild animals.

Then one day Brahmdev arrived there and asked Uma Devi, why she was doing such a difficult meditation. Then Uma Devi told Brahmdev that how she wanted to be Gauri. then by the advice of Brahmdev, Uma Devi left her dark image of incarnation and became Gauri. From Gauri A Divine Goddess Durga was born with eight hands. She was wearing ornaments and carrying weapons on hands. Then Brahmdev requested Goddess Durga to kill Sumbha and Nishumbha. For that Brahmdev also gave Goddess Durga a Lion as a protector. Then Brahmdev worshiped Goddess Durga by sacrificing other animals. Then that energy in Goddess Durga went to Bindyachal Mountain and killed Sumbha and Nishumbha.

Kindness over Lion:

From her old body Uma Devi creates Kali and ask to finish the work for Brahmdev. Then she tells Brahmdev, that the Lion who protected her in the Jungle is here's devotee. So Uma Devi says she wants to take him with her. Brahmdev then says this Lion must have done some noble work in the past, so that he could be your protector. After that Brahmdev vanishes from there. Uma Devi also returns to Mandarachal with the Lion, where Lord Shiva was staying.

Meeting of Lord Shiva and Gauri Devi:

Vayu Dev says, "Hey Rishis, when Gauri Devi returned to Mandarachal then Lord Shiva became very happy. He picked Gauri Devi and took her inside. Then Lord Shiva said to Gauri Devi, that now your anger must have gone. Now we should never fight with each other. After all we are the reason this world is. After that Gauri Devi told Lord Shiva that her anger was to kill those two demons. So she has already killed them therefore her anger is gone.

So my energy which used in killing those demons will benefit the humans, if they worship that energy, said Gauri Devi. Then Gauri Devi called her devotee Lion there and told Lord Shiva that this Lion protected her in the Jungle. So that Lion is a close devotee of her. Then Lord Shiva made that lion the doorkeeper, and he promoted the other doorkeeper to Palace guard. Then Lord Shiva himself decorated Gauri Devi with different ornaments and clothes.

Devotion of Upmanyou:

Vayu Dev says, "Hey Rishis, Upmanyou was a devotee of Lord Shiva from childhood. He was the son of great Rishi Byadrapadh. Later by the grace of Lord Shiva Upmanyou become one of the main devotee of Lord Shiva. By the grace of lord Shiva Upmanyou received all the knowledge of Veda and other holy scriptures. Because once when Upmanyou was a child he asked his mother for milk. Then his mother out of flour made a milk and gave it to Upmanyou. After drinking that milk Upmanyou said that milk is not good and he wants cow's milk. He also said he saw his brother drinking a milk so he also wants it. Then his mother told Upmanyou that they are poor and lives in a Jungle. So they have no money to buy cow. She had feed his brother a barrowed milk from others. She also told Upmanyou that by the grace of Lord Shiva, he can have milk. Then Upmanyou asked where Lord Shiva is. Then his mother told Upmanyou that Lord Shiva is everywhere. Then Upmanyou slept that night whispering Om Nama Shivaya Mantra. Around midnight he woke up and saw Lord Shiva standing at the door. He then approached him and Lord Shiva disappeared from there. Then Upmanyou went outside his to look for Lord Shiva. He started walking towards the Jungle looking for Lord Shiva. Then he heard the voice saying "Boy all your problem will be solved." After hearing that voice he became satisfied and started walking home. On the way he saw Shiva's temple. He went inside the temple and hugged Lord Shiva's idol and start whispering Om Nama Shivaya. He stayed there for three days hugging the idol of Lord Shiva and whispering Om Nama Shivaya.

His mother at home couldn't find him, so started worrying about him. Lord Shiva had just reached Mandarachal he just turned around and started walking back. Then Gauri Devi asked Lord Shiva if any of his devotee is calling him? Then Lord Shiva says, "Yes a small boy is calling me. Then Lord Shiva appeared before Upmanyou. Then Lord Shiva told Upmanyou, that he is his main devotee, so tell me your wish. then Upmanyou asked for Ocean of milk. Lord Shiva granted him that wish and also told him that from now on he will have no problem in life. After saying that Lord Shiva vanishes from there.

Vayu Dev says, "Basu Dev Krishna had taken birth on Earth. Then Krishna had gone to an Ashram to meditate to have a son. At the ashram Krishna meet Upmanyou. Upmanyou respected Krishna and he gave Krishna "Trayayus Jamdagne" Mantra.

After that for twelve months Upmanyou made Krishna to meditate. Then after one year Lord Shiva and Gauri Devi appeared before Krishna and blessed him for son. After that Krishna with his wife named Jambawati had a son named Samba.

Advice of Upmanyou:

Upmanyou says, "Hey Sri Krishna, the whole Universe is what Lord Shiva is. Brahmdev, Vishnu, Rudra they all are different incarnation of lord Shiva. Likewise Lord Shiva has five other idol as well. They are Ishan, Purus, Aghor, Bamdev, and Sadhojat. These five idols of Lord Shiva is popular. Among them Ishan is the main one. It controls the words of vocabulary. Ishan is also the area. Idol that stays Idol is Purus. Taking the support of intelligence is Aghor. Taking the support of ego is Bamdev. The idol that stays inside the heart of lord Shiva is Sadhojat.

Ishan is responsible for feeling and wind. Aghor is responsible for seeing. Bamdev is responsible for fluid in tongue. Likewise Lord Shiva has eight idols. They are Sarba, Bhav, Rudra, Ugra, Vim, Pashupati, Ishan and Mahadev. Therefore whole Universe is Lord Shiva. That's why devoting towards lord Shiva is beneficial to all.

Then Sri Krishna says, "Hey Maha Rishi, now please tell me how the influence of Male and Female is controlling this world."

Then Upmanyou says, "Hey Sri Krishna, both the male and female are all parts of part of Lord Shiva. Everything is energized by Shiv-Shiva.

Lord Shiva and Uma Devi is one. Shakti is part of Lord Shiva. The whole Universe is energized by Uma Devi's energy. With the help of her energy every work and act is done around the world. This energy creates Naad and from Naad a Bindu (Dot), From Bindu to Mahesower and from Mahesower knowledge (Vidya) is created. So in this world everything male is lord Shiva's incarnation and every female being is Goddess Uma Devi's incarnation.

Because of this relation of male with female in the world, everyone gets blinded by it and don't see the bigger picture of the Universal truth.

Among Rishi Munis found an option to know some effect of Lord, so they preach about the Lord. They usually call him Upar Brahma, Para Brahma, and Parmatma. They also call him Ananta (Unlimited), Mahadev. Knowledge and ignorance are both parts of Brahma. So is awareness and unaware. Lord Shiva is God of both the truth and false.

Description of Vyas Incarnation:

Sri Krishna says to Upmanyou, "Hey Maha Rishi, now give the knowledge of Ved." Upmanyou then says, "Hey Sri Krishna, when Shiva lord created the Universe then he appeared on it. After that from him Brahmdev was born. After that Rudra who was born from Brahmdev. Brahmdev then took permission from Rudra to create the world. Then Brahmdev created Som to do the Yegya. Then from Som he created heaven, earth, Sun, Yegya, Vishnu, Indra, and others. Then all those Gods asked Rudra, who he is? He is everything. Whoever surrender himself into lord Shiva will easily gain the knowledge of Shiva element.

Lord Shiva is the supreme personality. Nothing can harm or affect him. Maya, Intelligence, ego, nothing can harm him. Lord Shiva said he is the one. Who knows everything. There is no one far from him. After saying all these Rudra vanished.

Then Gods started praising lord Shiva again. This time he incarnated with eight hands and was situated on the Sun. then Gods offered water to that incarnation of Lord Shiva. Then lord Shiva told Goddess Parvati (Uma) different knowledge about life. Lord Shiva also gave different knowledge to Agastya, Brihaspati, Dadhichi, and Vyas Jee on different Kalpa. That way they all became incarnation of Lord Shiva. That's why all those incarnation throughout their life spread the knowledge of Ved throughout the world.

Sri Krishna again asks Upmanyou, in every Yug who did Lord Shiva made his disciples? Then Upmanyou says, "Hey Sri Krishna, in Baraha Kalpa lord Shiva had twenty eight disciples. All of them became Yog Acharya. All of them had four disciple each and all together they were one hundred twelve disciples. They all are devotee of lord Shiva. They all are knowledgeable in all sectors. They all devote themselves as disciple of lords Shiva. So after death they all can go to Shiva Loka. They don't have to suffer by going to hell.

Devotion towards Lord Shiva:

Goddess Parvati says to lord Shiva, How will you be pleased by Bhakti (Devotion)? Then lord Shiva said, "Hey Devi, by pronouncing my name I wouldn't please that easily. But if someone devotees me with full devoted emotion then I will be please quickly. Anyone who sings my glory with full devotion of emotion towards me I will be very please. Therefore to sing the glory of Lord Shiva with devoted feeling is the best way to worship.

Importance of Om Nama Shivaya Mantra:

Sri Krishna asks Upmanyou, "Hey Muni, please explain me the importance of "Om Nama Shivaya" Mantra.

Upmanyou then says, Ved and other scriptures also points out the importance of Omkar. This Mantra fulfils all wishes of the devotee. Main Mantra among all Mantra is OM Nama Shivaya. This Mantra is above all three Guna Sato, Rajo and Tamo. Shakti Brahma is situated within OM. Within this Mantra there are seventy million other Mantras hidden inside it. The person who doesn't believe in this Mantra goes to hell. The devotee who worships Shiva Linga with this Mantra goes to Shiva Loka after death.

Mantra for Kali Yug:

Goddess Parvati asks Lord Shiva, "Hey Nath, in Kali Yug how would a devotee devote himself to you? Because in Kali Yug all the religions will be destructed.

Then Lord Shiva says to Goddess Parvati, "Hey Devi, in Kali Yug my Om Nama Shivaya Mantra will be the most powerful Mantra. I will be easily please by devotee if he worships me with this Mantra. The devotee who worships me with this Mantra with pure feeling then he achieves Moksha. This Mantra is more powerful in Kali Yug then my any other Mantras. In Tretya and Duarpa Yug devotee had to do difficult meditation to perform a duty but in Kali Yug just by pronouncing this Mantra will do the work.

Types of Dikshya (Teachings):

Sri Krishna asks Upmanyou, "Hey Maha Rishi, tell me about different ways to have Dikshya (Education) to have Shiva Tatwa (Element)."

Upmanyou then says, Hey Sri Krishna, to clear six paths is known as Sanskar (Character), from which knowledge is gained and past sins are dissolved. This process is called Dikshya. There are three types of Dikshya. They are Shambhavi, Shakti, and Maitri. Shambhavi Dikshya is given by the grace of a Guru. From which all the sins are washed.

When Guru through Yug enters inside the body and give knowledge that is known as Shakti Dikshya. Dikshya given with Kriya Yug is known as Maitri Dikshya.

Guru first takes the test of a disciple before giving him Dikshya with Mantra. Disciple should also stand with his Guru and think Guru as lord Shiva himself.

Religion to Practice All the Time:

Sri Krishna ask Upmanyou, "Hey Maha Rishi, now I want to know about religion to practice every day as per Shiva Sastra. Please explain it to me."

Upmanyou says, "Hey Sri Krishna, everyday one should wake up early in the morning. Then one should meditate upon Lord Shiva and Goddess Parvati. After that one should start one's day. One should freshen up and clean one self. Then wear a clean clothes. Then one should with water pronounce the Shiva Mantra three times. Then offer the water to lord Shiva. Then one should make Tripunda (Three lines on forehead and arms). After that give Brahmins white and yellow clothes to wear. After that one should go the worshipping room and face south and meditate upon lord Shiva.

Way to Worship:

Upmanyou says, "Hey Sri Krishna, Nyas (Sacrifice) are of three types. They are Nyas creation, Nyas Situation, and Nyas continuity. Nyas situation is for domesticated disciples, Nyas creation is for Brhamacharis (Singles), and Nyas continuity is for Sanyasi.

Way to Worship Lord Shiva:

Upmanyou says, "Hey Sri Krishna, worshipping Lord Shiva is always beneficial. Even big sinners can wash away their sins by worshipping Lord Shiva. One can even without the Mantra worship lord Shiva. By worshipping Lord Shiva all problems will be solved. By worshipping Lord Shiva life will be successful. That's why one should worship lord Shiva, and should meditate to lord Shiva. There is no other religion as easy as worshipping Lord Shiva. After worshipping Lord Shiva distribute Prasad (Eatables) to females and other members of the house.

Avaran way of Worshipping:

Upmanyou says, "Hey Sri Krishna, first make five lines at the spot where you will worship Lord Shiva. Then on the middle of those lines place Shiv-Shiva there. On the right side of it establish God Ganesha and on the left side establish Kumar Kartikya. After that worship them. Then do Shakti worship there. Then with fire worship eight idols of Lord Shiva. After that establish Nandi on the north side and Mahakal on the south side. Then worship them.

On the fourth line worship Brahmdev. On the third line worship all nine planets. After that offer eatables to Lord Shiva and Goddess Parvati. After that worship Guru and take three circle of Lord Shiva and Goddess Parvati. Then offer your gratitude to Lord Shiva and Goddess Parvati. One should do Avaran worshipping at least once in their life time.

Benefits of Establishing Shiva Linga:

Upmanyou says, "Hey Sri Krishna, while worshipping Lord Shiva and Goddess Parvati one should offer water with Chandan and offer white flower. Making Shiva Linga as per the ritual with gold and other precious stones is beneficial to all. Then worship the Shiva Linga with Bel leaf. Then offer incense and take three circle of the Shiva Linga. Worshiping Shiva Linga like this will secure one's space in Shiva Loka.

All this Universe is inside the Lord Shiva. By establishing a Shiva Linga everything will situate on that Shiva Linga. All three Guna Sato, Rajo, and Tamo are created due to Linga. This Linga is unlimited. It can't be measured. Everything in the world is created from the Linga.

Before at the time Armageddon Vishnu went to sleep in the water and Brahmdev was born from the naval of Vishnu. Then when they saw each other they started fighting about who is superior. Then one huge Linga appeared before them. Then they gave their respect to that Linga. After that they tried to find out what that Linga is. So Brahmdev went towards the head of the Linga and Vishnu went towards the tail of the Linga. They travelled for one thousand years and still couldn't locate head or tail of the Linga. Then they figured it out that there is someone superior to them. So their ego disappeared.

Attraction of Brahmdev and Vishnu towards the Linga:

After seeing that Linga both Brahmdev and Vishnu became very attracted towards the Linga. Then start praising the Linga. Then Lord Shiva was pleased with them and said, "You two were thinking that you are Gods and superior. Therefore I appeared here in Linga form to destroy your egos. It is all my Lela. Now you two do your responsibilities and after saying that the Linga vanished from there.

How to create Shiva Linga:

Upmanyou says, "Hey Sri Krishna, now I will tell you about procedure of establishing Shiva Linga. On Shukla Pachya make a Shiva Linga. Then at the beginning Lord Ganesha should be worshiped. After that clean that Shiva Linga with cow's shed and water. After that dry up the Shiva Linga. After that start saying Mantras in Ved. After that all the waste from worshiping should be put on a River. Then put cloth over Shiva Linga. Then let Shiva Linga sleep on bed made for it. Then worship Lord Shiva and Goddess Parvati together. One should then follow the same ritual every day.

Way to do Yog:

Upmanyou says, "Hey Sri Krishna, now at the end I will teach you about the Yug. By which one is purified and finds the reason for everything. The air which operates the body is known as Pran. So measuring that air is called Pranayama. One should practice Pranayama every day and try to win over the air. By doing this one will erase all kinds diseases from the body. So while doing Pranayama one should also meditate upon lord Shiva.

Stories of Munis:

Sri Shoot Jee says, "Hey Rishis, like that Sri Upmanyou gave all the knowledge to Sri Krishna. Sri Krishna then gave the same knowledge to other Rishis. They then started praising Sri Krishna. After that those Rishis went to shower at Sarswoti River and from there they went to Kashi. There they showered at Ganga Jee and worshiped Vishwonath Jee. After that they saw a bright fire and on that fire there were Rishis then that fire slowly went inside the water of Ganga Jee in Kashi. So to know what that was they went to Brahmdev. They asked Brahmdev about that incident, then Brahmdev send them To Sumeru Mountain to know the answer.

Moksha of Munis:

Shoot Jee says, "Hey Rishis, by the advice of Brahmdev those Rishis went to Sumeru Mountain. There Sanat Kumar Jee was in deep meditation. All the Rishis gave their respect to Sanat Kumar and they waited right there. After some time Sanat Kumar Jee opened his eyes and saw the Rishis sitting there. Then the Rishis told Sanat Kumar Jee their story. At the same time Nandi (Bull, the vehicle of Lord Shiva) also arrived there. Then everyone gave their respect to Nandi. After that Nandi gave them the knowledge to achieve Moksha.

Shoot Jee then says, Hey Rishis, this great knowledge about Shiva Maha Puran was first told by Sanat Kumar Jee to Ved Vyas Jee. Ten Ved Vyas Jee gave this knowledge to me. Now I gave you all the knowledge of Shiva Maha Puran. This Shiva Maha Puran is the superior Puran. Listening to Shiva Maha Puran will award a person with all four rewards of Religion, Wealth, Lust, and Moksha.

After finishing the Shiva Maha Puran, Shoot Jee left. Also other Rishis fulfilled their wishes. After that they saw Kali Yug approaching so they all went to Kashi. Then they followed Pashupata Barta (Not thinking like animal). Then later they all achieved Moksha. They all started meditating upon lord Shiva after that.

Therefore one should at least hear the stories of Shiva Maha Puran once in their life. In Kali Yug one should daily read one story from Shiva Maha Puran, so that he gets all the benefit of life and Moksha at the end.

OM NAMA SHIVAYA

Shiva Maha Puran Completed.

Made in United States
Troutdale, OR
12/01/2023